PHILO-SOPHICAL EXPLO-RATIONS

PHILO-SOPHICAL EXPLO-RATIONS

FREEDOM, GOD, AND GOODNESS

STEVEN M. CAHN

PROMETHEUS BOOKS
Buffalo, New York

Published 1989 by Prometheus Books
700 East Amherst Street, Buffalo, New York 14215

Copyright © 1989 by Steven M. Cahn

Library of Congress Cataloging-in-Publication Data

Cahn, Steven M.
    Philosophical explorations : freedom, God, and goodness
        p. cm.
    Includes bibliographies.
    ISBN 0-87975-487-7 (pbk.)
    1. Liberty. 2. God. 3. Religion—Philosophy. 4. Ethics.
I. Title.
B105.L45C34   1988
100—dc 19   88-12430
                                                                     CIP

Printed in the United States of America

To
SIDNEY HOOK
and to the memory of
ERNEST NAGEL

Preface

Philosophical inquiry seeks to clarify our most fundamental beliefs and subject them to critical scrutiny. This volume concentrates on three such beliefs that have played a crucial role in the development of Western thought: freedom of the will, the existence of God, and the reasonableness of value judgments.

Part One, devoted to the concept of freedom, contains three chapters. The first provides an introduction to the traditional problem of freedom and determinism. The second contains a brief discussion of a familiar, but rarely explored, psychological phenomenon that may provide a clue to understanding human action. The third chapter presents a new puzzle about human freedom, offers two attempts to solve the puzzle, and concludes by rejecting these proposed solutions and challenging readers to think the matter through for themselves.

Part Two, which focuses on issues in philosophy of religion, is in four chapters. The first offers an introduction to the standard proofs and disproofs of the existence of God. The second offers a puzzle about the goodness of God, suggesting that every attempt to view evil as a part of a greater good can be met by viewing goodness as part of a greater evil. The third chapter is a defense of the claim that we can believe in God without being religious, while the fourth supports the view that we can be religious without believing in God.

Part Three, concerning values, has three chapters. The first is an introduction to the nature of moral judgments. The second attempts to discover one supreme moral principle that would provide the basis for resolving all ethical conflicts. The final chapter offers a puzzle about aesthetic judgment, one that challenges the appropriateness of a widely used criterion for evaluating works of art. Two replies to the puzzle are included, along with a rejoinder to them.

Sources referred to in the chapters form the second half of the book. These selections have been chosen to exemplify or amplify materials in the first half.

The nature of philosophy is best grasped by those who join in its quest to understand our basic commitments and their consequences. I hope, therefore, that readers will find in this volume a stimulus to their own philosophical reflections.

Acknowledgments

Chapters 1, 4, 6, 7, 8, and 9, are based on materials found in my book *A New Introduction to Philosophy* (New York: Harper & Row, 1971). Chapter 2 is reprinted with significant changes from *Philosophy and Phenomenological Research* 37, no. 4. Chapter 3 is reprinted with slight modifications from *Analysis* 25, no. 4. Richard Taylor is Leavitt-Spencer Adjunct Professor of Philosophy at Union College. Part A is reprinted by permission of the author from *Analysis* 26, no. 2. Arthur W. Collins is professor of philosophy at City College and the Graduate School of the City University of New York. Part B is reprinted with minor omissions from *Analysis* 26, no. 2. Yehoshua Bar-Hillel was professor of philosophy at the Hebrew University. Part C is reprinted with alterations from *Analysis* 26, no. 6. Chapter 5 is reprinted with significant changes from *Analysis* 37, no. 2. The puzzle presented in note 5 of chapter 8 is reprinted from *Analysis* 47, no. 3. Chapter 10 is reprinted by permission of The American Society for Aesthetics from the *Journal of Aesthetics and Art Criticism* 34, no. 1. L. Michael Griffel is professor of music at Hunter College and the Graduate School of the City University of New York. Parts A and B of chapter 10 are reprinted from the same issue with permission of the Society. Gordon Epperson is professor of music at the University of Arizona. Neil Courtney is a member of the Philadelphia Orchestra. Part C appears here for the first time.

Contents

Part One
Freedom

1

Freedom and Determinism

In 1924 the American people were horrified by a senseless crime of extraordinary brutality. The defendants were eighteen-year-old Nathan Leopold and seventeen-year-old Richard Loeb. They were the sons of Chicago millionaires, brilliant students who had led seemingly idyllic lives. Leopold was the youngest graduate in the history of the University of Chicago, and Loeb the youngest graduate in the history of the University of Michigan. Suddenly they were accused of the kidnapping and vicious murder of fourteen-year-old Bobby Franks, a cousin of Loeb's. Before the trial even began, Leopold and Loeb both confessed, and from across the country came an outcry for their execution.

The lawyer who agreed to defend them was Clarence Darrow, the outstanding defense attorney of his time. Since Leopold and Loeb had already admitted their crime, Darrow's only chance was to explain their behavior in such a way that his clients could escape the death penalty. He was forced to argue that Leopold and Loeb were not morally responsible for what they had done; that they were not to be blamed for their actions. But how could he possibly maintain that position?

Darrow's defense was a landmark in the history of criminal law. He argued that the actions of his clients were a direct and necessary result of hereditary and environmental forces beyond their control.[1] Leopold suffered from a glandular disease that left him depressed and moody. Originally shy with girls, he had been sent to an all-girls school to cure his shyness but had sustained deep psychic scars from which he never recovered. In addition, his parents instilled in him the belief that his wealth absolved him of any responsibility toward others. Pathologically inferior because of his diminutive size, and pathologically superior because of his wealth, he became an acute schizophrenic.

Loeb suffered from a nervous disorder that caused fainting spells. During his unhappy childhood he had often thought of committing suicide. He was under the control of a domineering governess and was

15

forced to lie and cheat to deceive her. His wealth led him to believe he was superior to all those around him, and he developed a fascination for crime, an activity in which he could demonstrate his superiority. By the time he reached college he was severely psychotic.

In his final plea Darrow recounted these facts. His central theme was that Leopold and Loeb were in the grip of powers beyond their control. They themselves were victims.

> I do not know what it was that made these boys do this mad act, but I do know there is a reason for it. I know they did not beget themselves. I know that any one of an infinite number of causes reaching back to the beginning might be working out in these boys' minds, whom you are asked to hang in malice and in hatred and in injustice, because someone in the past has sinned against them. . . . What had this boy to do with it? He was not his own father; he was not his own mother; he was not his own grandparents. All of this was handed to him. He did not surround himself with governesses and wealth. He did not make himself. And yet he is to be compelled to pay.[2]

Darrow's plea was successful, for Leopold and Loeb escaped execution and were sentenced to life imprisonment. Although they had committed crimes and were legally responsible for their actions, the judge believed they were not morally responsible, for they had not acted freely.

If the line of argument that Darrow utilized in the Leopold-Loeb case is sound, then not only were Leopold and Loeb not to blame for what they had done, but no person is ever to blame for any actions. As Darrow himself put it, "We are all helpless." But is Darrow's argument sound? Does the conclusion follow from the premises, and are the premises true?

We can formalize his argument as follows:

Premise 1: No action is free if it must occur.

Premise 2: In the case of every event that occurs, antecedent conditions, known or unknown, ensure the event's occurrence.

Conclusion: Therefore, no action is free.

Premise (1) assumes that an action is free only if it is within the agent's power to perform it and within the agent's power not to perform it. In other words, whether a free action will occur is up to the agent. If circumstances require the agent to perform a certain action or require the agent not to perform that action, then the action is not free.

Premise (2) is the thesis known as "determinism." Put graphically, it is the claim that if there were at any time a being who knew the position of every particle in the universe and all the forces acting on each particle, then that being could predict with certainty every future event. Determinism does not presume such a being exists; the being is only imagined in order to illustrate what the world would be like if determinism were true.

Darrow's conclusion, which is supposed to follow from premises (1) and (2), is that no person has free will. Note that to have free will does not imply being free with regard to all actions, for only the mythical Superman is free to leap tall buildings at a single bound. But so long as at least some of an agent's actions are free, the agent is said to have free will. What Darrow's argument purports to prove is that not a single human action that has ever been performed has been performed freely.

Does the conclusion of Darrow's argument follow from the premises? If premise (2) is true, then every event that occurs must occur, for its occurrence is ensured by antecedent conditions. Since every action is an event, it follows from premise (2) that every action that occurs must occur. But according to premise (1), no action is free if it must occur. Thus, if premises (1) and (2) are true, it follows that no action is free—the conclusion of Darrow's argument.

Even granting that Darrow's reasoning is unassailable, we need not accept the conclusion of his argument unless we grant the truth of his premises. Should we do so?

Hard determinism is the view that both premises of Darrow's argument are correct. In other words, a hard determinist believes that determinism is true and that, as a consequence, no person has free will.[3] Determinists note that whenever an event occurs, we all assume that a causal explanation can account for the occurrence of the event. Suppose, for example, you feel a pain in your arm and are prompted to visit a physician. After examining you, the doctor announces that the pain had no cause, either physical or psychological. In other words, you were supposed to be suffering from an uncaused pain. On hearing this diagnosis you would surely switch doctors. After all, no one may be able to discover the cause of your pain, but surely something is causing it. If nothing were causing it, you wouldn't be in pain. This same line of reasoning applies whether the event to be explained is a loud noise, a change in the weather, or an individual's action. If the event were uncaused, it wouldn't have occurred.

However, we may agree that the principle of determinism holds in the vast majority of cases, yet doubt its applicability in the realm of human action. While causal explanations may be found for rocks falling and birds flying, people are far more complex than rocks or birds.

The determinist responds to this objection by asking us to consider any specific action: for instance, your decision to read this book. You may suppose your decision was uncaused, but did you not wish to acquire information about philosophy? The determinist argues that your desire for such information, together with your belief that the information is found in this book, caused you to read. Just as physical forces cause rocks and birds to do things, so human actions are caused by desires and beliefs.

If you doubt this claim, the determinist can call attention to our success in predicting people's behavior. For example, a store owner who reduces prices can depend on increasing visits by shoppers; an athlete who wins a major championship can rely on greater attention from the press. Furthermore, when we read novels or see plays, we expect to understand why the characters act as they do, and an author who fails to provide such explanations is charged with poor writing. The similarity of people's reactions to the human condition also accounts for the popularity of the incisive psychological insights of a writer such as La Rochefoucauld, the French aphorist. We read one of his maxims, for instance, "When our integrity declines, our taste does also,"[4] and nod our heads with approval, but are we not agreeing to a plausible generalization about the workings of the human psyche?

Granted, people's behavior cannot be predicted with certainty, but the hard determinist reminds us that each individual is influenced by a unique combination of hereditary and environmental factors. Just as each rock is slightly different from every other rock and each bird is somewhat different from every other bird, so human beings differ from each other. But just as rocks and birds are part of an unbroken chain of causes and effects, so human beings, too, are part of that chain. Just as a rock falls because it breaks off from a cliff, so people act because of their desires and beliefs. And just as a rock has no control over the wind that causes it to break off, so people have no control over the desires and beliefs that cause them to act. In short, we are said to have no more control over our desires and beliefs than Leopold and Loeb had over theirs. If you can control your desire for food and your friend cannot, the explanation is that your will is of a sort that can control your desire and your friend's will is of a sort that cannot. That your will is of one sort and your friend's will of another is not within the control of either of you. As one hard determinist has written, "If we can overcome the effects of early environment, the ability to do so is itself a product of the early environment. We did not give ourselves this ability; and if we lack it we cannot be blamed for not having it."[5]

At this point in the argument an antideterminist is apt to call attention to recent developments in physics that have been interpreted by some thinkers as a refutation of determinism. They claim that work in quantum mechanics demonstrates that certain subatomic events are uncaused and inherently unpredictable. Yet some physicists and philosophers of science argue that determinism has not been refuted, since the experimental results can be understood in causal terms.[6] The outcome of this dispute, however, seems irrelevant to the issue of human freedom, since the events we are discussing are not subatomic, and indeterminism on that level is compatible with the universal causation of events on the much larger level of human action.

Here, then, is a summary of hard determinism: According to this view, determinism is true and no person has free will. Every event that occurs is caused to occur, for otherwise why would it occur? Your present actions are events caused by your previous desires and beliefs, which themselves are accounted for by hereditary and environmental factors. These are part of a causal chain extending back far before your birth, and each link of the chain determines the succeeding link. Since you obviously have no control over events that occurred before your birth, and since these earlier events determined the later ones, it follows that you have no control over your present actions. In short, you do not have free will.

The hard determinist's argument may appear plausible, yet few of us are inclined to accept its shocking conclusion. We opt, therefore, to deny one of its two premises. *Soft determinism* is the view that the conclusion is false because premise (1) is false. In other words, a soft determinist believes both that determinism is true and that human beings have free will. The implication of the position is that an action may be free even if it is part of a causal chain extending back to events outside the agent's control. While this view may at first appear implausible, it has been defended throughout the centuries by many eminent philosophers, including Thomas Hobbes, David Hume, John Stuart Mill, and A. J. Ayer (see source #2).

An approach employed explicitly or implicitly by many soft determinists has come to be known as "the paradigm-case argument." Consider it first in another setting, where its use is a classic of philosophical argumentation.

In studying physics we learn that ordinary objects like tables and chairs are composed of sparsely scattered, minute particles. This fact may lead us to suppose that such objects are not solid. As Sir Arthur Eddington, the noted physicist, put it, a "plank has no solidity of substance. To step on it is like stepping on a swarm of flies."[7]

Eddington's view that a plank is not solid was forcefully attacked by the British philosopher L. Susan Stebbing. She pointed out that the word "solid" derives its meaning from examples such as planks.

> For "solid" just is the word we use to describe a certain respect in which a plank of wood resembles a block of marble, a piece of paper, and a cricket ball, and in which each of these differs from a sponge, from the interior

of a soap-bubble, and from the holes in a net. . . . The point is that the common usage of language enables us to attribute a meaning to the phrase "a solid plank"; but there is no common usage of language that provides a meaning for the word "solid" that would make sense to say that the plank on which I stand is not solid.⁸

In other words, a plank is a paradigm case of solidity. Anyone who claims that a plank is not solid does not know how the word "solid" is used in the English language. Note that Stebbing is not criticizing Eddington's scientific views, but only the manner in which he interpreted them.

The paradigm-case argument is useful to soft determinists; for in the face of the hard determinist's claim that no human action is free, soft determinists respond by pointing to a paradigm case of a free action, for instance, a person walking down the street. They stipulate that the individual is not under the influence of drugs, is not attached to ropes, is not sleepwalking, and so on; in other words, they refer to a normal, everyday instance of a person walking down the street. Soft determinists claim that the behavior described is a paradigm case of a free action, clearly distinguishable from instances in which a person is, in fact, under the influence of drugs, attached to ropes, or sleepwalking. These latter cases are not examples of free actions, or are at best problematic examples, while the case the soft determinists cite is clear and seemingly indisputable. Indeed, according to soft determinists, anyone who claims the act of walking down the street is not free does not know how the word "free" is used in English. Thus people certainly have free will, for we can cite obvious cases in which they act freely.

How do soft determinists define a "free action"? According to them, actions are free if the persons who perform them wish to do so and could, if they wished, not perform them. If your arm is forcibly raised, you did not act freely, for you did not wish to raise your arm. If you were locked in a room, you would also not be free, even if you wished to be there, for if you wished to leave, you couldn't.

Soft determinists emphasize that once we define "freedom" correctly, any apparent incompatibility between freedom and determinism will disappear. Consider some particular action I perform that is free in the sense explicated by soft determinists. Granting that the action is one link in a causal chain extending far back beyond my birth, nevertheless, I am free with regard to that action, for I wish to perform it, and if I did not wish to, I would not do so. This description of the situation is consistent with supposing that my wish is a result of hereditary and environmental factors over which I have no control. The presence of such factors is, according to the soft determinist, irrelevant to the question of whether my action is free. I may be walking down a particular street because of my desire to buy a coat and my belief that I am heading toward a clothing store, and this desire and belief may themselves be caused by any number of other factors. But, since I desire to walk down the street and could walk down some other street if I so desired, it follows that I am freely walking down the street. By this line of reasoning soft determinists affirm both free will and determinism, finding no incompatibility between them.

Soft determinism is an inviting doctrine, for it allows us to maintain a belief in free will without having to relinquish the belief that every event has a cause. Soft determinism, however, is open to serious objections that have led some philosophers to abandon the position.

The fundamental problem for soft determinists is that their definition of "freedom" does not seem in accordance with the ordinary way in which we use the term. Note that soft determinists and hard determinists offer two different definitions of "freedom." According to the hard determinist, an action is free if it is within my power to perform it and also within my power not to perform it. According to the soft determinist, an action is free if it is such that if I wish to perform it I may, and if I wish not to perform it I also may. To highlight the difference between these definitions, consider the case of a man who has been hypnotized and rolls up the leg of his pants as if to cross a stream. Is his action free? According to the hard determinist, the man's action is not free, for it is not within his power to refrain from rolling up the leg of his pants. According to the soft determinist's definition of "freedom," the action would be considered free, for the agent desires to perform it, and if he didn't desire to, he wouldn't. But a man under hypnosis is not free. Therefore, the soft determinist's definition of "freedom" seems unsatisfactory.

Perhaps this objection to soft determinism is unfair, since the desires of the hypnotized man are not his own but are controlled by the hypnotist. The force of the objection to soft determinism, however, is that the soft determinist overlooks whether a person's wishes or desires are themselves within that individual's control. The hard determinist emphasizes that my action is free only if it is up to me whether to perform it. But, in order for an action to be up to me, I need to have control over my own wishes or desires. If I do not, my desires might be controlled by a hypnotist, a brainwasher, my family, hereditary factors, or so on, and thus I would not be free. Soft determinists do not appear to take such possibilities seriously, since, according to them, I would be free even if my desires were not within my control, so long as I was acting according to my desires and could act differently if my desires were different. But could my desires have been different? That is the crucial question. If my desires could not have been different, then I could not have acted in any other way than I did. And that is the description of a person who is not free.

By failing to consider the ways in which a person's desires can be controlled by external forces beyond the individual's control, soft determinists offer a definition of "freedom" that I find not in accord with our normal use of the term. They may, of course, define terms as they wish, but we are interested in the concept of freedom relevant to questions of moral responsibility. Any concept of freedom implying that hypnotized or brainwashed individuals are morally responsible for their actions is not the concept in question.

What of the soft determinist's claim that a person's walking down the street is a paradigm case of a free action? Although I agree that the paradigm-case argument can sometimes be used effectively, the soft determinist's appeal to it does not seem convincing. To see why, imagine that we traveled to a land in which the inhabitants believed that every woman born on February 29 was a witch, and that every witch had the power to cause droughts. If we refused to believe that any woman was a witch, the philosophically sophisticated inhabitants might try to convince us by appealing to the paradigm-case argument, claiming that anyone born on February 29 is a paradigm case of a witch.

What would we say in response? How does this appeal to a paradigm case differ from Susan Stebbing's appeal to a plank as a paradigm case of solidity? No one doubts that a plank can hold significant weight and is, in that sense, solid. But, until women born on February 29 demonstrate supernatural powers and are in that sense witches, the linguistic claim alone has no force.

Are soft determinists appealing to an indisputable instance when they claim that a person's walking down the street is a paradigm case of a free action? Not at all, for as we saw in the trial of Leopold and Loeb, such apparently free actions may not turn out to be judged as free. By appealing to a disputable example as a paradigm case, soft determinists are assuming what they are supposed to be proving. They are supposed to demonstrate that actions such as walking down the street are examples of free actions. Merely asserting that such actions are free is to overlook the hard determinist's argument that such actions are not free. No questionable instance can be used as a paradigm case, and walking down the street is, as Darrow demonstrated, a questionable example of a free action. So, again, soft determinism appears to have a serious weakness.

Remember that the hard determinist argues that since premises (1) and (2) of Darrow's argument are true, so is the conclusion. Soft determinists argue that premise (1) is false. If they are mistaken, then the only way to avoid hard determinism is to reject premise (2). That position is known as "libertarianism."[9]

The *libertarian* agrees with the hard determinist that an action is not free if it must occur. For the libertarian as well as for the hard determinist, I am free with regard to a particular action only if it is within my power to perform the action and within my power not to perform it. But do persons ever act freely? The hard determinist believes that people are never free, since in the case of every action antecedent conditions, known or unknown, ensure the action's occurrence. Libertarians refuse to accept this conclusion, but find it impossible to reject premise (1) of Darrow's argument. So their only recourse is to reject premise (2). As Sherlock Holmes noted, "When you have eliminated the impossible, whatever remains, however improbable, must be the truth."[10] The libertarian thus denies that every event has a cause.

But why is the libertarian so convinced that people sometimes act freely? Consider an ordinary human action: for instance, raising your hand at a meeting to attract the speaker's attention. If you are attending a lecture and the time comes for questions from the audience, you believe it is within your power to raise your hand and also within your power not to raise it. The choice is yours. Nothing forces you to ask a question, and nothing prevents you from asking one. What could be more obvious? If this description of the situation is accurate, then hard determinism is incorrect, for you are free with regard to the act of raising your hand.

The heart of the libertarian's position is that innumerable examples of this sort are conclusive evidence for free will. Indeed, we normally accept them as such. We assume on most occasions that we are free with regard to our actions, and, moreover, we assume that other persons are free with regard to theirs. If a friend agrees to meet us at six o'clock for dinner and arrives an hour late claiming to have lost track of time, we blame her for her tardiness, since we assume she had it within her power to act otherwise. All she had to do was glance at her watch, and assuming no special circumstances were involved, it was within her power to do so. She was simply negligent and deserves to be blamed, for she could have acted conscientiously. But to believe she could have acted in a way other than she did is to believe she was free.

How do hard determinists respond to such examples? They argue that such situations need to be examined in greater detail. In the case of our friend who arrives an hour late for dinner, we assume she is to blame for her actions, but the hard determinist points out that some motive impelled her to be late. Perhaps she was more interested in finishing her work at the office than in arriving on time for dinner. But why was she more interested in finishing her work than in arriving on time? Perhaps because her parents instilled in her the importance of work but not of promptness. Hard determinists stress that whatever the explanation for her lateness, the motive causing it was stronger than the motive impelling her to arrive on time. She acted as she did because her strongest motive prevailed. Which motive was the strongest, however, was not within her control, and so she was not free.

The hard determinist's reply may seem persuasive. How can I deny that I am invariably caused to act by my strongest motive? But analysis reveals that the thesis is tautological, immune from refutation, but devoid of empirical content. For no matter what example of a human action is presented, a defender of the thesis could argue that the person's action resulted from the strongest motive. If I take a swim, taking a swim must have been my strongest motive. If I decide to forgo the swim and read a book instead, then reading a book must have been my strongest motive. How do we know that my motive to read a book was stronger than my motive to take a swim? Because I read a book and did not take a swim. If this line of argument appears powerful, the illusion will last only so long as we do not ask how we are to identify a person's strongest motive. For the only possible answer appears to be that the strongest motive is the motive that prevails, the motive that causes the person to act. If the strongest motive is the motive causing the person to act, what force is there in the claim that the motive causing a person to act is causing the person to act? No insight into the complexities of human action is obtained by trumpeting such an empty redundancy.

Thus, the hard determinist does not so easily succeed in overturning the examples of free actions offered by the libertarian. But both hard and soft determinists have another argument to offer against the libertarian's position. If the libertarian is correct that free actions are uncaused, why do they occur? Are they inexplicable occurrences? If so, to act freely would be to act in a random, chaotic, unintelligible fashion. Yet it is unreasonable to hold people morally blameworthy for inexplicable actions. If you are driving a car and, to your surprise, you find yourself turning the wheel to the right, we can hardly blame you if an accident occurs, for what happened was beyond your control.

So determinists argue that libertarians are caught in a dilemma. If we are caused to do whatever we do, libertarians assert we are not morally responsible for our actions. Yet if our actions are uncaused and inexplicable, libertarians again must deny our moral responsibility. How then can libertarians claim we ever act responsibly?

To understand the libertarian response, consider the simple act of a man's picking up a telephone receiver. Suppose we want to understand what he is doing and are told he is calling his stockbroker. The man has decided to buy some stock and wishes his broker to place the appropriate order. With this explanation, we now know why this man has picked up the telephone. Although we may be interested in learning more about the man or his choice of stocks, we have a complete explanation of his action, which turns out not to be random, chaotic, or unintelligible. We may not know what, if anything, is causing the man to act, but we do know the reason for the man's action. The libertarian thus replies to the determinist's dilemma by arguing that an action can be uncaused yet understandable, explicable in terms of the agent's intentions or purposes.

Now contrast the libertarian's description of a particular action with a determinist's. Let the action be your moving of your arm to adjust your television set. A determinist claims you were caused to move your arm by your desire to adjust the set and your belief that you could make this adjustment by turning the dials. A libertarian claims you moved your arm in order to adjust the set.

Note that the libertarian explains human actions fundamentally differently from the way in which we explain the movements of rocks or rivers. If we speak of a rock's purpose in falling off a cliff or a river's purpose in flowing south, we do so only metaphorically, for we believe that rocks and rivers have no purposes of their own but are caused to do what they do. Strictly speaking, a rock does not fall in order to hit the ground, and a river does not flow in order to reach the south. But libertarians are speaking not metaphorically but literally when they say that people act in order to achieve their purposes. After all, not even the most complex machine can act as a person does. A machine can break down and fail to operate, but only a human being can protest and stop work on purpose.

Is the libertarian's view correct? I doubt anyone is justified in answering that question with certainty, but if the libertarian is right, human beings are often morally responsible for their actions. They deserve praise when acting admirably and blame when acting reprehensibly. Darrow may have been correct in arguing that Leopold and Loeb were not free agents, but if the libertarian is right, the burden of proof lay with Darrow, for he had to demonstrate that these boys were in that respect unlike the rest of us.

But what if the libertarian is not correct? What if all human actions are caused by antecedent conditions, known or unknown, that ensure their occurrence? Then moral responsibility would vanish, but even so people could be held legally responsible for their actions. Just as we need to be safeguarded against mad dogs, so we need protection from dangerous people. Thus, even if no person were morally responsible, we would still have a legal system, courts, criminals, and prisons. Remember that Darrow's eloquence did not free his clients; indeed, he did not ask that they be freed. Although he did not blame them for their actions, he did not want those actions repeated. To Darrow, Leopold and Loeb were sick men who needed the same care as sick persons with a contagious disease. After all, in a world without freedom, events need not be viewed as agreeable; they should, however, be understood as necessary.

NOTES

1. The following information is found in Irving Stone's *Clarence Darrow for the Defense* (Garden City, N.Y.: Garden City, 1943), pp. 384-91.

2. See source #1.

3. The expressions "hard determinism" and "soft determinism" were coined by William James in his essay "The Dilemma of Determinism," reprinted in *Essays on Faith and Morals* (Cleveland and New York: World, 1962).

4. *The Maxims of La Rochefoucauld,* trans. Louis Kronenberger (New York: Random House, 1959), #379.

5. John Hospers, "What Means This Freedom?" in *Determinism and Freedom in the Age of Modern Science,* ed. Sidney Hook (New York: Collier Books, 1961), p. 138.

6. For a detailed discussion of the philosophical implications of quantum mechanics, see Ernest Nagel's classic work, *The Structure of Science* (New York: Harcourt Brace Jovanovich, 1961), chap. 10.

7. A. S. Eddington, *The Nature of the Physical World* (New York: Macmillan, 1928), p. 342.

8. L. Susan Stebbing, *Philosophy and the Physicists* (New York: Dover, 1958), pp. 51-52.

9. For a defense of libertarianism, see source #3.

10. Arthur Conan Doyle, "The Sign of Four," in *The Complete Sherlock Holmes* (New York: Doubleday, 1953), 1: 118.

2

A Note on Random Choices

The libertarian claim that the doctrine of free will can be true only if determinism is false has often been attacked on the grounds that "what is random is no more free than what is caused."[1] As A. J. Ayer argues:

> Either it is an accident that I choose to act as I do or it is not. If it is an accident, then it is merely a matter of chance that I did not choose otherwise; and if it is merely a matter of chance that I did not choose otherwise, it is surely irrational to hold me morally responsible for choosing as I did. But if it is not an accident that I choose to do one thing rather than another, then presumably there is some causal explanation of my choice; and in that case we are led back to determinism.[2]

I want to call attention to a common phenomenon that has not often been the subject of philosophical concern, but that on examination suggests that a random act, although seemingly uncaused, need be neither accidental nor irresponsible.

We are frequently called on to make a conscious choice from among alternatives that are exactly equal in their degree of attractiveness or unattractiveness: "Pick a card." "Choose a number from 1 to 10." "Park your car in any of the available spaces." "Have a cupcake." Normally none of us has any difficulty making such a random choice. But how do we manage to perform this seemingly simple task? How do we decide which card to pick or which number to choose?

At a party you are offered a bowl of apples. You reach out, choose one, take it in your hand, and eat it. The following conversation ensues:

Host: "Why did you choose that one?"

Guest: "I just picked one, any one. You said, 'Take one.' So I did."

Host: "But why did you take that one? You could have taken any of the others. Don't they look as good? What led you to make that particular choice?"

Guest: "I don't know. I just chose."

At the store you buy one box of corn flakes rather than another, although other boxes appear equally wholesome. In the park you sit on one bench rather than another, although others would serve equally well. While writing a philosophical paper, you choose "Jones" as an example of a proper name, although "Smith" would be equally appropriate. None of these decisions causes you any anguish; they are all made with ease.

Can such random choices be explained? Of course, we can explain a person's deciding to spend money on corn flakes rather than prunes—although some philosophers would say such an explanation must be ultimately causal in nature, while others would say the appropriate explanation would be irreducible in terms of the agent's reasons or purposes. But can we explain a person's decision to buy one particular box of corn flakes rather then another? To assert we can seems no more than an expression of faith; for what evidence supports the claim?

On the one hand, to suppose that each time I am asked to choose a number, a causal explanation of why I picked that number can be provided, is to adhere to determinism, but to extrapolate wildly beyond available empirical data. On the other hand, to assume the choice can be explained in terms of my intentions is to be committed to the view that if we have no reason to prefer one choice to another, then we cannot choose at all. But we have no trouble making a random choice even in circumstances in which we would find it impossible, before or after the fact, to think of any reason to prefer one of the alternatives. Indeed, if we had to postpone such a choice until we could think of a reason to prefer one alternative, our lives would come to a virtual standstill. Should I listen to this record or that one? Should I open this letter or that letter first? Should I walk home this way or that?[3] Without the ability to make random choices, we would be caught in a nightmare of indecision.

I believe we possess the ability to make random choices. We are not condemned to the fate of Buridan's Ass, the animal featured in medieval debate who died while, equally pressed by hunger and thirst, he stood motionless midway between a bundle of hay and a pail of water. What we would do in such a situation is make a random choice. Faced with equally attractive or unattractive alternatives, we are not bludgeoned into inactivity by some need for a decision principle. We simply choose. And to refer to such a random choice as either accidental or irresponsible would surely be misleading.

The British philosopher P. H. Nowell-Smith is thus mistaken when he equates a random occurrence with "an Act of God, or a miracle."[4] He even denies that a random occurrence would be an action at all, but, as we have seen, a random choice is an ordinary sort of action that each of us performs frequently. Indeed, not only are random choices actions, they appear to be good candidates, although not the only ones, for membership in that class of actions we ordinarily designate as "free."

NOTES

1. A. C. MacIntyre, "Determinism," *Mind* 66, no. 261 (January 1957): 30.
2. See source #2.
3. See William James's intriguing discussion of his choice whether to walk home by Divinity Avenue or Oxford Street in "The Dilemma of Determinism," pp. 155–57.
4. P. H. Nowell-Smith, *Ethics* (Baltimore: Penguin, 1954), p. 282.

3

Time, Truth, and Ability
A Puzzle concerning Freedom

Steven M. Cahn and Richard Taylor
("Diodorus Cronus"*)

We shall here be concerned with statements of the form *"M does A at t,"* wherein *M* designates a specific person, *A* a specific action, and *t* a specific time. We shall refer to these as R-statements. Thus, "Someone raised his hand at noon last Tuesday," "Stilpo raised his hand," and "Stilpo did something at noon last Tuesday" are not R-statements; but "Stilpo raised his right hand at noon last Tuesday" is an R-statement.

Let us assume that it sometimes at least makes sense to speak of an agent's being able to render an R-statement true, as distinguished, for example, from simply *discovering* that it is true; and similarly, that it sometimes makes sense to speak of his being able to render an R-statement false. Thus, Stilpo could render it true that he is running at a certain time simply by running at that time, and this would be something quite different from his then merely discovering—observing, noting, etc.—that he is running. He could, of course, render the same statement false in a variety of ways—by standing still, for instance, or by lying down, and so on. We, on the other hand, could not in any similar way render *that* R-statement true. We could only discover by some means that it is true, or that it is false—by looking at Stilpo at the time in question, for instance, to *see* whether he is then running.

---

* Diodorus Cronus was a fourth-century B.C. philosopher of the Megarian School that influenced the early Stoics. Although no Megarian writings are extant, we know that Diodorus defended fatalism, the thesis that logic alone implies that no human being ever acts freely. Perhaps the argument presented here is of a sort he would have favored, and in that spirit the essay was originally published under his name.

Further, let us assume that it sometimes at least makes sense to speak of *asking* someone to render an R-statement true. This, of course, is only an application of the general principle that, in the case of something that someone is able to do, it sometimes makes sense to ask him to do it. To illustrate, suppose that Crates has a bet with Metrocles that Stilpo will pass through the Diomean Gate at noon on the following day (call that day D). Now it surely seems to make sense that Crates might ask, and perhaps even bribe, Stilpo to do just that—to pick just that time to pass through the gate—and thus render true the R-statement "Stilpo passes through the Diomean Gate at noon on day D." That a request or even a bribe would not be out of place in such circumstances suggests both that it sometimes makes sense to speak of an agent's rendering an R-statement true, and that it sometimes makes sense to ask someone—namely, the agent referred to in such a statement—to do it.

Now it is easy enough to state, in general terms, what one has to do in order to render a given R-statement true. He has to do *precisely* what the statement in question says he does, at precisely the time the statement says he does it. The *only* way Stilpo can render it true that he passes through the Diomean Gate at a specific time is to pass through the gate at just that time. Similarly, the *only* way he can render it false is to refrain from passing through the gate at just that time. For someone to be *able* to render an R-statement true, then, consists simply of his being able to do something that is *logically* both necessary and sufficient for the truth of the statement to the effect that he does the thing in question at the time in question. Nothing else suffices, and this will need to be borne in mind.

Finally, we shall assume that, in case one speaks truly in uttering a particular R-statement at a particular time, then one also speaks truly in uttering the same R-statement at any other time. If, for example, one were to speak truly in saying that Stilpo is running at noon on a given Tuesday, one would also speak truly if one said the same thing again a week later, or at any other time. This, of course, is only an application of the orthodox assumption that complete statements, or the utterances of them, are not converted from true to false, or from false to true, just by the passage of time. There are some statements, to be sure, like "Stilpo is running," that are not, as they stand, true every time they are uttered, since it is not always the case that Stilpo is running. But that is not an R-statement. If one adds to it an explicit reference to the time at which Stilpo is alleged to be running—say, at noon on a given Tuesday—then it becomes an R-statement. It also thereby becomes a statement that is true every time it is uttered, in case it is true at all, for one can on Wednesday still say truly that Stilpo was running at noon on the day preceding, in case he was, even though

Stilpo may in the meantime have stopped running. This assumption, it should be noted, does not imply that *truth* and *falsity* are "properties" of "propositions" that might be gained or lost through the passage of time, nor does it imply that they are not. Some say that they are, others that they are not, and still others that such a notion is meaningless to begin with; but we, at least, prefer to take no stand on that somewhat metaphysical point.

Now let us consider three times, t_1, t_2, and t_3, all of them being *past*, and t_1 being earlier than t_2, which is earlier than t_3. Consider, then, the R-statement (S):

Stilpo walks through the Diomean Gate at t_2

and assume that statement, tenselessly expressed so as to avoid ambiguity in what follows, to be *true*. What we want to consider is: which, if any, of the following, which are not R-statements but are statements concerning Stilpo's abilities, are also true?

1. Stilpo was at t_3 able to render S false.

2. Stilpo was at t_3 able to render S true.

3. Silpo was at t_1 able to render S false.

4. Stilpo was at t_1 able to render S true.

5. Stilpo was at t_2 able to render S false.

6. Stilpo was at t_2 able to render S true.

Now the first of these is quite evidently false. If, as assumed, it is true that Stilpo was walking through the gate at t_2, then there is absolutely nothing he (or anyone) was able to do at t_3 that could render the statement false. It was, it would seem natural to say, by that time, *too late* for that. He was perhaps able at t_3 to refrain from passing through the gate again, of course, and he was perhaps able to regret that he had walked through it, to wish he had not, and so on, but his doing any of those things would not have the least tendency to render S false. Or we might think that he was at t_3, able to find conclusive evidence that he had *not* walked through the gate; but that is not in fact anything that he was able to do, for he had already walked through the gate, and hence there was at t_3 no conclusive evidence to the contrary that he could possibly find.

The second statement seems also to be clearly false. S is, we said, true. So if anyone were, at t_2 (or any other time), to assert S, he would then be speaking truly. No sense, then, can be made of Stilpo's subsequently undertaking to *render* it true. It is in this case not just too late for him to do anything about that; it is also superfluous. What he wants to do—to render S true—he has already done.

The truth or falsity of the third statement is not quite so obvious, but it certainly appears to be false, and for the same kind of reason that (1) is false. That is, if it is true that Stilpo was walking through the gate at t_2, then it is difficult to see what he (or anyone) was able to do at t_1 that might render *S* false. (Analogous to the foregoing remarks, one might say, though it seems less natural to do so, that it was at that time *"too early"* for that.) Stilpo was perhaps able at t_1, to refrain from then and there walking through the gate, to be sure, and perhaps he did then refrain, but that does not in the least affect the truth of S, which says nothing about what he was doing at t_1. Or we might think that he was, at t_1, able to find some conclusive evidence or indication that he was not going to walk through the gate at t_2, but that again is not anything he was able to do; for he did walk through the gate at t_2, and hence there was at t_1 no conclusive indication to the contrary that he could possibly have found.

To have been able at t_1 to render S false, Stilpo would have to have been able at t_1 to do something that would have been *logically* sufficient for the falsity of S. But nothing that he might have done at t_1 has the least logical relevance to the truth or falsity of S. We might, to be sure, suppose that he was able at t_1 firmly to resolve not to walk through the gate at t_2, but his making such a resolve would not be sufficient for the falsity of S. In fact, it has no logical relevance to S, which is, in any case, true.

Perhaps, then, Stilpo was able at t_1 to do something that would have been causally or physically sufficient for the falsity of S—to commit suicide, for example. Actually, this suggestion is irrelevant, for we have said that one renders an R-statement false only by doing something that is *logically* sufficient for its falsity. But even if it were relevant, it would not do. What is behind this suggestion is, obviously, that it is physically impossible that Stilpo should be walking through the gate at t_2 in case he killed himself at t_1. This is of course true—but if so, then it is *also* true that it was physically impossible that Stilpo should have killed himself at t_1 in case he was walking through the gate at t_2—and we have said from the start that he *was* then walking through the gate. The only conclusion, then, is that (3) is false, even on this enlarged and still irrelevant conception of what is involved in rendering an R-statement false.

The fourth statement appears false for reasons similar to those given for the falsity of (2). Namely, that S is true, or such that if anyone had uttered S at t_1 he would then have spoken truly. No sense, then, can be made of Stilpo's being able to do something at t_1 to *render* it true.

There would have been no point, for example, in his passing through the gate at t_1, for that would certainly not by itself render it true that he was still passing through the gate at t_2. Similarly, it would not have been enough for him simply to have resolved at t_1 to pass through the gate at t_2, for that would have been entirely compatible with the falsity of S, which in any case neither says nor implies anything whatsoever about Stilpo's resolutions. Men do not always act upon their resolves anyway, and there is, in any case, no logical necessity in their doing so. Besides, anything Stilpo might do at t_1 would be superfluous, even if it were not pointless, for one can no more render true a statement that is true than he can render hard a piece of clay that is hard. He can only verify that it *is* true, and this, we have seen, is something quite different. Anything Stilpo does at t_1, or is able to do then, is entirely wasted.

The fifth statement likewise appears to be false. If, as we are assuming, it is true that Stilpo was passing through the gate at t_2, then it is quite impossible to see what he might be able then and there to do, in addition to passing through the gate, which would, if done, render that statement false. Indeed, it is logically impossible that there should be any such supplementary action, for no matter what it was, it would have no tendency to render S false. Even if Stilpo were to declare most gravely and emphatically that he was not passing through the gate, this would not render it false that he was—it would only render him a liar. A condition logically sufficient for the truth of S—namely, Stilpo's walking through the gate—already obtains at t_2 and can by no means be conjoined with another condition logically sufficient for the falsity of that statement. Now Stilpo might, to be sure, suddenly *stop* walking through the gate, which we can for now assume that he is able to do, but this would not in the least alter the truth of S. On the contrary, unless he were walking through the gate at t_2, and unless, accordingly, S were true, he could not then *stop* walking. His ceasing to walk would only render it false that he was walking shortly after t_2; and this is hardly inconsistent with S.

The sixth statement, finally, appears, unlike the others, to be quite evidently true in one seemingly trivial sense, but nonsensical in another. The sense in which it is true is simply this: that if S is true, then it follows that Stilpo was able to be walking through the gate at t_2, that being, in fact, precisely what he was doing. It is not clear, however, what sense can be attached to his being able to render true what is true, just as it is not clear what sense could be made of someone's rendering hard some clay that is already hard.

If a piece of clay is hard, we cannot sensibly ask anyone to *render* it hard. Similarly, if Stilpo is walking through the gate, we cannot sensibly ask him to render it true that he is walking through the gate. We cannot sensibly ask him to *be* walking through the gate, for he is already doing that, and our request would be otiose and absurd, like asking a man who is sitting to be sitting, or one who is talking to be talking. We cannot ask him to *continue* walking through the gate, for that would not be to the point. It would, if done, only render it true that he was still walking through the gate at some time *after* t_2, which is not what we are after. And obviously, there is nothing else we could ask him to do which is anywhere to the point.

The only conclusion we can draw is that, of the six statements before us, those that make clear sense are all false, and the only one that is true makes only trivial and dubious sense. More generally, we can say that while it might, as we assumed at the beginning, make sense to speak of being able to render an R-statement true, or being able to render such a statement false, men can in fact only render true those R-statements that are true and can only render false those that are false, and that these latter two conceptions themselves make very dubious sense.

3A

On Dating Abilities and Truths

Arthur W. Collins

Diodorus Cronus has it that I am unable to render any R-statements true except those that are true anyway, and this is at best a degenerate sense of "ability," an ability to do things already done. This is a bleak conclusion rendered bleaker by the reflection that if I have any abilities whatever, then I surely have the ability to render R-statements true since R-statements are just those that describe people doing things.

An R-statement is a statement "of the form 'M does A at t,' wherein M designates a specific person, A a specific action, and t a specific time." The following, "Stilpo walks through the Diomean gate at t_2," is the R-statement to which Diodorus Cronus devotes most attention and which he does, and we shall, designate S. "To render a statement true" is an odd expression, and I think Diodorus Cronus employs it primarily because it enables him to reach pessimistic conclusions concerning human abilities. No doubt, however, we can understand rendering an R-statement true: we would understand someone who proposed to pay Stilpo in order to get him to render S true. The pessimistic conclusion is reached by supposing that Stilpo does in fact walk through the Diomean gate at t_2, thus that S is true, and then asking for t_2, and for t_1 and t_3, times earlier and later than t_2 respectively, whether Stilpo had at each of these times the ability to render S true (or false). It turns out that Stilpo cannot have the ability to render S either true or false at t_3, "too late"; or at t_1, "too early"; and at t_2 he cannot have the ability to render S false because by hypothesis Stilpo is walking through the gate at t_2, the very thing that makes S true; and therefore Stilpo is reduced to the ability at t_2 to render S true at t_2, an ability he cannot fail to exercise, since S is true anyway, and an ability the imputation of which Diodorus Cronus himself finds either "trivial" or "nonsensical."

Is it Stilpo's ability in the trivial or nonsensical sense on which we would rely in proposing to bribe him? Plainly a lot has gone wrong here. We are led astray in part by the unstated premise: if Stilpo has the ability to render S true, then he must have that ability at, before or after t_2. I think the pattern here is: if the butler could have dropped the arsenic into the teapot, then he must have been able to do it before entering, while he was in the drawing room, or after he left. This natural analogy is out of place here. S says that Stilpo does something at t_2. What he does is exactly what he is required to do in order to render S true. It follows, and not at all paradoxically, that Stilpo cannot be said to render S true at times other than t_2. This is no limitation on Stilpo's abilities. Strictly, it does not make sense to speak of being able to render S true at any time at all, much less at specific times before and after t_2. Rendering S true requires, and only requires, walking through the gate at t_2. If it made sense to speak of being able to render S true before or after t_2, it would make sense to speak of walking through the gate at t_2, before, or after t_2. Just as there is no sense in talking of walking through the gate at t_2, at times other than t_2, so there is no sense in speaking of walking through the gate at t_2, at t_2. And this latter is what rendering S true at t_2 would have to mean. Compare

I had the ability to walk through the gate yesterday but today I do not, because I have sprained my ankle,

and

I had the ability to walk through the gate yesterday but today I do not, because it is not yesterday.

The latter can only be a joke based on a redundant dating: I only had the ability to walk through the gate yesterday, yesterday. Aside from this perverse redundancy, the concept of ability is strained here. As a consequence of the passage of time *per se* I only lose opportunities, not abilities. I lose an ability only if more than time passes, if, for example, health, strength, or coordination pass too.

By the same token, it is perverse to say that before t_2 it is too early for Stilpo to be able to render S true, and after t_2, too late. I think that there is no natural way of using "render true" here, but if we chose, we could, incurring no logical burden, say that Stilpo is able to render S true, even speaking after t_2 and supposing S false. This would be the right thing to say if we wanted to emphasize Stilpo's abilities in contrast with his opportunities for exercising them. Stilpo himself might say at t_3, "Of course I am able to render S true, and I would too, if only it were t_2 (again)."

Having seen how the dating of abilities operates in Diodorus Cronus's pessimistic argument, let us now consider his dating of truths. In defense of the claim that Stilpo was not able to render S true at t_3, we find,

> S is, we said, true. So if anyone were, at t_2 (or any other time), to assert S, he would then be speaking truly. No sense, then, can be made of Stilpo's subsequently undertaking to *render* it true. It is in this case not only too late for him to do anything about that; it is also superfluous. What he wants to do—to render S true—he has already done.

Now why is it too late? Because Stilpo has already walked through the gate and because S is already true. There are two different senses in which it is asserted to be too late for Stilpo to render S true here. First, t_3 is too late for rendering S true because t_2 has already passed. (Our actions cannot affect the past.) Second, t_3 is too late for rendering S true because S is already true at t_3. (There is no sense in undertaking to render true what is true already.) To be sure of the difference here, notice the following divergence: in the former sense, t_1 is not too late for rendering S true, for t_2 is still to come. In the latter sense, however, t_1 is too late just as t_3 is. For even at t_1 S is already true, as S is at any time whatever, supposing it to be true at all. Since at any t, S is already true, it is always too late to do anything about S. Again, a redundant dating obfuscates. The opportunity for rendering S true that Stilpo might be supposed to have is eliminated by dating not only the action, at t_2, but also dating the truth of S. The truth of S only becomes relevant to Stilpo's ability by making it too late for him to act, too late because S is already true: S was true before, in particular at t_2. There is no rendering true left to be done. "S is, if true, always already true," would be at best a mystifying way of saying that truth is timeless, but in this context it amounts to assimilating all time to past time. The idea of being already true is being used as if it were like "already eaten." "I can't eat it, it's already eaten." But, in contrast, nothing has *happened* yet and Stilpo need feel no inhibition, although it is "already" true that Stilpo will walk through the gate tomorrow.

Paradoxical conclusions here depend to a considerable extent on taking too literally "to render true." This is a flimsy metaphor, flimsy because in Diodorus Cronus's sense, to render a statement true is not to do anything to a statement, not, for example, to tamper with its truth value. Compare "Render that statement true," and "Render that statement in German." In another possible sense, perhaps less flimsy, one could even render a false statement true, say, by negating it or changing a word. In this sense, it would be obvious that the impossibility of rendering true a statement "already" true has nothing to do with time.

3B

Et Tu, Diodorus Cronus?

Yehoshua Bar-Hillel

In a recent article Diodorus Cronus tried to show, among other amazing results, that the statement (made by someone at time t_3)

(1) Stilpo was able at t_1 to render S false

(where S is the statement "Stilpo walks through the Diomean Gate at t_2," and where t_1 is earlier than t_2, and t_2 earlier than t_3) must be false, if Stilpo was indeed walking at t_2 through that fateful gate.

Unfortunately, Diodorus Cronus (DC) arrived at this truly astonishing conclusion only after a whole series of fallacies, some of which will be exposed here.

S has the form

(2) M does A at t,

"wherein M designates a specific person, A a specific action, and t a specific time." DC calls statements of this form R-statements. R-statements are context independent, so that the statement "M does A at t" is true if and only if M does A at t. S, in particular, is true if and only if Stilpo walks through the Diomean Gate at t_2. In what seems to be an innocuous paraphrase, one may then also say that Stilpo, by walking through the Diomean Gate at t_2, *renders* S true, and this is then also clearly the only way in which Stilpo can render S true.

Having said, in effect, that much, DC continues: "For someone to be able to render an R-statement true, consists simply of his being able to do something which is *logically* both necessary and sufficient for the truth of the statement to the effect that he does the thing in question

39

at the time in question." Very benevolently interpreted, this is an extra-ordinarily cumbersome paraphrase of the truism, "For someone to be able, at t_1, to render, at t_2, an R-statement (with time-reference t_2) true, consists of his being able, at t_1, to do something, at t_2, that renders this R-statement true." However, by consistently omitting, by inadvertency or negligence, the time adverbs, DC manages to fall very quickly into the trap he created for himself by his elliptical formulation. He clearly replaces in his mind the truism by "For someone to be able, at t_1, to render an R-statement (with time-reference t_2) true consists in his being able, at t_1, to do something, at t_1(!), that renders this R-statement true," and the road to hell is wide open. This replacement may well have happened in three easy stages: "For Stilpo to be able, at t_1, to render S true consists in his being able, at t_1, to do something, at t_2, that renders S true" (truism) → "For Stilpo to be able, at t_1, to render S true consists in his being able, at t_1, to do something that renders S true" (ellipsis of a truism which—if one knows how to read it!—is still equivalent to that truism) → "For Stilpo to be able, at t_1, to render S true" consists in his being able "to do something, at t_1, that renders S true" (so long as the second occurrence of "at t_1" is enclosed by commas, this can still be interpreted, with extreme benevolence, as equivalent to the original truism) → "For Stilpo to be able, at t_1, to render S true consists in his being able to do something at t_1 that renders S true." (Omitting the commas now makes the benevolent interpretation psychologically well-nigh impossible.) Though DC himself had insisted that for Stilpo to render S true, the only thing for him to do is to walk, at t_2, through the Diomean Gate, DC now has to face the self-created problem of determining an act Stilpo can perform at t_1 to the same effect. He therefore first arrives at the curious formulation quoted above and then takes two pages to demolish it. By falling now into the same trap from the opposite direction (if I may be allowed to use this wild simile), DC arrives at the conclusion that (1) cannot possibly be true.

But on his way to this conclusion, he manages to commit a further fallacy. By a seemingly utterly innocent linguistic transformation, DC manages to turn the triviality, "Stilpo is unable, at any time prior to t_2, to do *something that renders* S false" (since the only way in which Stilpo can do this is by not performing, at t_2, the act A) into the fatalistic monstrosity, "Stilpo is unable, at any time prior to t_2, to do *something to render* S false." Not even committing suicide will do, as DC is very careful to expound. The simple truth is, of course, that there are innumerable acts that Stilpo can perform, prior to t_2, to render S false—committing suicide at t_1 only being a particularly radical one, while also certainly being particularly effective—just as there are innumerable acts that Stilpo can perform, at t_1, to render S true, though, by the definition stipulated by DC himself (and perhaps also by common usage), none of these acts renders S false (or true, respectively).

Let us summarize: If someone advocates an atemporal use of "is true" (and I for one should applaud, particularly in logico-philosophical contexts), he should refrain from using, in the same context, the phrase "to render a statement true," since this phrase almost automatically implies that what has been rendered true was not so before. If, nevertheless, anyone wants to use this phrase, *e.g.*, by saying that M. by performing act A at time t, renders the statement "M performs act A at time t" true, he has no right to find fault with the expression "M renders an R-statement true," since, for certain kinds of statements, this means neither more nor less than that M performs the act described in this statement. Nor should he find any fault with the expression "M is able at t_1 to render true, at t_2, the statement 'M performs A at t_2' " (where t_1 is prior to t_2). He may even, at his own risk, omit "at t_2" from this expression, but it is then up to him to beware of interpreting the resulting ellipsis as "M is able at t_1 to render ture, at t_1, the statement 'M performs A at t_2.' " Nor is there anything faulty with "M is able, at t_1, to do something, at t_1, in order to render true the statement 'M performs A at t_2.' " He must of course distinguish carefully between this faultless formulation and the nonsensical formulation of the preceding sentence, and this in spite of the fact that in order to render the statement "M performs A at t" true, M has to do something at t, namely to perform A. If someone, be he a reincarnated Diodorus Cronus, manages to confuse all these things, then we should not be surprised if he arrives at very strange results indeed. Fatalism remains in need of stronger arguments.

3C

An Unanswered Paradox

Steven M. Cahn

A paradox purports to prove that seemingly absurd conclusions can be logically drawn from seemingly innocuous premises. The challenge of a paradoxical argument is thus not met merely by noting that its conclusions are absurd or by providing another argument that uses different premises to reach opposing conclusions. Nevertheless, these strategies are employed by Arthur Collins and Yehoshua Bar-Hillel in their attacks on the paradox presented by Diodorus Cronus.

Diodorus is concerned with "R-statements" of the form "M does A at t," wherein M designates a specific person, A a specific action, and t a specific time. He then introduces the notion of "rendering an R-statement true" and notes that for someone to render a given R-statement true, he "has to do *precisely* what the statement in question says he does, at *precisely* the time the statement says he does it." Diodorus also assumes that "in case one speaks truly in uttering a particular R-statement at a particular time, then one also speaks truly in uttering the same R-statement at any other time."

Diodorus considers the R-statement (S) "Stilpo walks through the Diomean Gate at t_2," t_2 being some specific past time. We are asked to assume that S is true and then consider when, if ever, Stilpo has it within his power to render S true, and when, if ever, Stilpo has it within his power to render S false. Diodorus finds that (1) at t_3, any specific time after t_2, it is "too late" for Stilpo to render S true or false; (2) at t_1, any specific time before t_2, it is "too early" for Stilpo to render S true or false; and (3) at t_2 Stilpo is, by hypothesis, already walking through the gate, and so he cannot render S false and he can only render S true in a "trivial and dubious sense."

The paradoxical conclusion of Diodorus's argument is thus that "people can in fact only render true those R-statements that are true, and can only render false those that are false, and that these latter two conceptions themselves make very dubious sense." This conclusion is surely radical, for it amounts to the claim that the only actions we can perform are those we do perform.

Arthur Collins claims that Diodorus's paradoxical conclusion results from two errors: (1) his dating of abilities, and (2) his dating of truths. Collins claims first that "we are led astray by the unstated premise: if Stilpo has the ability to render S true then he must have the ability at, before, or after t_2." Collins claims this premise is misleading because "just as there is no sense in talking of walking through the gate at t_2, at times other than t_2, so there is no sense in speaking of walking through the gate at t_2, at t_2. And this latter is what rendering S true at t_2 would have to mean." Collins admits that Stilpo renders S true and that, therefore, he has the ability to render S true, but claims that Stilpo does not have this ability at any particular time.

This claim, however, is untenable. If you have the ability to perform a specific action (and that is what it means to be able to render a given R-statement true), then you must have that ability at a specific time. If there is no time at which you have the ability to perform a specific action, then you cannot perform that action. Collins admits that Stilpo has the ability to render S true at t_2 and that he, in fact, exercises that ability at t_2. But you cannot exercise an ability you do not possess. Therefore, at t_2 Stilpo has the ability to render S true.

In the face of this obvious objection to his position, Collins alters his view and argues that although Stilpo *has* the ability at t_2 to render S true at t_2, to say so is a "perverse redundancy." But, as Collins himself notes, "if I have any abilities whatever then I surely have the ability to render R-statements true since R-statements are just those that describe people doing things." That one can render an R-statement true *only* in a "redundant" sense is one of the conclusions of Diodorus's paradox. To refer to this conclusion as "perverse" is not to answer the paradox but to acknowledge it.

Collins then notes that there are two senses in which Stilpo cannot render S true at t_3: "First, t_3 is too late for rendering S true because t_2 has already passed. (Our actions cannot affect the past.) Second, t_3 is too late for rendering S true because S is already true at t_3. (There is no sense in undertaking to render true what is true already.)" In this second sense, Collins notes, it is too late at t_1, *or at any time,* to render S true, for S is already true at any given time.

The obvious conclusion is that for at least two good reasons Stilpo cannot render S true at t_3. But Collins claims that since Diodorus's argument implies that "it is always too late to do anything about S," the argument is clearly mistaken since "it amounts to assimilating all time to past time."

Admittedly, Diodorus's paradox leads to the conclusion that it is "always too late" to do anything about S. But to point out the implausibility of this conclusion is again merely to acknowledge the paradox. Diodorus has not assimilated all time to past time. He has assumed that if one speaks truly in uttering an R-statement at some future time, then one also speaks truly in uttering the same R-statement at some past time. To point out that the past and future have this feature in common is not to equate them any more than pointing out that all humans are mortal and all pigs are mortal is to equate humans and pigs.

Yehoshua Bar-Hillel claims that Diodorus's paradoxical conclusion is due to his equating the innocuous statement "For someone to be able, at t_1, to render S true consists in his being able, at t_1, to do something at t_2 that renders S true" with the erroneous statement "For someone to be able, at t_1, to render S true consists in his being able, at t_1, to do something at t_1 that renders S true." This move supposedly leads Diodorus "to turn the triviality, 'Stilpo is unable, at any time prior to t_2, to do *something that renders* S false' . . . into the fatalistic monstrosity, 'Stilpo is unable, at any time prior to t_2, to do *something to render* S false.' " This "monstrosity," Bar-Hillel claims, is clearly false, since "there are innumerable acts that Stilpo can perform, prior to t_2, to render S false . . . though, by the definition stipulated by Diodorus Cronus himself (and perhaps also by common usage), none of these acts render S false."

It is all well and good for Bar-Hillel to assure us that if we adopt his definition of "render false" then Stilpo has it within his power at t_1 to render S false; but according to Diodorus's definition of "render false" Stilpo does not; and as Bar-Hillel himself concedes, Diodorus's definition reflects ordinary usage.

To render an R-statement false one must avoid doing what the R-statement says one does. The R-statement S says that Stilpo walks through the Diomean Gate at t_2. For Stilpo to render S false then, he must *not* walk through the Diomean Gate at t_2. Diodorus's question is: When does Stilpo have the ability to render S false, i.e, when does he have the ability not to walk through the Diomean Gate at t_2? The seemingly obvious answer is that he has this ability at t_2, but as Diodorus points out, at t_2 Stilpo is, by hypothesis, already walking through the gate and so does not then have the ability not to walk through the gate. Perhaps then Stilpo has this ability at t_1. But at t_1 it is in one sense, as Bar-Hillel agrees, too early to render S false and in another sense, as Collins points out, too late to render S false. So we reach the paradoxical conclusion of Diodorus's argument: Stilpo never has the ability to render S false.

How does Bar-Hillel propose to avoid this conclusion? He argues that although Stilpo cannot at t_1 do something *that* renders S false, viz., not walk through the gate at t_2, it is obvious he can do something *to* render S false, e.g., commit suicide at t_1. Since he can do something *to* render S false, it follows that at some time he can do something *that* renders S false, and thus, Bar-Hillel claims, Diodorus's conclusion is shown to be erroneous.

Bar-Hillel, however, has merely presented another argument to show that the conclusion of Diodorus's paradox is false. The challenge, however, is to demonstrate why Diodorus's argument itself is unsound. Diodorus claims that at no time does Stilpo have the ability to do something *that* renders S false. Since he never has that ability, it follows that he never has the ability to do something *to* render S false. Diodorus's argument can be refuted only by pointing out a specific time at which Stilpo has the ability to do something *that* renders S false. Bar-Hillel has not succeeded at this task, nor is it easy to see how anyone could. Therein lies the force of Diodorus's paradox.[1]

NOTE

1. This paradox can be viewed as a reductio ad absurdum of the assumption that every true statement has always been true. For a full-scale attack on this supposition, see my *Fate, Logic, and Time* (1967; rpt., Atascadero, Calif.: Ridgeview, 1982).

Part Two

God

4

Does God Exist?

A theist believes God exists. An atheist believes God does not exist. An agnostic believes the available evidence is insufficient to decide the matter. Which of these positions is the most reasonable?

The first step in answering this question is to determine what is to be meant by the term "God." The word has been used in various ways, ranging from the Greek concept of the Olympian gods to John Dewey's concept of the "active relation between ideal and actual."[1] Let us adopt the more usual view, common to many religious believers, that "God" refers to an all-good, all-powerful, eternal Creator of the world. The question then is whether a Being of that description exists.

Throughout the centuries various arguments have been put forth to prove the existence of God. One of the best known is the cosmological argument, which rests on the assumption that everything that exists is caused to exist by something else. For example, a house is caused to exist by its builder, and rain is caused to exist by certain meteorological conditions. But if everything that exists is caused to exist by something else, then the world itself must be caused to exist by something else. This "something else" is God.[2]

Although the cosmological argument may have an initial plausibility, a major difficulty with it is that if everything that exists is caused to exist by something else, then the cause of the world's existence is itself caused to exist by something else. In that case the cause of the world's existence is not God, for God is an all-powerful, eternal Being who does not depend on anything else for His existence. A defender of the cosmological argument might try to surmount this difficulty by claiming that the cause of the world's existence is not caused to exist by something else but is self-caused, that is, the reason for its existence lies within itself. However, if we admit the possibility that something is self-caused, the argument crumbles, for if the cause of the world's existence can be self-caused, why cannot the world be self-caused? In that case no need would arise to postulate an external cause of the world's existence, for this cause was postulated only to explain the existence of the world, and if the reason for the world's existence lies within itself, then no further explanation for its existence is required.

In a last-ditch attempt to salvage the cosmological argument, a defender might argue simply that something must have started everything, and that this "something" is God. Yet even if we grant the claim that something must have started everything (and this claim could be questioned by appealing to the mathematical notion of an infinite series), it hardly follows that the "something" is all-good, all-powerful, or eternal. Perhaps the first cause is evil, or perhaps it ceased to exist after a brief life. No such possibilities are excluded by the cosmological argument, and so the argument is not successful.

A second classic proof for the existence of God is the ontological argument. This argument, which was defended by such eminent philosophers as Descartes, Spinoza, and Leibniz, makes no appeal to empirical evidence but purports to demonstrate that the very nature of God implies His existence.[3]

The argument has various versions, but its basic structure remains the same. God is defined as a Being who possesses every perfection. It is more perfect to exist than not to exist. Thus, since God possesses every perfection, and existence is a perfection, God must exist.

Although this argument has been ably defended, it is open to the devastating criticism, stated succinctly by Kant, that existence is not an attribute. In other words, the definition of anything remains the same regardless of whether that thing exists. For example, the definition of a unicorn would not be altered if we discovered a living unicorn, just as our definition of a whooping crane would not be altered if whooping cranes became extinct. In short, whether unicorns or whooping cranes exist does not affect the meaning of the terms "unicorn" and "whopping crane."

To clarify the point, imagine a ferocious tiger. Now imagine a ferocious tiger that exists. What more is there to imagine in the second case than in the first? Our concept of a ferocious tiger remains the same whether or not any ferocious tigers exist.

Applying this insight to the ontological argument, we can see why the argument is unsound. Since the definition of a thing remains the same whether or not the thing exists, it follows that the definition of "God" remains the same whether or not He exists. Thus, existence cannot be part of the definition of God. God may be defined as a Being who possesses all perfections, but existence is not a perfection, since existence is no attribute at all. To assert that something exists is not to ascribe a perfection to the thing but to state a fact about the world. What we mean by the term "God" is one matter; whether God exists is another. The ontological argument confuses the two matters and thereby goes awry.

Even if the ontological argument were sound, its abstruseness would impede its popular appeal. The next argument we shall consider, the teleological argument, is easily understood and highly plausible.

Defenders of this argument invite us to look around at the world in which we live. They point out that it possesses a highly ordered structure, just like an extraordinarily complex machine. Each part of the machine is adjusted to all the other parts with wondrous precision, and the more we investigate the working of the world, the more we are amazed at its intricate patterns. For instance, the human eye, which so many of us take for granted, is a mechanism of such enormous complexity that its design is breathtaking. But doesn't a design require a designer? The magnificent order of our world cannot be a result of pure chance, but must be the work of a Supreme Mind that is responsible for the order. That Supreme Mind is God.

Although this argument has persuasive power, it suffers from several fatal flaws. Note first that any world would exhibit some order. Were you at random to drop ten coins on the floor they would exhibit an order. An order, therefore, does not imply an orderer. If we use the term "design" to mean " a consciously established order," then a design implies a designer. But the crucial question is whether our world exhibits mere order or design.

If the world were just like a machine, as the teleological argument assumes, then since a machine has a design and a designer, so would the world. Is it obvious that the world is just like a machine? In his classic book *Dialogues Concerning Natural Religion*, Hume argues that our experience is too limited for us to accept such an analogy. Hume notes that although the world bears some slight resemblance to a machine, the world is also similar to an animal in that "[a] continual circulation of matter in it produces no disorder; a continual waste in every part is incessantly repaired; the closest sympathy is perceived throughout the entire system; and each part or member, in performing its proper offices, operates both to its own preservation and to that of the whole."[4] Hume further points out that the world is somewhat like a vegetable, since neither has sense organs or brains, although both exhibit life and movement. But whereas any machine requires a designer of the machine, animals and vegetables come into being very differently from machines. Hume does not intend to prove that the world came into being as an animal or vegetable does, but he wishes to show that the world is not sufficiently like an animal, a vegetable, or a machine to permit us to draw reasonable conclusions from such weak analogies. Lacking such an analogy, the teleological argument collapses, for we are left with no reason to believe that the world exhibits a design rather than an order.

However, as Hume pointed out, even if we were to accept the analogy the argument fails. Let us grant, he says, that like effects prove like causes. If the world is like a machine, the cause of the world is like the cause of a machine. Machines are usually built after many trials; so the world was probably built after many trials. Machines are usually built by many workers; so the world was probably built by many deities. Those who build machines are often inexperienced, careless, or foolish; so the gods, too, may be inexperienced, careless, or foolish. As Hume suggests, perhaps this world "was only the first rude essay of some infant deity, who afterwards abandoned it, ashamed of his lame performance." Or perhaps "it is the work only of some dependent, inferior deity, and is the object of derision to his superiors." It might even be "the production of old age and dotage in some superannuated deity, and ever since his death has run on at adventures, from the first impulse and active force which it received from him." By suggesting such possibilities Hume demonstrates that even if we grant an analogy between the world and a machine and agree that the world was designed as a machine is designed, we are not committed to believing that the world's design is due to one all-good, all-powerful, eternal Designer.

What, then, is the source of order? The world may have gone through innumerable structural changes until a stable pattern was reached, and the existence of such complex phenomena as the human eye may be a result of the process of natural selection whereby forms of life that cannot adjust to their environment disappear, while forms of life that can adjust survive. Such an explanation of the world's order not only requires no recourse to the hypothesis of a Supreme Designer, but has also been confirmed by biological research since the time of Darwin.

This reply to the teleological argument may appear conclusive, but some of the argument's proponents have responded that the existence of God is not implied merely by the order in the world but, as Berkeley put it, by the "surprising magnificence, beauty, and perfection" of that order.[5] In other words, such a perfect world as the one in which we live could not possibly be either the work of an inferior deity or the outcome of impersonal natural processes. Only an all-good, all-powerful Creator could have produced such a flawless masterpiece.

This defense of the teleological argument, however, rests on the highly dubious premise that the world is perfect. In fact, the evidence against this view is overwhelming. Just consider droughts, floods, famines, hurricanes, tornadoes, earthquakes, and the innumerable varieties of disease that plague us. Is it a perfect world in which babies are born deformed, small children are bitten by rats, and young people die from leukemia? And what of the evils people cause each other? The savageries of war, the indignities of slavery, and the torments of injustice and treachery extend far beyond the limits of our imagination. In short, the human condition is of such a nature that, as Hume observed, "The man of a delicate, refined temper, by being so much more alive than the rest of the world, is only so much more unhappy."

We need not go on long enumerating the ills of our world, before the teleological argument loses its last vestige of plausibility. Indeed, human misery poses a serious problem even for the theist who abandons the teleological argument; for why should we suffer evils if, as theists affirm, our world was created by an all-good, all-powerful Being? An all-good Being would do everything possible to abolish evil. An all-powerful Being would be able to abolish evil. So if an all-good, all-powerful Being existed, evil would not. But evil exists. Therefore, it would seem that an all-good, all-powerful Being doesn't.

Until this point, those who do not believe in the existence of God have been on the defensive, attempting to refute arguments that purport to prove the existence of God. Now it is those who believe in the existence of God who are on the defensive, for they must reply to the challenge known as "the problem of evil": How is it possible for evil to exist in a world created by an all-good, all-powerful Being? As Epicurus put it, is God willing to prevent evil, but not able? Then He is impotent. Is He able, but not willing? Then He is malevolent. Is He both able and willing? Whence then is evil?

Numerous attempts have been made to provide a theodicy, a defense of God's goodness in the face of evil. The most promising approach begins by distinguishing two types of evil: moral and physical. Moral evils are those for which human beings are responsible, evils such as murder, theft, and oppression. Physical evils are those for which human beings are not responsible, evils resulting from such natural phenomena as typhoons, locusts, and viruses.

Moral evils are justified by the hypothesis that God has given us free will, the power to do both good and evil. Which we do is up to us. God could have ensured that we always act rightly, but if He had done so, He would have had to take away our free will, since a person who is forced to act rightly is not free. God is all-powerful, but He cannot perform an act whose description is contradictory, for such an act is no act at all. For example, since to speak of a square circle makes no sense, it is no limitation on God's ability that He cannot draw a square circle. Similarly, it is no limitation on God's ability that he cannot create free persons who must always do what is right, for, by definition, a free person is one who does not always have to do what is right. God, therefore, had to choose between creating beings who always did what was right and creating beings who were free to do both right and wrong. In His wisdom He chose the latter, since it constituted the greater good. Thus, all moral evils are justified as necessary concomitants of the best possible world God could have created, namely, a world in which persons have free will.

Physical evils may be justified in one of two ways. According to one approach, physical evils provide the opportunity for human beings to develop moral attributes. If the world were a paradise without hardships and dangers, it would not be possible for people to acquire the strength of character that results from standing firm in the face of difficulties. According to this view, the world was not intended as a pleasure palace but as an arena in which human beings grapple with their weaknesses and in so doing acquire the strength that will serve them well in some future life. An alternative approach to physical evils explains them as resulting from the free actions of the Devil, whose freedom is a greater good than would be his performing right actions involuntarily.

Does this two-pronged reply to the problem of evil succeed in blunting its force? To some extent. Those who pose the problem claim that it is logically impossible that an all-good, all-powerful Being would permit the existence of evil. As we have seen, it is possible under certain circumstances that an all-good, all-powerful Being would have to allow evil to exist, for if the evil were a necessary component of the best possible world, then a Being who wished to bring about the best possible world would have to utilize whatever evil was necessary to the achievement of that goal. Thus, no contradiction is involved in asserting that a world containing evil was created by an all-good, all-powerful Being.

Yet is there any reason to believe that we live in the best possible world and that all the evils are logically necessary? I would answer this question as Bertrand Russell did. He was once asked what his reaction would be if, after death, he found himself in the presence of God. Russell replied that this possibility was extremely unlikely. His questioner persisted, "What would you say to God if, contrary to all you believe, you were to find yourself in His presence?" Russell replied, "I would tell Him He should have given us more evidence."

Those who believe in the existence of God despite the lack of such evidence may possibly be rewarded in a hereafter for their display of tenacity. But no less likely is the possibility that those who do not believe in the existence of God will be rewarded for their adherence to rationality.

NOTES

1. John Dewey, *A Common Faith* (New Haven: Yale, 1934), p. 51.
2. For a defense of the cosmological arguments, see source #4.
3. For a defense of the ontological argument, see source #5.
4. See source #6.
5. George Berkeley, *A Treatise Concerning the Principles of Human Knowledge* (New York: Liberal Arts, 1957), p. 97.

5

Cacodaemony
A Puzzle about God

For many centuries philosophers have grappled with what has come to be known as "the problem of evil." Succinctly stated, the problem is: Could a world containing evil have been created by an omnipotent, omniscient, omnibenevolent being?

Considering the vast literature devoted to this issue, it is perhaps surprising that there has been little discussion of an analogous issue that might appropriately be referred to as "the problem of goodness." Succinctly stated, the problem is: Could a world containing goodness have been created by an omnipotent, omniscient, omnimalevolent being?

This chapter has two aims. The first is to provide a reasonable solution to the problem of goodness. Traditional theists find the hypothesis of creation by a benevolent deity far more plausible than the hypothesis of creation by a malevolent demon, and they may, therefore, believe the problem of goodness to be irrelevant to their commitments. My second aim is to demonstrate that this belief is mistaken.

Before proceeding, it would be well to restate the problem of goodness in more formal fashion.

(1) Assume that there exists an omnipotent, omniscient, omnimalevolent Demon who created the world.

(2) If the Demon exists, there would be no goodness in the world.

(3) But there is goodness in the world.

(4) Therefore, the Demon does not exist.

Since the conclusion of the argument follows from the premises, those who wish to deny the conclusion must deny one of the premises. No demonist (the analogue to a theist) would question premise (1), so in

55

order to avoid the conclusion of the argument, an attack would have to be launched against either premise (2) or premise (3).

What if a demonist attempted to deny premise (3)? Suppose it were claimed that goodness is an illusion, that there is nothing of this sort in the world. Would this move solve the problem?

I think not, for such a claim is either patently false or else involves a distortion of the usual meaning of the term "good." If the word is being used in its ordinary sense, then acts of kindness, expressions of love, and creations of beauty are good. Since obviously such things do occur, there is goodness in the world.

If one insists that such things are not good, then the expression "good" is being used eccentrically, and the claim loses its import. It is as though one were to defend the view that all persons are pigs by defining "persons" as "omnivorous hoofed mammals of the family Suidae." Such "persons" are not persons at all. Similarly, a supposedly omnimalevolent Demon who cherishes personal affection and great works of art is certainly not omnimalevolent and is probably no demon.

Premise (3) can thus be adequately defended, and if demonists are to find an answer to the problem of goodness, they must attack premise (2). How can there be goodness in the world if the creator is omnimalevolent and possesses the power and the knowledge to carry out evil intentions? To paraphrase Epicurus, is the Demon willing to prevent good, but not able? Then he is impotent. Is he able, but not willing? Then he is benevolent. Is he both able and willing? Whence then is goodness?

At this point it may appear to be a hopeless task to justify the Demon's malevolence in the face of the fact of goodness, an enterprise appropriately referred to as "cacodaemony" (the analogue of theodicy). But sophisticated demonists would realize there is much play left in their position. They would not agree that just because there is goodness in the world, it could not have been created by the omnimalevolent Demon. After all, isn't it possible that whatever goodness exists is logically necessary for this to be the most evil world that the Demon could have created? Not even an omnipotent being can contravene the laws of logic, for such a task is senseless, and so if each and every good in the world were logically tied to the achievement of the greatest evil, the omnimalevolent Demon, in order to bring about the greatest possible evil, would have been forced to allow the existence of these goods.

The demonist thus rejects premise (2) of the argument and argues instead for premise (2′):

(2′) If the Demon exists, then every good in the world is logically necessary in order for this to be most evil world that the Demon could have created.

Now if we substitute premise (2′) for premise (2) in the original argument, that argument falls apart, for the conclusion no longer follows from the premises. One can affirm without contradiction both the existence of an omnipotent, omniscient, omnimalevolent Demon who created the world and the existence of goodness in the world, so long as one also affirms that every good is logically necessary in order for this to be the most evil world the Demon could have created. Demonists thus appear to have escaped the force of the problem of goodness.

Things are not so simple, for now demonists are faced by yet another argument that challenges their belief.

(1) Assume that there exists an omnipotent, omniscient, omnimalevolent Demon who created the world.

(2) If the Demon exists, then every good in the world is logically necessary in order for this to be the most evil world that the Demon could have created.

(3) But there is strong reason to believe that not every good in the world is logically necessary in order for this to be the most evil world the Demon could have created.

(4) Therefore, there is strong reason to believe that the Demon does not exist.

This second argument, unlike the first, does not claim that belief in the Demon is illogical; rather, it claims that such belief is unreasonable. Beautiful mountain ranges, spectacular sunsets, the plays of Shakespeare, and the quartets of Beethoven do not seem in any way to enhance the evils of the world. Acts of altruism, generosity, and kindheartedness certainly do not appear to increase the world's sinister aspects. In other words, this argument challenges demonists to suggest plausible reasons for their view that every good in the world makes possible a world containing even greater evils than would be possible without these goods.

The reader will, of course, have observed that thus far the discussion of the problem of goodness exactly parallels traditional discussions of the problem of evil; all the arguments and counterarguments that have been presented are equally applicable *mutatis mutandis* to either problem. What may be somewhat surprising, however, is that classic arguments in defense of the view that every evil in the world makes possible a world containing even greater goods can be exactly paralleled by arguments in defense of the view that every good in the world makes possible a world containing even greater evils. To illustrate this point, I shall proceed to construct a cacodaemony along the identical lines of the well-known theodicy constructed by John Hick.[1]

We begin by dividing all goods into two sorts: moral goods and physical goods. Moral goods are those human beings do for each other; physical goods are those to be found in the human environment.

The justification of moral goods proceeds by logically tying the existence of such goods to human free will. Surely, performing a bad act freely is more evil than performing such an act involuntarily. The Demon could have ensured that human beings would always perform bad actions, but such actions would not have been free, since the Demon would have ensured their occurrence.[2] Because the actions would not have been free, their performance would not have produced the greatest possible evil, since greater evil can be produced by free persons than by unfree ones. The Demon, therefore, had to provide human beings with freedom, so that they might perform their bad actions voluntarily, thus maximizing evil.

As for the justification of physical goods, we should not suppose that the Demon's purpose in creating the world was to construct a mere chamber of tortures in which the inhabitants would be forced to endure a succession of unrelieved pains. The world can be viewed, instead, as a place of "soul-breaking," in which free human beings, by grappling with the exhausting tasks and challenges of their existence in a common environment, can thereby have their spirits broken and their wills-to-live destroyed.

This conception of the world can be supported by what, following Hick, we may call "the method of negative cacodaemony." Suppose, contrary to fact, that this world were so arranged that nothing could ever go well. No one could help anyone else, no one could perform a courageous act, no one could complete any worthwhile project. Presumably, such a world could be created through innumerable acts of the Demon that would continually alter the laws of nature as necessary.

It is evident that our present ethical concepts would be useless in such a world, for "ought" implies "can," and if no good acts could be performed, it would follow that none ought to be performed. The whole notion of "evil" would seem to drop out, for to understand and recognize evils we must have some idea of goods. Consequently, such a world, however efficiently it might promote pains, would be ill-adapted for the development of the worst qualities of the human personality.

At this point, this cacodaemony, just as Hick's theodicy, points forward in two ways to the subject of life after death. First, although there are many striking instances of evil being brought forth from good through a person's reaction to it (witness the pollution of beautiful lakes or the slashing of great paintings), still there are many other cases in which the opposite has happened. Therefore, it would seem that any demonic purpose of soul-breaking at work in earthly history must continue beyond this life if it is ever to achieve more than a very partial and fragmentary success.

Second, if we ask whether the business of soul-breaking is so evil as to nullify all the goodness to be found in human life, the demonist's answer must be in terms of a future evil great enough to justify all that has happened on the way to it.

Have we now provided an adequate cacodaemony? It is, I think, just as strong as Hick's theodicy, but neither in my view is successful. Nor do I see any plausible ways of strengthening either one. What reason is there to believe in an afterlife of any particular sort? What evidence is there that the world would be either better without the beauty of a sunset or worse without the horrors of bubonic plague? What evidence is there either that the free will of a Socrates achieved greater evil than would have been achieved by his performing wrong actions involuntarily or that the free will of a Hitler achieved greater good than would have been achieved by his performing right actions involuntarily?

The hypothesis that all the good in the world is a necessary part of this worst of all possible worlds is not contradictory; nevertheless, it is highly unlikely. Similarly, the hypothesis that all the evil in the world is a necessary part of this best of all possible worlds is not contradictory; but it, too, is highly unlikely. If this is neither the worst of all possible worlds nor the best of all possible worlds, then it could not have been created by either an all-powerful, all-evil demon or an all-powerful, all-good diety. Thus, although the problem of goodness and the problem of evil do not show either demonism or theism to be impossible views, they show them both to be highly improbable. If demonists or theists can produce any other evidence in favor of their positions, they may be able to increase the plausibility of their views, but unless they can produce such evidence, the reasonable conclusion appears to be that neither the Demon nor God exists.[3]

NOTES

1. See source #7.
2. I here assume without argument that freedom and determinism are incompatible. Those who believe they are not face more difficulty in resolving the problem of goodness (or the problem of evil).
3. Regarding the claim that evidence is irrelevant to theism, see source #8.

6

God without Religion

Philosophical proofs for the existence of God have a long and distinguished history. Almost every major Western philosopher has been seriously concerned with defending or refuting such proofs, and many contemporary philosophers continue to exhibit keen interest in them.

We might expect that religious believers would be vitally interested in discussions of this subject, that when a proof of God's existence is presented and eloquently defended, believers would be most enthusiastic, and that when a proof is attacked and persuasively refuted, believers would be seriously disappointed. Such is not the case. Religious believers seem remarkably uninterested in philosophical proofs for the existence of God. They seem to consider discussion of such proofs a sort of intellectual game, without relevance to religious belief or activity. Soren Kierkegaard, for example, wrote, "Whoever therefore attempts to demonstrate the existence of God . . . [is] an excellent subject for a comedy of the higher lunacy!"[1] The same essential point was made in a less flamboyant manner by one of this century's foremost contributors to Jewish thought Mordecai M. Kaplan, who remarked that the "immense amount of mental effort to prove the existence of God . . . was in vain, since unbelievers seldom become believers as a result of logical arguments."[2]

In what follows I seek to explain why religious believers have so little interest in philosophical proofs for the existence of God. I believe this lack of interest is reasonable, and that whatever the philosophical relevance of the proofs, they have little or no relevance to religion.

Suppose we assume, contrary to what most philosophers believe, that the ontological, cosmological, and teleological proofs are all sound. Let us grant the existence of the most perfect conceivable Being, a Being who is all-good and is the designer and creator of the universe. What implications can be drawn from this fact that would be of relevance to human life? In other words, what difference would it make in our lives if God existed?[3]

60

Some people would feel more secure in the knowledge that the universe had been planned by an all-good Being. Others would feel insecure, realizing the extent to which their very existence depended on the will of this Being. In any case, most people, either out of fear or respect, would wish to act in accordance with the divine moral code.

Note, however, that the proofs for the existence of God provide us with no hint whatever as to what we ought to do so as to please or obey Him. We may affirm that God is all-good and yet have no way of knowing the highest moral standards. We may be sure only that whatever these standards are, God always acts in accordance with them. Some might assume that God has implanted within us the correct moral standards, but this assumption seems doubtful in view of the wide variance in the standards to which people adhere. Which of these, if any, is correct is disputable, and no appeal to a proof for the existence of God casts the least light on the matter.

For example, assuming God exists, is murder immoral? Some would argue that since God created humanity, it is immoral to murder, since it is immoral to destroy what God in His infinite wisdom and goodness has created. This argument, however, fails on several grounds. First, if God created humanity, He also created germs, viruses, and disease-carrying rats. Does it follow from the assumption that God created these things that they ought not be eliminated? Second, if God arranged for us to live, He also arranged for us to die. Does it follow that by committing murder we are assisting the work of God? Third, God provided us with the mental and physical capacity to commit murder. Does it follow that He wishes us to exercise this ability? Clearly, the attempt to deduce moral precepts from God's existence is but another case of trying to do what Hume long ago pointed out to be logically impossible, viz., the deduction of normative judgments from factual premises. No such deduction is valid, and, therefore, any moral principle is consistent with the existence of God.

Since the proofs for God's existence afford no means of distinguishing good from evil, no person can be sure of how to obey God. We may hope that our actions are in accord with His standards, but no test is available to check. Some seemingly good people suffer ills, while some seemingly evil people achieve happiness. Perhaps in a future life these apparent injustices are rectified, but we have no way of ascertaining which people are ultimately rewarded and which ultimately punished.

Those who believe in God's existence typically have been eager to learn His will, and historically they tended to rely on those individuals who claimed to possess such insight. Diviners, seers, and priests were given positions of great influence. Competition among them was severe, for no one was sure which oracle to believe. Assuming that God made no effort to reveal His will by granting any of these oracles truly superhuman powers (though each oracle claimed such powers), no one could distinguish the genuine prophet from the fraud.

In any case, prophets died, and all their supposedly superhuman powers disappeared with them. What was required for practical purposes was a permanent record of God's will as revealed to His special prophet. This need was eventually met by the writing of holy books in which God's will was permanently revealed.

But there were many such books. Which was to be believed? Which moral code was to be followed? Which prayers were to be recited? Which rituals were to be performed? Proofs for the existence of God are silent on these crucial matters.

The only direct avenue to the divine will is to undergo a personal experience in which one senses the presence of God and apprehends which of the putative holy books is the genuine one. But to avoid being deceived, to be sure it is God whose presence is being experienced and whose will is being apprehended, one must undergo a self-validating experience that carries its own guarantee of infallibility.

Those who undergo what they believe to be such experiences are convinced which holy book is genuine, and, consequently, which actions, prayers, and rituals God approves. Notice they have thereby assured themselves of the existence of God, for unless they have actually experienced God's presence, they cannot be certain that the message they have received is true. They, therefore, have no further need for a proof of the existence of God.

Those who do not themselves undergo what they believe to be self-validating experiences may accept the validity of another's. They thereby accept the holy book that has been revealed as genuine as well as God's existence, since unless they believed this other person had experienced the presence of God, they would not accept this individual's view as to which is the genuine book.

But suppose one does not accept any person's claim to a self-validating experience. Perhaps one doubts the logical possibility of such an experience[4] or is uncertain who, if anyone, has undergone it. In that case, one is thrown back on the resources of reason, coming to share Sidney Hook's view that "Whether an actual angel speaks to me in my beatific vision or whether I only dreamed he spoke, the truth of what he says can only be tested in the same way as I test what my neighbor says to me. For even my neighbor may claim to be a messenger of the Lord."[5] But then adherence to a supernatural religion is unjustified.

So is it surprising that religious believers are uninterested in philosophical proofs for the existence of God? Not at all. Those who believe in God-based or personal experience are certain not only that God exists but also what He wills. To them a philosophical proof for the existence of God is useless. If the proof is sound, it merely confirms what they already know on the stronger evidence of a self-validating experience. If the proof is unsound, it casts no doubt on such an experience.

Who then is concerned with philosophical proofs for the existence of God? First are those who suppose that if such proofs are shown to be unsuccessful, religion is undermined. This belief, I have argued, is erroneous.

A second group interested in the proofs are those who believe that if they are invalid, our moral commitments are undermined. This claim underlies the so-called moral argument for the existence of God, according to which only those who believe in the existence of God have reason to commit themselves to moral values. This argument is unsound, for belief in the existence of God is compatible with any and all positions on moral issues. Only if one can learn the will of God can moral implications be derived from His existence.

The third group interested in the proofs are those who discuss them purely for the sake of clarifying the philosophical issues involved. Such analysis is commendable but should not be used as arguments for and against religion. Religious belief and activity may be rationally attacked or defended, but to refute philosophical proofs for the existence of God is not to attack religion, and to support philosophical proofs for the existence of God is not to defend religion.

NOTES

1. *Philosophical Fragments*, tr. by David F. Swenson (Princeton: Princeton University Press, 1936), chap. 3, p. 34.

2. *The Future of the American Jew* (New York: Macmillan, 1948), p. 171.

3. I am not concerned here with the implications of God's omniscience and omnipotence for free will. These divine attributes can be understood so as not to entail the loss of freedom, and for the purposes of this chapter I shall assume such an interpretation.

4. Such doubts are forcefully expressed in C. B. Martin's *Religious Belief* (Ithaca, N.Y.: Cornell University Press, 1959), chap. 5.

5. Sidney Hook, *The Quest for Being* (New York: St. Martin's, 1961), pp. 130-31.

7

Religion without God

Most of us suppose that all religions are akin to the one we happen to know best. But this assumption can be misleading. For example, many Christians believe that all religions place heavy emphasis on an afterlife, although the central concern of Judaism is life in this world, not the next. Similarly, many Christians and Jews are convinced that a person who is religious must affirm the existence of a supernatural God. They are surprised to learn that religions such as Jainism or Theravada Buddhism deny the existence of a Supreme Creator of the world.

How can there be a nonsupernatural religion? To numerous theists as well as atheists, the concept appears contradictory. I propose to show, however, that nothing in the theory or practice of religion—not ritual, not prayer, not metaphysical belief, not moral commitment—necessitates a commitment to traditional theism. In other words, one may be religious while rejecting supernaturalism.

Let us begin with the concept of ritual. A ritual is a prescribed symbolic action. In the case of religion, the ritual is prescribed by the religious organization, and the act symbolizes some aspect of religious belief. Those who find the beliefs of supernaturalistic religion unreasonable or the activities of the organization unacceptable may come to consider any ritual irrational. Yet although particular rituals may be based on irrational beliefs, nothing is inherently irrational about ritual.

Consider the simple act of two people shaking hands when they meet. This act is a ritual, prescribed by our society and symbolic of the individuals' mutual respect. The act is in no way irrational. Of course, if people shook hands in order to ward off evil demons, then shaking hands would be irrational. But that is not the reason people shake hands. The ritual has no connection with God or demons but indicates the attitude one person has toward another.

It might be assumed that the ritual of handshaking escapes irrationality only because the ritual is not prescribed by any specific organization and is not part of an elaborate ceremony. To see that this assumption is false, consider the graduation ceremony at a college. The graduates and faculty all wear peculiar hats and robes, and the participants stand and sit at appropriate times. However, the ceremony is not at all irrational. Indeed, the rites of graduation day, far from being irrational, are symbolic of commitment to the process of education and the life of reason.

At first glance, rituals may seem a comparatively insignificant feature of life; yet they are a pervasive and treasured aspect of human experience. Who would want to eliminate the festivities associated with holidays such as Independence Day or Thanksgiving? What would college football be without songs, cheers, flags, and the innumerable other symbolic features surrounding the game? Those who disdain popular rituals typically proceed to establish their own distinctive ones, ranging from characteristic habits of dress to the use of drugs, symbolizing a rejection of traditional mores.

Religious persons, like all others, search for an appropriate means of emphasizing their commitment to a group or its values. Rituals provide such a means. Granted, supernaturalistic religion has often infused its rituals with superstition, but nonreligious rituals can be equally as superstitious as religious ones. For instance, most Americans view the Fourth of July as an occasion on which they can express pride in their country's heritage. With this purpose in mind, the holiday is one of great significance. However, if the singing of the fourth verse of "The Star-Spangled Banner" four times on the Fourth of July were thought to protect our country against future disasters, then the original meaning of the holiday would soon be lost in a maze of superstition.

A naturalistic (i.e., nonsupernaturalistic) religion need not utilize ritual in a superstitious manner, for such a religion does not employ rituals in order to please a benevolent deity or to appease an angry one. Rather, naturalistic religion views rituals, as one of its exponents has put it, as "the enhancement of life through the dramatization of great ideals."[1] If a group places great stress on justice or freedom, why should it not utilize ritual in order to emphasize these goals? Such a use of ritual serves to solidify the group and to strengthen its devotion to its expressed purposes. These are strengthened all the more if the ritual in question has the force of tradition, having been performed by many generations who have belonged to the same group and have struggled to achieve the same goals. Ritual so conceived is not a form of superstition; rather, it is a reasonable means of strengthening religious commitment and is as useful to naturalistic religion as it is to supernaturalistic religion.

Having considered the role of ritual in a naturalistic religion, let us next turn to the concept of prayer. It might be thought that naturalistic religion could have no use for prayer, since prayer is supposedly addressed to a supernatural being, and proponents of naturalistic religion do not believe in the existence of such a being. But this objection oversimplifies the concept of prayer, focusing attention on one type while neglecting an equally important but different sort.

Supernaturalistic religion makes extensive use of petitionary prayer, prayer that petitions a supernatural being for various favors. These may range all the way from the personal happiness of the petitioner to the general welfare of all society. Since petitionary prayer rests on the assumption that a supernatural being exists, such prayer clearly has no place in a naturalistic religion.

However, not all prayers are prayers of petition. Some prayers are prayers of meditation. These are not directed to any supernatural being and are not requests for the granting of favors. Rather, these prayers provide the opportunity for persons to rethink their ultimate commitments and rededicate themselves to live up to their ideals. Such prayers may take the form of silent devotion or may involve oral repetition of certain central texts. Just as Americans repeat the Pledge of Allegiance and reread the Gettysbury Address, so adherents of naturalistic religion repeat the statements of their ideals and reread the documents that embody their traditional beliefs.

It is true that supernaturalistic religions, to the extent that they utilize prayers of meditation, tend to treat these prayers irrationally, by supposing that if the prayers are not uttered a precise number of times under certain specified conditions, then the prayers lose all value. Yet prayer need not be viewed in this way. Rather, as the British biologist Julian Huxley wrote, prayer "permits the bringing before the mind of a world of thought which in most people must inevitably be absent during the occupatons of ordinary life: . . . it is the means by which the mind may fix itself upon this or that noble or beautiful or awe-inspiring idea, and so grow to it and come to realize it more fully.[2]

Such a use of prayer may be enhanced by song, instrumental music, and various types of symbolism. These elements, fused together, provide the means for adherents of naturalistic religion to engage in religious services akin to those engaged in by adherents of supernaturalistic religion. The difference between the two services is that those who attend the latter come to relate themselves to God, while those who attend the former come to relate themselves to their fellow human beings and to the world in which we live.

We have so far discussed how ritual and prayer can be utilized in naturalistic religion, but to adopt a religious perspective also involves metaphysical beliefs and moral commitments. Can these be maintained without recourse to supernaturalism?

If we use the term "metaphysics" in its usual sense, referring to the systematic study of the most basic features of existence, then a metaphysical system may be either supernaturalistic or naturalistic. The views of Plato, Descartes, and Leibniz are representative of a supernaturalistic theory; the views of Aristotle, Spinoza, and Dewey are representative of a naturalistic theory.

Spinoza's *Ethics*, for example, one of the greatest metaphysical works ever written, explicitly rejects the view that any being exists apart from Nature itself. Spinoza identifies God with Nature as a whole and urges that the good life consists in coming to understand Nature. In his words, "our salvation, or blessedness, or freedom consists in a constant and eternal love toward God."[3] Spinoza's concept of God, however, is explicitly not the supernaturalistic concept of God, and Spinoza's metaphysical system thus exemplifies not only a naturalistic metaphysics, but also the possibility of reinterpreting the concept of God within a naturalistic framework.

Can those who do not believe in a supernaturalistic God commit themselves to moral principles, or is the acceptance of moral principles dependent on acceptance of supernaturalism? Some have assumed that those who reject a supernaturalistic God are necessarily immoral, for their denial of the existence of such a God leaves them free to act without fear of Divine punishment. This assumption, however, is seriously in error.

The refutation of the view that morality must rest upon belief in a supernatural God was provided more than two thousand years ago by Socrates in Plato's *Euthyphro*.[4] Socrates asked the following question: Are actions right because God says they are right, or does God say actions are right because they are right? This question is not a verbal trick; on the contrary, it poses a serious dilemma for those who believe in a supernatural deity. Socrates was inquiring whether actions are right due to God's fiat or whether God is Himself subject to moral standards. If actions are right due to God's command, then anything God commands is right, even if He should command torture or murder. If one accepts this view, then it makes no sense to say that God Himself is good, for since the good is whatever God commands, to say that God commands rightly is simply to say that He commands as He commands, which is a tautology. This approach makes a mockery of morality, for might does not make right, even if the might is the infinite might of God. To act morally is not to act out of fear of punishment; it is not to act as one is commanded to act. Rather, it is to act as one ought to act. How one ought to act is not dependent on anyone's power, even if the power be Divine.

Thus actions are not right because God commands them; on the contrary, God commands them because they are right. What is right is independent of what God commands, for what He commands must conform with an independent standard in order to be right. Since one could act in accordance with this independent standard without believing in the existence of a supernatural God, it follows that morality does not rest upon supernaturalism. Consequently, naturalists can be highly moral (as well as immoral) persons, and supernaturalists can be highly immoral (as well as moral) persons. This conclusion should come as no surprise to anyone who has contrasted the life of Buddha, an atheist, with the life of the monk Torquemada, organizer of the Spanish Inquisition.

We have now seen that naturalistic religion is a genuine possibility, since reasonable individuals may perform rituals, utter prayers, accept metaphysical beliefs, and commit themselves to moral principles without believing in supernaturalism. Indeed, one can even do so while maintaining allegiance to Christianity or Judaism. Consider, for example, those Christians who accept the "Death of God"[5] or those Jews who adhere to Reconstructionist Judaism.[6]

Such options are philosophically respectable. Whether to choose any of them is for each reader to decide.

NOTES

1. Jack Cohen, *The Case for Religious Naturalism* (New York: Reconstructionist Press, 1958), p. 150.

2. Julian Huxley, *Religion Without Revelation* (New York: New American Library, 1957), p. 141.

3. Spinoza, *Ethics*, ed. James Gutmann (New York: Hafner, 1957), pt 5, prop. 36, note.

4. See source #9.

5. See John H.T. Robinson, *Honest to God* (Philadelphia: Westminster, 1963).

6. See Mordecai M. Kaplan, *Judaism as a Civilization* (New York: Schocken, 1967).

Part Three
Goodness

8

Morality and Rationality

We live in an age beset by a mood of moral uncertainty. Even ethical principles held tenaciously by previous generations have been called into question. In the face of such challenge, how can moral judgments be rationally justified?

Some have supposed that just as there are scientific truths, so there are moral truths. Just as it is true that water freezes at 0° C and boils at 100° C, so it is true that murder is wrong and honesty right. Laws of nature are true at any time and at any place; similarly, it is said, moral laws are true for any person in any situation. As the truth of factual statements can be tested by an appeal to scientific method, so the truth of ethical judgments can be tested by an appeal to that moral sense possessed by every human being. Faced with an instance of unmitigated cruelty, for example, do we not all acknowledge that it is evil? As the Scottish philosopher Thomas Reid argued: "Every man in his senses believes his eyes, his ears, and his other senses. . . . And he has the same reason, and indeed, is under the same necessity of believing the clear and unbiased dictates of his conscience, with regard to what is honorable and what is base."[1]

But, suppose the dictates of one person's conscience should differ from those of another. One conscience may dictate that capital punishment is inhumane, while another dictates that such retribution is sometimes appropriate. How can we reasonably decide between these incompatible views? It might be argued that one conscience is biased while the other is not. How are we to know which is which? Each of us could appeal to our own conscience, but perhaps ours is biased. We could take a poll and determine the majority's opinion, but the majority may possess biased consciences. We could distinguish a biased from an unbiased conscience by determining whether capital punishment is immoral, but this procedure would be circular. So the appeal to conscience alone does not provide a way to reason about ethics.

Faced with this apparent dead end, some have argued that moral judgments are neither true nor false, but merely expressions of individual preference. On this view, to defend the morality of capital punishment is only to indicate your preference for it; to assert its immorality is merely to express your feelings against it. As it is fruitless to argue whether red or blue is a better color, so it is futile to discuss whether capital punishment is moral or immoral. Both views are tenable, since reason cannot decide between opposing moral sentiments.

This theory suffers from a major flaw, for we do sometimes convince others that they are holding incorrect moral positions, and we do so by presenting arguments in behalf of our view. We do not debate whether red or blue is a better color, for such a dispute would be pointless. But we do argue about whether capital punishment ought to be abolished, and people on occasion change their views as a result of such discussion. So it would seem that moral judgments are not mere emotional outpourings but are either true or false. Yet we have already recognized the difficulties with this theory.

To break through the impasse, let us consider how the concepts of "good" and "bad" function in a nonmoral context. Then we can seek to apply these findings in the moral sphere.

Suppose, for instance, you participate in a softball league and are told by your friend Ferguson that a fellow named Benson is an excellent ball player. You invite him to join your team, but he turns out to be woefully inadequate. He drops balls thrown to him, lets grounders go through his legs, and regularly strikes out. You tell Ferguson that his recommendation of Benson was a mistake. Either Ferguson does not know what a good player is or someone has misled him about Benson's capabilities, for obviously, Benson is not a good player.

Notice that when you say Benson is not a good player you are not merely expressing your emotions or appealing to the dictates of your conscience. Rather, you are indicating that he hits poorly and fields inadequately. To defend your view, you would point to Benson's batting and fielding averages. Although disagreement may persist as to whether a player who bats .250 and commits a number of errors is good, surely an individual who bats .100 and commits errors in every game is not good, while one who bats .400 and hardly ever commits an error is good. In other words, the distinction between good and bad players is clear, despite the possibility of borderline cases.

It would make no sense to claim that although Benson hits and fields well, he still lacks one attribute essential to an all-star, namely, goodness, because if he could hit and field well, then he would be a good player. Goodness is not an attribute apart from these abilities, but a shorthand way of referring to them.

Suppose when you tell Ferguson that Benson is not a good player,

Ferguson replies that you are mistaken, for he has watched Benson in practice and has seen him hit the ball over the fence and field flawlessly. How would you respond? You would not say that since value judgments are mere matters of preference, you can think of no reasonable way to decide whether Benson plays well. Nor would you appeal to Ferguson's conscience to try to persuade him. You would explain that sometimes an individual performs well in practice but not in league games. In support of this view you might indicate that in the first ten games of the season, Benson batted .075 and committed twenty-two errors. Ferguson would no doubt be amazed at these statistics but would surely agree that although Benson is impressive in practice, he does not play well under game conditions. Here then is an example of a disagreement about a value judgment resolved by a reasoned examination of factual evidence.

What if Ferguson is not so cooperative? Suppose he refuses to agree that a good player hits and fields well but claims instead that the essence of a good player is to look good, that is, to be attractive, graceful, and appealing to the opposite sex. Since Benson fits this description, he is, according to Ferguson, a good player.

The disagreement may now appear irresolvable, but your criteria for a good player are not arbitrary, and you need to explain why you have chosen them. You play softball to win, and a good player helps achieve that goal. The key to winning is hitting and fielding well, not looking good. Hence you judge a good player on performance, not appearance.

If Ferguson plays to win and believes players who look good are victorious more often than those who hit and field well, then your disagreement is resolvable by an appeal to the record books. But if Ferguson plays to gain popularity, then players who look good may be of greater value to him than those who hit and field well. In that case, the resolution of your disagreement would depend on determining whether your disparate goals are a means to some common end. If so, your disagreement would be resolvable by deciding the factual question about the most effective means of achieving that end. If you had no common end, you would have no reasonable way to reach agreement.

Do value terms function in moral contexts as they do in nonmoral ones? Let us next consider an ethical disagreement and observe whether the pattern of argument is analogous.

Suppose Thorndike and Williams, citizens of the country of Freedonia, become embroiled in a dispute over whether Freedonia ought to attack the country of Sylvania.[2] Thorndike argues that Freedonia ought to bombard Sylvania, for its leaders are committed to the conquest of Freedonia and will soon possess the necessary armaments to carry out this conquest. Williams, however, claims that it would be immoral for

Freedonia to initiate the horrors of war, and that the nation has sufficient resources to repel any attack.

The first step in the analysis is to determine whether the disputants disagree about the most effective means of achieving shared ends. If the two both believe that Freedonia should defend its independence and cause no unnecessary suffering, while they are not of one mind about whether Sylvania would or could undertake a successful offensive, then their judgment as to whether Freedonia should launch a preemptive strike—a matter of the most serious moral moment—depends on factual considerations, including the size of Sylvania's forces and the plans of its leaders.

Such a reduction of a moral disagreement to a factual one does not promise a quick and easy solution, for many factual disputes are enormously complex. But at least the analysis makes clear that the dispute is not merely a matter of personal preference or individual conscience, but is in principle resolvable by reason.

Suppose Thorndike and Williams do not agree that Freedonia should retain its sovereignty. While Thorndike supposes that a good policy could help ensure the country's independence, Williams considers Freedonia's government illegitimate, since it denies citizens basic freedoms. He, therefore, considers a good policy to be one that would contribute to the triumph of Sylvania.

So the two differ about the nature of a good policy. Do they disagree about the most effective means of achieving shared ends or about the ends themselves? If we assume the two agree that a government that guarantees freedom of speech, freedom of assembly, freedom of the press, and freedom of religion is morally preferable to one that does not, then their ethical disagreement as to whether Freedonia should go to war is reducible to the factual disagreement about whether the citizens of Freedonia lack basic freedoms possessed by the citizens of Sylvania. If the political situation is as Thorndike supposes, then his views on initiating war would be accepted by Wiliams; if the political situation is as Williams supposes, his views would be accepted by Thorndike. The nature of the political situation, however, is not a matter of personal preference or individual conscience but a factual issue open to rational resolution through empirical investigation.

Imagine, however, that Thorndike and Williams do not agree that a government is good if it guarantees freedom of speech, freedom of assembly, freedom of the press, and freedom of religion. Thorndike holds this view, but Williams believes a government ought to guarantee other freedoms, for instance, freedom from military service. Can this disagreement be decided rationally? The pattern of possible resolution is clear. If they agree on the ends for which governments are established, then their disagreement as to what sort of governmental authority is morally justifiable can be reduced to a factual disagreement as to how these ends can most effectively be achieved. If the two share no further ends, their disagreement will not yield to rational resolution.

What of the popular saying that "ends do not justify means"? This adage may serve to remind us that means as well as ends require justification, yet taken literally the adage is false, for the only possible justification for one's means are one's ends.

Consider "Speedy," a man whose only aim in life is to win a particular automobile race. Assume that as the race nears its end, an accident occurs. Cars overturn and drivers are left sprawled on the track directly in the path of Speedy's oncoming car. If he slows down to avoid running over them, he will lose the race. Faced with the choice between killing the injured drivers or slowing down and losing the race, Speedy decides to continue ahead at full speed.

His decision is surely regrettable, but not because ends do not justify means. Speedy's end, if accepted, would justify his means. He aims to win the race, and if we agreed that all other aims should be subordinated to this one, then we would accept the need for any action Speedy took to win the race. But we do not share his end, since we place the value of preserving human life far above the value of winning a race. Thus, we deplore his action.

Contrast Speedy with a physician who advises a patient to undergo a series of painful injections in order to avoid a fatal disease. The physician expresses regret that the injections are necessary but justifies them by the end they will achieve. Indeed, how else could they be justified? These two examples differ only in that in the physician's case the end is appropriate, while in Speedy's case it is not. In both cases the end, if accepted, would justify the means.

How likely is it that we will agree about our overarching ends? The chances are greater than might be supposed, for each person desires happiness and relies on the cooperation of others in order to achieve it. As a contemporary philosopher has emphasized:

> We cannot conceive of a being like ourselves, who desire his own happiness, and the happiness of his family and friends (if not the happiness of the whole of mankind), who needs the company of his fellows, who is easily injured by their hostile acts, and who cannot continue to exist unless they cooperate with him—we cannot conceive of a being such as this approving of promise-breaking, dishonesty, and deliberate callousness to the interests of others.[3]

In short, our mutual dependence leads to our approving principles that facilitate cooperation.

Those who reject such rules, who favor persecution and cruelty for its own sake, hardly qualify as persons. In any case, we must guard ourselves against such beings, for they are threats to us all. No political leaders have ever come to power by promising that they seek to bring about a golden age characterized by increased hatred, violence, and oppression. Even the worst of dictators must mouth the usual moral sentiments in order to gain popular support. Thus disputants in a moral disagreement are likely to agree at some point on broad aims, and for this reason moral disagreements can usually be reduced to factual ones.

How would we know in any particular case that such a reduction was impossible? The only way would be to consider the disputants' proposed ends and the reasoning offered in their defense. So long as each is defended as a means to a further end, the analysis would continue. At some point, however, conflicting ends may be proposed for which no reasons are offered. An individual may declare something good and when challenged to defend the claim be able to reply only, "Well, it just is good," or "I just prefer it." Let us refer to such moral judgments, not defended by any reasons, as "fundamental moral judgments." If such conflicting judgments are reached, the dispute will not yield to rational resolution.

Returning now to the issue with which we began: are moral judgments factual claims or expressions of personal preference? As it turns out, they are typically statements of proposed means to preferred ends, and, therefore, open to empirical testing. As to fundamental moral judgments, which are rarely, if ever, reached in moral disputes, these are not defended rationally, and so we can view them as either ethical intuitions or personal preferences. In either case, arguing about them is of no avail.

One final observation. In considering the nature of moral judgments, I have avoided the terms "objective" and "subjective," for they are notoriously ambiguous. Indeed, faced with the foggy question "Are moral judgments objective or subjective?" I would reply: "I don't know what you mean by those terms, but the vast majority of moral disagreements, and virtually all that are significant, are open to rational resolution."[4,5]

NOTES

1. Thomas Reid, *Essays on the Active Powers of the Human Mind* (Cambridge, Mass.: M.I.T., 1969), p. 237.

2. The names of the countries are borrowed from the Marx Brothers' classic film *Duck Soup*.

3. Jonathan Harrison, "Empiricism in Ethics," *The Philosophical Quarterly*, 2 (1952): 306.

4. For a different, although related, approach to the issue of whether ethical disagreements can be rationally resolved, see source #10.

5. Readers are invited to apply rationality to morality in considering the following puzzle concerning divesture: Suppose I hold one hundred shares of stock in a company that has embarked on a policy I consider immoral. I therefore wish to divest myself of those one hundred shares. In order for me to sell them, someone must buy them. But the buyer would be purchasing one hundred shares of "tainted" stock. And I would have abetted the buyer in this immoral course of action. Granted, the prospective buyer might not believe the stock "tainted," but that consideration would be irrelevant to me, since I am convinced that, knowingly or unknowingly, the buyer would be doing what is immoral. Surely I should not take any steps that would assist or encourage the buyer in such deplorable conduct. Nor should I try to release myself from a moral predicament by entangling someone else. How then is principled divestiture possible?

9

A Supreme Moral Principle?

Many thinkers have sought one basic principle that could serve as the ultimate ethical guide, requiring us to perform all the actions we ought to perform and forbidding us from performing all the actions we ought not to perform. Which are the leading candidates for such a moral touchstone?

One common to various religious traditions is the Golden Rule. Its positive formulation, attributed to Jesus, is: "whatever you wish that men would do to you, do so to them."[1] The negative formulation, which appeared five hundred years earlier, is attributed to Confucius and was later proposed by the Jewish sage Hillel. The latter put it as follows: "What is hateful to you, do not to your neighbor."[2] Is either of these the supreme moral principle?

Consider first the positive formulation. Granted, we usually ought to treat others as we would wish them to treat us. For instance, we ought to go to the aid of an injured person, just as we would wish that person to come to our aid if we were injured. But if we always followed this rule, the results would be unfortunate. Consider masochists, who derive pleasure from being hurt. Were they to act according to the principle in question, their duty would be to inflict pain, thereby doing to others as they wish done to themselves. Similarly, consider a person who enjoys receiving telephone calls, regardless of who is calling. The principle would require the individual to telephone everyone, thereby reciprocating preferred treatment. Indeed, strictly speaking, it would be impossible to fulfill the positive formulation of the Golden Rule, for we wish so many others to do so much for us, we would not have time to do all that is necessary to treat them likewise. Indeed, as the contemporary philosopher Walter Kaufmann noted, "anyone who tried to live up to Jesus' rule would become an insufferable nuisance."[3]

In this respect the negative formulation of the Golden Rule is preferable, for it does not imply that we have innumerable duties toward everyone else. Neither does it imply that masochists ought to inflict pain on others, nor that those who enjoy receiving telephone calls ought themselves to make calls. However, while the negative formulation does not require these actions, neither does it forbid them. It enjoins us not to do to others what is hateful to ourselves, but pain is not hateful to the masochist and calls are not hateful to the telephone enthusiast. Thus, the negative formulation of the Golden Rule, although superior in a sense to the positive formulation, is not the supreme moral principle, since it does not prohibit actions that ought to be prohibited.

Let us next consider two other standards of conduct, each of which has sometimes been thought to be the supreme moral principle. One of these was originally formulated by Immanuel Kant, who argued that the moral worth of an action is to be judged not by its consequences but by the nature of the maxim (the principle) that motivates the action. Thus, right actions are not necessarily those with favorable consequences but those performed in accordance with correct maxims. But which maxims are correct? According to Kant, only those that can serve as universal laws, since they are applicable to every person at any time without exception. In other words, you should act only on a maxim that can be universalized without contradiction.

To see what Kant had in mind, consider a specific example he used to illustrate his view. Suppose you need to borrow money, but it will be lent to you only if you promise to pay it back. You realize, however, that you will not be able to honor the debt. Is it permissible for you to promise to repay the money, knowing you will not keep that promise? Kant proposed that the way to determine whether such an action is permissible is to universalize the maxim in question and see whether it leads to contradiction. The maxim is: Whenever I am short of money, I shall borrow it, promising to pay it back even if I know I shall not do so. Can this maxim be universalized without contradiction? Kant argued that it cannot.

> For supposing it to be a universal law that everyone when he thinks himself in a difficulty should be able to promise whatever he pleases, with the purpose of not keeping his promise, the promise itself would become impossible, as well as the end that one might have in view in it, since no one would consider that anything was promised to him, but would ridicule all such statements as vain pretenses.[4]

In other words, to make promises with no intention of keeping them would lead to the destruction of the practice of promising. Thus, since the maxim in question cannot be universalized without contradiction, it is not morally acceptable and, consequently, any action it motivates is immoral. According to Kant, then, the supreme moral principle is:

"Act only on that maxim whereby thou canst at the same time will that it should become a universal law."

Unfortunately, this principle prohibits actions that ought to be permitted. Although we might agree that the maxim of making insincere promises cannot be universalized, we can easily imagine cases in which a person ought to make a promise without any intention of keeping it. Suppose, for example, you and your family will starve to death unless you obtain food immediately, and a very wealthy person offers to provide the food if you will promise repayment within twenty-four hours. Surely we would say, contrary to Kant's principle, under these circumstances you ought to act on a maxim that cannot be universalized and make a promise you have no intention of keeping.

Kant's insistence that proper maxims admit of no exceptions leads him not only to approve morally repugnant actions, but also to sanction some that are inconsistent. Maxims he approves may conflict, and in that case adherence to one involves the violation of another. In the preceding case, for instance, were you to act in accord with the maxim of never making insincere promises, you would violate another maxim affirmed by Kant, that of aiding those who are in distress. He argues that both maxims admit of no exceptions, but since it is impossible always to abide by both, Kant's position leads to contradiction.

Perhaps his proposal fails because it concentrates exclusively on the reason for an action and fails to take into account its results. So, let us next consider a principle that focuses on consequences, that defended by John Stuart Mill. He was a leading advocate for the ethical position known as utilitarianism, according to which an action is right in so far as it promotes the happiness of mankind, and wrong in so far as it promotes unhappiness. By the term "happiness" Mill means pleasure and the absence of pain. By the term "mankind" he means all persons, each valued equally. So Mill's supreme moral principle is: Act in such a way as to produce the greatest pleasure for the greatest number of people, each person's pleasure counting equally.

This principle avoids the pitfalls of Kant's view, for whereas he admitted no exceptions to moral rules and was thus led to condemn insincere promises that saved human lives, the utilitarian principle is flexible enough to allow for any exceptions that increase overall happiness. Although Mill would agree that insincere promises are usually wrong, since they are apt to cause more pain than pleasure, he would allow that in some cases, such as that of the starving family, an insincere promise is morally justifiable, for it would lead to greater overall happiness than any alternative.

The flexibility of the utilitarian principle is an advantage but also a fatal flaw, for it permits action that ought to be prohibited. Consider, for example, inhabitants of a city who each week abduct a stranger and place the unfortunate in an arena to wrestle a lion. When the inhabitants of the city are challenged to justify this practice, they reply that although one person suffers much pain, thousands of spectators obtain greater pleasure from this form of entertainment than from any other, and so the spectacle is justified on utilitarian grounds. Clearly Mill's principle here yields an unacceptable implication. And other cases along similar lines likewise illustrate the laxity of utilitarianism. The sheriff who hangs an innocent person in order to satisfy the vengeance of the townspeople may maximize pleasure but nevertheless acts irresponsibly. So, too, does the teacher who agrees with students' views in order to curry their favor.[5]

One way to try to salvage the utilitarian principle is to argue that not all pleasures are of equal quality, that, for example, the pleasure of spectators at a lion arena is less valuable than that enjoyed by those at a piano recital. As Mill put it, "It is better to be a human being dissatisfied than a pig satisfied; better to be Socrates dissatisfied than a fool satisfied. And if the fool, or the pig, are of a different opinion, it is because they only know their own sides of the question. The other party to the comparison knows both sides."[6]

This move is dubious, for some individuals, knowing both sides of the question, would prefer to witness a struggle between human and lion rather than between human and keyboard. And even if only one knowledgeable individual had such taste, why should that person's view be disregarded? Furthermore, Mill's principle cannot be salvaged by the claim that attendance at a piano recital develops sensitivity whereas a visit to a lion arena dulls it, for, according to utilitarianism, actions are good to the extent that they produce pleasure, not to the extent that they produce sensitivity.

Perhaps, given the complexities of the human condition, any search for a supreme moral principle is doomed to failure, but the analysis so far has at least succeeded in calling attention to one fundamental feature of morality. The positive and negative formulations of the Golden Rule, the Kantian principle, and utilitarianism all serve as reminders that a moral person is obligated to be sensitive to the feelings of others. This insight motivates not only the biblical injunction to treat our fellow human beings as we wish to be treated, but also the utilitarian insistence that each person's happiness is to count neither more nor less than another's. The same theme is central to Kant's view, a point he made explicit by claiming that his supreme moral principle could be reformulated as follows: "So act as to treat humanity, whether in thine own person or in that of any other, in every case as an end and never as means only."

The moral point of view thus involves taking into account interests apart from our own. Do we ever do so? According to the theory known as egoism, all human behavior is motivated only by selfishness. On this view all individuals act solely in an effort to increase their own pleasure; people are kind to others only if they believe that such kindness will eventually redound to their own benefit. Thus no person would ever be a moral agent, for no one would ever act from genuinely altruistic considerations. Is egoism correct?

On the surface the theory seems clearly mistaken. Consider, for instance, a doctor who is devoted to serving the poor and has no interest whatever in publicizing this work. Doesn't such a case refute egoism?

A defender of the theory is apt to reply that this doctor only appears to be acting altruistically but is, in fact, acting selfishly, deriving pleasure from ministering to others. The egoist claims that the doctor is as selfish as the rest of us, but whereas we enjoy owning cars and attending parties, the doctor enjoys living a simple life and providing medical aid to the poor. All of us seek to maximize our pleasure, but since we differ in what we enjoy, we act in different ways. Nevertheless, the underlying motive in every case is self-interest.

The egoistic line of argument is impervious to counterexamples, but this invulnerability reveals the theory as vacuous, a reflection not of empirical evidence but of an arbitrary decision to use words idiosyncratically. The egoist declares us selfish if we act to fulfill our own desires. How are those identified? According to the egoist, we desire to do whatever we actually do, even if we are sacrificing ourselves for others. But then to say that we act as we desire is to say merely that we act as we act, which is a tautology. If we are declared selfish simply because we act as we act, then, of course, we all act selfishly, but such a definition is obviously a misuse of the term "selfish." As the American philosopher James Rachels notes: "The mere fact that I am acting on my wants does not mean that I am acting selfishly; it depends on *what it is* that I want."[7] An unselfish person cares about the welfare of others, whereas a selfish person does not. The tautology that all of us act as we act does not obliterate the distinction between an unselfish and a selfish person, no matter how the meaning of words is distorted. Thus the egoist's challenge to morality fails.

While most of us sometimes act altruistically, why should we do so on those occasions when our self-interest dictates otherwise?

This final question rests on the dubious assumption that we can ever be sure that acting morally is contrary to our own advantage. While that is how an immoral action may at first appear, as David Hume noted, "Knaves, with all their pretended cunning and abilities, [are] betrayed by their own maxims; and while they purpose to cheat with moderation and secrecy, a tempting incident occurs—nature is frail—and they give in to the snare, whence they can never extricate themselves without a total loss of reputation and the forfeiture of all future trust and confidence with mankind."[8] In short, immorality invariably threatens self-interest, and rarely, if ever, can this menace be sufficiently minimized to render the risk worthwhile.

What if someone wishes to take the chance and is unmoved by altruistic considerations? Can we reason further? Perhaps in such a case we can only repeat the words of La Rochefoucauld: "To virtue's credit we must confess that our greatest misfortunes are brought about by vice."[9] In sum, when sympathy is missing, morality rests on practicality.

NOTES

1. *The Holy Bible: Revised Standard Version* (New York: Thomas Nelson and Sons, 1952), Matthew 7:12.

2. *The Babylonian Talmud* (London: Soncino, 1938), Shabbath, 31a.

3. Walter Kaufmann, *The Faith of a Heretic* (New York: Doubleday, 1963), p. 212.

4. See source #11.

5. This latter example is elaborated in my *Saints and Scamps: Ethics in Academia* (Totowa, N.J.: Rowman & Littlefield, 1986).

6. See source #12.

7. See source #13.

8. David Hume, *An Enquiry Concerning the Principles of Morals* (New York: Liberal Arts, 1957), p. 103.

9. *The Maxims of La Rochefoucauld,* #183.

10

The Strange Case of John Shmarb
An Aesthetic Puzzle

Steven M. Cahn and L. Michael Griffel

One morning Art Freund opened his newspaper and was astonished to come upon the following headline: "FIND MANUSCRIPT OF BRAHMS'S FIFTH SYMPHONY: LOST WORK UNCOVERED IN VIENNA HOME." The accompanying story reported that a grandson of a former student of Brahms, rummaging through an old family trunk, had unearthed some dusty pages that turned out to be an original Brahms manuscript: a fifth symphony completed just prior to the composer's death in 1897. It had never been performed or published, and, in fact, Brahms seems never to have even mentioned it to anyone. According to the newspaper, members of the illustrious Vienna music circle, having seen the score, enthusiastically agreed that the work was a worthy companion to its four famous predecessors.

But they were no more enthusiastic than Art, who firmly resolved to attend the premiere of the Fifth Symphony in Vienna on May 7, the anniversary of Brahms's birth. Only with great difficulty did Art manage to obtain a ticket, for all the most celebrated members of the music world were to be in attendance on this momentous occasion.

When that great day finally arrived, Art's expectations were fully realized. The music was magnificent and the audience response overwhelming. Critics spoke with impassioned, unqualified admiration for the new masterpiece. The *Times* reported:

> The four extended movements of the Symphony are each of the highest order and exemplify many of the composer's finest traits. The intense agitation and propulsion of the opening allegro appassionata, the lilting Vien-

nese charm of the andante, the scherzo's cross-rhythms and explosive climaxes, the all'ongarese melodies of the theme and variations finale all testify to the strong Brahmsian character of the piece. But the special significance of the composition is its unusual tendencies toward a cyclical structure, most apparent in the use of the first-movement theme to link the end of the scherzo with the finale. In addition, the main theme of the second movement returns as a counterpoint to the final variation of the last movement. Interestingly, the work is marked by the use of many more non-functional harmonic progressions than one encounters in Brahms's other symphonies. This feature gives the work a forward-moving restlessness and enormous impact.

A story later in the week announced that the first recording of the Fifth Symphony would be released at the end of the year by the Berlin Philharmonia. When Art arrived home, he found in his mailbox publicity releases from leading American orchestras advising subscribers that performances of the new masterpiece would be scheduled immediately upon publication of the eagerly awaited score, already in progress.

Several weeks later Art was shocked by another headline: "BRAHMS'S FIFTH SYMPHONY A FAKE: MUSIC WORLD A-GHAST." Incredibly, the symphony had actually been the handiwork of a young American composer, John Shmarb, who had called a press conference to announce his achievement. He explained that after managing to obtain authentic paper and ink of the nineteenth century, he had forged Brahms's handwriting and arranged to have the manuscript found in the old trunk. When asked why he had concocted such an elaborate hoax, young Shmarb replied:

> For the last ten years, publishers and critics and musicologists have been dismissing my work as inconsequential because they claimed all I did was copy nineteenth-century music. Well, I finally got fed up. They weren't being fair to my music. Now that the world has judged my work as it would judge the work of any nineteenth-century composer, my genius has been acknowledged. I am not imitating Brahms. I am simply composing as a contemporary of Brahms might have. I find it natural to write in the Romantic vein and want to continue to do so. A great work is a great work, whether composed by Brahms or by Shmarb.

Response to Shmarb's words was swift and unanimously harsh. One German critic typified the attitude of many by denouncing Shmarb as an unscrupulous fraud. "The outrage of it all! Having us waste our time on such worthless music is criminal. Shmarb has shown himself to be a musical charlatan." A leading American avant-garde composer commented: "Shmarb has always been incapable of utilizing his natural abilities. His output is merely derivative. Another sad case of misdirected and misused talent." Word soon followed that the Berlin Philharmonia had eliminated the symphony from its recording schedule, that plans to publish the work had been abandoned at considerable cost to the publisher, and that all announced performances had been cancelled.

Art was greatly disheartened at these disclosures, for his cherished experience of attending the premiere of a major Brahms work had been turned into participation in a hoax. But the more he thought about the situation, the more upset he became, for he gradually realized that an even greater disappointment was that he would never again hear that symphony he had so much enjoyed. Shmarb's words ran through his mind: "A great work is a great work." He wondered why the same critics who had praised the symphony earlier now condemned it as worthless. For, he thought, did the great Brahms symphony suddenly become a poor work just because it was written by Shmarb in 1968? Suppose it had been written by Stravinsky in 1928 or by Bruckner in 1888? Would it be a finer composition or more enjoyable? Is it impossible to judge the merit of an anonymous composition because the composer and date are unknown? Why cannot a composer be permitted to choose for himself the style in which he wishes to compose, whether that style is original in its time, typical of its time, or typical of an earlier time? Stylistic originality has been the gift of only a few composers in the history of music. Most works, indeed most of the outstanding and best-loved musical compositions, have been written in an established idiom. Stylistic originality can be a virtue, but it is not a necessity in the creation of great art. Inventiveness within a style, though more common than radical stylistic originality, is nevertheless deserving of equal consideration. Inventiveness within a particular style is possible for any composer writing at any time within that style.

After all, certain styles, such as that of the late Romantic period, are beloved by audiences around the world. Why must they hear only old works, composed centuries ago, in those styles? Why can they not hear compositions written by contemporary composers in classic styles that have endured the test of time?

The more Art pondered the matter, the more disturbed he was by the public response to Shmarb's symphony. He very much wanted to hear the work again and have the opportunity to confirm his judgment that it was a masterpiece. Surely, he thought, listening to the music itself is the only sensible way to evaluate it. What other way could possibly be appropriate?

10A

Some Further Thoughts

Gordon Epperson

Let us suppose that Shmarb was, indeed, gifted enough to pull off such a spectacular forgery, skillful enough to convince the critical intelligentsia that here was yet another masterwork by Brahms himself. Can we agree that "a great work is a great work," no matter who writes it?

One is reminded of Mark Twain's remark that the Shakespearean plays were written by Shakespeare or someone else of the same name. If it were proved that Francis Bacon wrote the entire canon, "Shakespeare" would no doubt be retained as a pseudonym. The plays are self-validating, and though uneven, like every artist's work, they bear a recognizable stamp, a stylistic consistency. Have we a modern counterpart to Shakespeare (as Brahms appears to have had in Shmarb!) who can give us further works in the language of the Elizabethan period? Do we want, and need, more "Shakespearean" plays, even if written by someone else: or, for that matter, brand-new Van Goghs and Cezannes?

Painters often copy the works of masters as an exercise in technique; no creativity is claimed, though a fluent executant may fool the experts occasionally or even produce, as John Shmarb did with his symphony, something that passes for an original. An artist lacking creative spark may exploit such skill for money or even (for still more money) foist his forgeries upon the public. But for a composer of Shmarb's self-proclaimed genius this would be profoundly unsatisfying: he wishes to be recognized, and listened to, as Shmarb, not as Brahms.

But Shmarb cannot have it both ways. If he writes a "masterpiece" that has the attributes of Brahms's work, he is exploiting those characteristics of the earlier composer's oeuvre that discerning listeners recognize and esteem, musical traits of pronounced individuality, even idiosyncrasy. It just won't do to speak of the Romantic ambience as though it were a style manipulated by Dvorak, Tchaikovsky, and Brahms in virtually the same way. Their vocabularies had much in common, to be sure; but what Art Freund describes as *inventiveness within a style* is precisely what establishes the creative originality of each composer. The "musical idiom" of Romanticism was never *established*, but was, instead, in constant flux, exhibiting myriad facets. This appears dramatically in Beethoven's musical peregrinations, which begin in the "classical" style he absorbed early in life, and ended with the far-out introspections—still Beethoven—of the last quartets.

The authors of "The Strange Case" say, through their spokesman Art Freund, that stylistic originality has been the gift of only a few composers in the history of music. A giant computer might, if all the relevant data were available, confirm the statement; but it would be necessary first to determine what constitutes originality. Would not "inventiveness within a style" qualify? An absence of such inventiveness would make a composer indistinguishable from a host of other indistinguishable contemporaries. But is it true, as the authors claim, that stylistic originality has been the gift of only a few composers in the history of music? It is true that we hear many examples of newly uncovered Baroque and late eighteenth-century music that show no arresting individuality and that can be assigned anonymously to one period or the other. But this is *not* true of Bach and Handel, or of Haydn and Mozart. Which composers, then, of "most of the outstanding and best-loved musical compositions" do the authors have in mind?

Maybe Professors Cahn and Griffel are thinking of radical *novelty,* when they speak of stylistic originality. (This is crucial and requires clarification: what *kind* of novelty? Tonality? Texture? Formal structure? Instrumentation?) Radical novelty, however defined, can probably be absent or minimal even in certain inventive composers. Brahms himself, so often described a few decades ago as a "classical Romanticist" because of his alleged conservatism, is a good example of this, though savants speak of the characteristic Brahmsian "sound" that derives from a complex of factors, not least of these being his personal harmonic vocabulary, the vigor and independence of thematic lines, and, in his ensemble works, his particular "blend" of voices. Brahms's rhythmic style, though, is quite original: even—I am tempted to say—inimitable, but we're giving Shmarb the benefit of the doubt. Brahms can hardly be mistaken for one of his contemporaries; no "established idiom" is *that* homogeneous.

Well, Shmarb was mistaken for Brahms. What of his symphony, which was played only once? We know that it was a frankly imitative work; otherwise the deception could not have been perpetrated. How does his neglected and controversial (though derivative) masterpiece fit into the Shmarb canon: early, middle, late? Mature? We know that

Shmarb has written other works and that because he creates out of inner necessity he will continue to compose, regardless of critical rejection or the lack of public response. (Nicolas Slonimsky's *Lexicon of Musical Invective* is convincing testimony to the fallibility of critics and the lonely struggles of misunderstood and underestimated artists.) Shmarb will be glad for the support that Professors Cahn and Griffel afford him through Art Freund, but even without that endorsement he has faith in his music and its power to endure; he recognizes his own genius. He may, like Charles Ives, have to wait for the recognition of others, possibly for a long time.

But Brahms's music, only forty years ago—though he was already long dead—was not nearly so popular with the general public as it is now. A Brahms festival in Cincinnati in the late thirties was considered a bit steep by many avid music lovers: too much of a good thing, too demanding . . . and this in a city with strong German musical traditions. In those days Brahms was more widely known for his Hungarian dances (in the Americas, at any rate) than for the *Requiem* or his four symphonies.

Shmarb must be patient.

There is a difference, however, between Shmarb and earlier neglected composers, in that most of them were, in one way or another, explorers: some of them inventive *within* a style, if you will, while others were iconoclasts. Shmarb—and we surely wish to do him justice—appears to cultivate (and to rearrange) the already known.

Art Freund would like to know why audiences today cannot hear compositions, written by living composers, in styles that have withstood the test of time. But they *can:* traditional tonality is still viable, to say nothing of such enduring paradigms as sonata-form in its various manifestations. Leonard Meyer calls attention to the great variety of musical idioms that now coexist, more or less in equilibrium, and suggests that this is what we can continue to expect: a fluctuating stasis, with no single style assuming sovereignty or invalidating others. (Meyer believes we are approaching certain "outer limits" in the search for radical novelty: aural, functional limits.) Composers, some of whom exhibit a bewildering eclecticism, can literally ransack the ages.

Romantic composers still inhabit the earth. Samuel Barber, who has often been called "Brahmsian" because of his stylistic affinities with that master, is one of them. Yet Barber would never be mistaken for Brahms; he sings with his own voice. Barber is "inventive," though the influence of his predecessors is evident. Every composer is influenced similarly, even—or perhaps especially—when he "breaks away" from one or more essential features of his musical patrimony, as evidenced in Schoenberg's rejection of tonal centers.

What about Shmarb? Even if he avoids experimentation there must be uniqueness, of some kind, in his music—unless he and Art Freund are wrong in their estimate of his abilities—that saves it from cliche, from slavish imitation, and makes it worth listening to. If he had, in truth, composed "simply as a contemporary of Brahms might have," nobody would have been taken in. What was required, to bring off the hoax, was a clever forgery.

None of this is intended to imply that Art Freund has no case. The landscape of professional music is a political quagmire. There are powerful coteries, mandarins who determine what prizes are awarded and to whom. Avant-garde composers promulgate a party line subject to mysterious changes; only a true believer would engage in the assiduous maneuvering required to keep in step.

John Shmarb cannot qualify, probably, for any kind of grant; not now, anyway. His symphony is shelved. Not having heard his music, I must take Art's word for it that the neglect of this composer is a loss for us all. Shmarb must endure, and see injustice done; he should also, as a fervent classicist, invoke his daemon.

10B

An Epilogue and Further Reflections

Neil Courtney

As Art Freund continued to brood about the control over his rights as a concert goer wielded by the "illustrious Vienna music circle," the *Times*'s music critic, and the management of the leading American orchestras, his sense of powerlessness overwhelmed him. He became listless on his job and once, while out driving, unable to find anything on the good-music station but some dodecaphonic choral music (it was actually only poorly performed Gesualdo), he ran a stop sign.

That night as he listened to a recording of Delius's *Walk to the Paradise Garden,* it came to him that there must be thousands like him, many in high places, who felt deprived of a new romantic work. He took a leave of absence from his job, withdrew his life savings, and launched a vigorous campaign on their behalf. With the sympathetic support of The Friday Morning Music Club and ASOL (the American Symphony Orchestra League), he achieved a minor miracle. Within two seasons, Shmarb's First—formerly Brahms's Fifth—was included in every major orchestra's season in the Western world and Japan.

Unfortunately, repeated hearings did not enhance the original evaluations of the work's worth, and it quickly passed from the repertoire despite the efforts of the critics, who in a desperate attempt to rescue their reputations continued to review the piece in the most favorable terms.

There are two assumptions in the original "Strange Case" that have been extended into the Epilogue. The first is that some sort of elite conspiracy of critics, program makers, and influential contemporary composers wields a kind of international control over what the average concert goer gets to hear. While there are numerous influences on program selection, not the least of which are record companies (whose main hope of making money seems to lie in continued mining of the rich vein of nineteenth-century Romantic music with the same blind conviction of its inexhaustibility as other miners of natural resources for profit seem to have), it is clearly observable that most programs reflect audience acceptance. Boards of directors of major symphony orchestras are largely composed of conservative wealthy individuals or business persons whose aims and purposes do not necessarily coincide with the aims of those who seek to continue great symphonic music in our culture. Reasons for their being on these boards aside, the result is a reflection of their conservative musical tastes and their conservative business practices, which dictate that costs must be held to a minimum and programs must attract the most paying customers possible. These priorities overwhelm the influences of any critic-composer conspiracy—a conspiracy that represents, at most, very little economic clout.

Another bit of paranoia related to the "conspiracy theory" is the "they're-going-to-put-something-over-on-me-and-then-laugh-at-me" syndrome expressed by the more insecure concert goer. This can be observed at concerts of extremely modern or avant-garde music, and accounts for the listener only being able to half-participate in the performance because the other half of his brain is telling him that if he shows signs of liking it, someone is sure to tell him afterwards that the piece was actually composed by a computer, or by a committee from the staff of *National Lampoon*. Once again, the result is more of the old, familiar tunes rather than an encouragement of a more adventurous spirit in programming.

There is a solution to this particular problem which has worked well for some. If one tries to remain open to like or dislike anything one hears without regard for the opinions of experts or the threat of making oneself vulnerable to a hoax, the result could be a larger measure of satisfaction at a very small risk of humiliation. It is not that bad to be fooled occasionally. A long career in a major symphony orchestra has helped this observer to develop a healthy disregard for critics' opinions of *anything,* for critics are usually wrong about most aspects of a performance, with the possible exception of historical data, which they frequently crib from the program notes.

The second assumption is somewhat more difficult to deal with. It is that a composer today could write a symphony that would be stylistically undetectable as counterfeit. Only if this assumption were true could Shmarb's symphony take its place as an equal with the four symphonies of Brahms. The Epilogue rejects the assumption for several reasons.

The argument could be made that during Brahms's lifetime there were very few composers writing symphonies that could stand as equals to Brahms's. Tchaikovsky, Dvorak, Bruckner, or Mahler would probably qualify, and yet each of those composers' symphonies is so obviously of a style easily identifiable with the composer that there could be no question of its originator. In other words, during Brahms's own time there was no one who approached him in his greatness in his own personal Brahmsian voice. What are the chances of a composer from a different century and culture not only successfully imitating Brahms's style, but creating a masterwork while doing it?

This brings us to the strongest argument against the likelihood of a contemporary composer succeeding in composing a great symphony in the style of Brahms. Any composer who specifically and severely limited himself to the re-creation of someone else's style to the extent that his own style was indistinguishable from it would be so limiting his own creative vision that it almost certainly would be impossible for him to create a "great" work of art, as the four Brahms symphonies certainly are.

The composers of the Romantic period, which was characterized by, among other things, a search for new forms and new means of expression, did not achieve their greatness by confining their musical expression. They were freer than any previous composers to experiment and to find solutions in entirely new ways. This freedom is one of the characteristics of the period, and what the Romantic composers wrote was their ultimate expression of this freedom.

A composer of today who had already heard *Ein Heldenleben, La Mer, Le Sacre du Printemps, Pierrot Lunaire, Wozzeck, Intégrales,* or *Threnody for the Victims of Hiroshima,* to mention only a few of the compositions that have expanded our aural consciousness, and was able to repress and rigorously exclude all this from his experience for the purpose of sounding like another composer would almost certainly produce a work more expressive of its limitations than of its freedom and creativity.

John Shmarb was lucky to get his symphony past the sycophants and self-deceiving opinion makers the first time. He would never survive extended exposure to true music lovers.

10C

Coda

Steven M. Cahn

Apart from its musical structure, what do we know of Shmarb's Symphony? Only that critics and audiences admired it greatly and, because of factors in part external to the music, thought it a composition by Brahms. Yet, although never having heard the work, Epperson disparages it as "imitative" and "derivative," while Courtney calls its admirers "sycophants" and assures us it "would never survive extended exposure to true music lovers."

Both these commentators appear certain that great composers display such individuality that no piece by one could be thought to have been written by anyone else. This claim has historically been proven false. Debates have raged for decades over the authenticity of various musical, artistic, and literary works sometimes attributed to one of the masters. Might we not hear a section of the incomparable Mozart C-Minor Piano Concerto and suppose it written by Beethoven? Haven't sophisticated listeners sometimes confused a scene by Rossini with one by Donizetti? Indeed, all "true music lovers" have had the experience of turning on the radio in the middle of a lovely selection and mistaking its composer.

So if Shmarb's Symphony was thought to have been written by Brahms, why is the piece necessarily inferior? Before making a judgment, I would want to hear the music. To do otherwise, as Epperson eventually puts it, would be an aesthetic "injustice."

Sources

[1]

Compulsion

Clarence Darrow

No one knows what will be the fate of the child he gets or the child she bears; the fate of the child is the last thing they consider. This weary old world goes on, begetting, with birth and with living and with death; and all of it is blind from the beginning to the end. I do not know what it was that made these boys do this mad act, but I do know there is a reason for it. I know they did not beget themselves. I know that any one of an infinite number of causes reaching back to the beginning might be working out in these boys' minds, whom you are asked to hang in malice and in hatred and injustice, because someone in the past has sinned against them.

I am sorry for the fathers as well as the mothers, for the fathers who gave their strength and their lives for educating and protecting and creating a fortune for the boys that they love; for the mothers who go down into the shadow of death for their children, who nourish them and care for them, and risk their lives, that they may live, who watch them with tenderness and fondness and longing, and who go down into dishonor and disgrace for the children that they love.

All of these are helpless. We are all helpless. But when you are pitying the father and the mother of poor Bobby Franks, what about the fathers and mothers of these two unfortunate boys, and what about the unfortunate boys themselves, and what about all the fathers and all

Reprinted from *The Plea of Clarence Darrow, August 22nd, 23rd, and 25th, in Defense of Richard Loeb and Nathan Leopold, Jr., On Trial for Murder* (Chicago: Ralph Fletcher Seymour, 1924).

Clarence Darrow (1859-1938) used his superb legal skills to defend numerous unpopular clients and causes.

the mothers and all the boys and all the girls who tread a dangerous maze in darkness from birth to death?

Do you think you can cure it by hanging these two? Do you think you can cure the hatreds and the maladjustments of the world by hanging them? You simply show your ignorance and your hate when you say it. You may here and there cure hatred with love and understanding, but you can only add fuel to the flames by cruelty and hate.

What is my friend's idea of justice? He says to this court, whom he says he respects—and I believe he does—Your Honor, who sits here patiently, holding the lives of these two boys in your hands:

"Give them the same mercy that they gave to Bobby Franks."

Is that the law? Is that justice? Is this what a court should do? Is this what a state's attorney should do? If the state in which I live is not kinder, more humane, more considerate, more intelligent than the mad act of these two boys, I am sorry that I have lived so long.

I am sorry for all fathers and all mothers. The mother who looks into the blue eyes of her little babe cannot help musing over the end of the child, whether it will be crowned with the greatest promises which her mind can image or whether he may meet death upon the scaffold. All she can do is to rear him with love and care, to watch over him tenderly, to meet life with hope and trust and confidence, and to leave the rest with fate.

*   *   *

I do not claim to know how it happened; I have sought to find out. I know that something, or some combination of things, is responsible for this mad act. I know that there are no accidents in nature. I know that effect follows cause. I know that, if I were wise enough, and knew enough about this case, I could lay my finger on the cause. I will do the best I can, but it is largely speculation.

The child, of course, is born without knowledge.

Impressions are made upon its mind as it goes along. Dickie Loeb was a child of wealth and opportunity. Over and over in this court Your Honor has been asked, and other courts have been asked, to consider boys who have no chance; they have been asked to consider the poor, whose home had been the street, with no education and no opportunity in life, and they have done it, and done it rightfully.

But, Your Honor, it is just as often a great misfortune to be the child of the rich as it is to be the child of the poor. Wealth has its misfortunes. Too much, too great opportunity and advantage, given to a child has its misfortunes, and I am asking Your Honor to consider the rich as well as the poor (and nothing else). Can I find what was wrong? I think I can. Here was a boy at a tender age, placed in the hands of a governess, intellectual, vigorous, devoted, with a strong ambition for the welfare of this boy. He was pushed in his studies, as plants are forced in hothouses. He had no pleasures, such as a boy should have, except as they were gained by lying and cheating.

Now, I am not criticizing the nurse. I suggest that some day Your Honor look at her picture. It explains her fully. Forceful, brooking no interference, she loved the boy, and her ambition was that he should reach the highest perfection. No time to pause, no time to stop from one book to another, no time to have those pleasures which a boy ought to have to create a normal life. And what happened? Your Honor, what would happen? Nothing strange or unusual. This nurse was with him all the time, except when he stole out at night, from two to fourteen years of age. He, scheming and planning as healthy boys would do, to get out from under her restraint; she, putting before him the best books, which children generally do not want; and he, when she was not looking, reading detective stories, which he devoured, story after story, in his young life. Of all of this there can be no question.

What is the result? Every story he read was a story of crime. We have a statute in this state, passed only last year, if I recall it, which forbids minors reading stories of crime. Why? There is only one reason. Because the legislature in its wisdom felt that it would produce criminal tendencies in the boys who read them. The legislature of this state has given its opinion, and forbidden boys to read these books. He read them day after day. He never stopped. While he was passing through college at Ann Arbor he was still reading them. When he was a senior he read them, and almost nothing else.

Now, these facts are beyond dispute. He early developed the tendency to mix with crime, to be a detective; as a little boy shadowing people on the street; as a little child going out with his fantasy of being the head of a band of criminals and directing them on the street. How did this grow and develop in him? Let us see. It seems to be as natural as the day following the night. Every detective story is a story of a sleuth getting the best of it: trailing some unfortunate individual through devious ways until his victim is finally landed in jail or stands on the gallows. They all show how smart the detective is, and where the criminal himself falls down.

This boy early in his life conceived the idea that there could be a perfect crime, one that nobody would ever detect; that there could be one where the detective did not land his game—a perfect crime. He had been interested in the story of Charley Ross, who was kidnaped. He was interested in these things all his life. He believed in his childish way that a crime could be so carefully planned that there would be no detection, and his idea was to plan and accomplish a perfect crime. It would involve kidnapping and involve murder.

*   *   *

There had been growing in Dickie's brain, dwarfed and twisted—as every act in this case shows it to have been dwarfed and twisted—there had been growing this scheme, not due to any wickedness of Dickie Loeb, for he is a child. It grew as he grew; it grew from those around him; it grew from the lack of the proper training until it possessed him. He believed he could beat the police. He believed he could plan the perfect crime. He had thought of it and talked of it for years—had talked of it as a child, had worked at it as a child—this sorry act of his, utterly irrational and motiveless, a plan to commit a perfect crime which must contain kidnapping, and there must be ransom, or else it could not be perfect, and they must get the money.

The State itself in opening this case said that it was largely for experience and for a thrill, which it was. In the end the State switched it onto the foolish reason of getting cash.

Every fact in this case shows that cash had almost nothing to do with it, except as a factor in the perfect crime; and to commit the perfect crime there must be a kidnapping, and a kidnapping where they could get money, and that was all there was of it. Now, these are the two theories of this case, and I submit, Your Honor, under the facts in this case, that there can be no question but that we are right. This fantasy grew in the mind of Dickie Loeb almost before he began to read. It developed as a child just as kleptomania has developed in many a person and is clearly recognized by the courts. He went from one thing to another—in the main insignificant, childish things. Then, the utterly foolish and stupid and unnecessary thing of going to Ann Arbor to steal from a fraternity house, a fraternity of which he was a member. And, finally, the planning for this crime. Murder was the least part of it; to kidnap and get the money, and kill in connection with it—that was the childish scheme growing up in these childish minds. And they had it in mind for five or six months—planning what? Planning where every step was foolish and childish; acts that could have been planned in an hour or a day; planning this, and then planning that, changing this and changing that; the weird actions of two mad brains.

Counsel have laughed at us for talking about fantasies and hallucinations. They had laughed at us in one breath, but admitted in another. Let us look at that for a moment, Your Honor. Your Honor has been a child. I well remember that I have been a child. And while youth has its advantages, it has its grievous troubles. There is an old prayer, "Though I grow old in years, let me keep the heart of a child." The heart of a child—with its abundant life, its disregard for consequences, its living in the moment, and for the moment alone, its lack of responsibility, and its freedom from care.

The law knows and has recognized childhood for many and many a long year. What do we know about childhood? The brain of the child is the home of dreams, of castles, of visions, of illusions and of delusions. In fact, there could be no childhood without delusions, for delusions are always more alluring than facts. Delusions, dreams and hallucinations are a part of the warp and woof of childhood. You know it and I know it. I remember, when I was a child, the men seemed as tall as the trees, the trees as tall as the mountains. I can remember very well when, as a little boy, I swam the deepest spot in the river for the first time. I swam breathlessly and landed with as much sense of glory and triumph as Julius Caesar felt when he led his army across the Rubicon. I have been back since, and I can almost step across the same place, but it seemed an ocean then. And those men whom I thought so wonderful were dead and left nothing behind. I had lived in a dream. I had never known the real world which I met, to my discomfort and despair, and that dispelled the illusions of my youth.

The whole life of childhood is a dream and an illusion, and whether they take one shape or another shape depends not upon the dreamy boy but on what surrounds him. As well might I have dreamed of burglars and wished to be one as to dream of policemen and wished to be one. Perhaps I was lucky, too, that I had no money. We have grown to think that the misfortune is in not having it. The great misfortune in this terrible case is the money. That has destroyed their lives. That has fostered these illusions. That has promoted this mad act. And, if Your Honor shall doom them to die, it will be because they are the sons of the rich.

Do you suppose that if they lived up here on the Northwest Side and had no money, with the evidence as clear in this case as it is, that any human being would want to hang them? Excessive wealth is a grievous misfortune in every step in life. When I hear foolish people, when I read malicious newspapers talking of excessive fees in this case, it makes me ill. That there is nothing bigger in life, that it is presumed that no man lives to whom money is not the first concern, that human instincts, sympathy and kindness and charity and logic can only be used for cash. It shows how deeply money has corrupted the hearts of most men.

Now, to get back to Dickie Loeb. He was a child. The books he read by day were not the books he read by night. We are all of us molded somewhat by the influences around us, and of those, to people who read, perhaps books are the greatest and the strongest influences.

I know where my life has been molded by books, among other things. We all know where our lives have been influenced by books. The nurse, strict and jealous and watchful, gave him one kind of book; by night he would steal off and read the other.

Which, think you, shaped the life of Dickie Loeb? Is there any kind of question about it? A child. Was it pure maliciousness? Was a boy of five or six or seven to blame for it? Where did he get it? He got it where we all get our ideas, and these books became a part of his dreams and a part of his life, and as he grew up his visions grew to hallucinations.

He went out on the street and fantastically directed his companions, who were not there, in their various moves to complete the perfect crime. Can there be any sort of question about it?

Suppose, Your Honor, that instead of this boy being here in this court, under the plea of the State that Your Honor shall pronounce a sentence to hang him by the neck until dead, he had been taken to a pathological hospital to be analyzed, and the physicians had inquired into his case. What would they have said? There is only one thing that they could possibly have said. They would have traced everything back to the gradual growth of the child.

That is not all there is about it. Youth is hard enough. The only good thing about youth is that it has no thought and no care; and how blindly we can do things when we are young!

Where is the man who has not been guilty of delinquencies in youth? Let us be honest with ourselves. Let us look into our own hearts. How many men are there today—lawyers and congressmen and judges, and even state's attorneys—who have not been guilty of some mad act in youth? And if they did not get caught, or the consequences were trivial, it was their good fortune.

We might as well be honest with ourselves, Your Honor. Before I would tie a noose around the neck of a boy I would try to call back into my mind the emotions of youth. I would try to remember what the world looked like to me when I was a child. I would try to remember how strong were these instinctive, persistent emotions that moved my life. I would try to remember how weak and inefficient was youth in the presence of the surging, controlling feelings of the child. One that honestly remembers and asks himself the question and tries to unlock the door that he thinks is closed, and calls back the boy, can understand the boy.

But, Your Honor, that is not all there is to boyhood. Nature is strong and she is pitiless. She works in her own mysterious way, and we are her victims. We have not much to do with it ourselves. Nature takes this job in hand, and we play our parts. In the words of old Omar Khayyam, we are only:

> *But helpless pieces in the game He plays*
> *Upon this checkerboard of nights and days;*
> *Hither and thither moves, and checks, and slays,*
> *And one by one back in the closet lays.*

What had this boy to do with it? He was not his own father; he was not his own mother; he was not his own grandparents. All of this was handed to him. He did not surround himself with governesses and wealth. He did not make himself. And yet he is to be compelled to pay.

There was a time in England, running down as late as the beginning of the last century, when judges used to convene court and call juries to try a horse, a dog, a pig, for crime. I have in my library a story of a judge and jury and lawyers trying and convicting an old sow for lying down on her ten pigs and killing them.

What does it mean? Animals were tried. Do you mean to tell me that Dickie Loeb had any more to do with his making than any other product of heredity that is born upon the earth?

At this period of life it is not enough to take a boy—Your Honor, I wish I knew when to stop talking about this question that always has interested me so much—it is not enough to take a boy filled with his dreams and his fantasies and living in an unreal world, but the age of adolescence comes on him with all the rest.

But what does he know? Both these boys are in the adolescent age. Both these boys, as every alienist in this case on both sides tells you, are in the most trying period of the life of a child—both these boys, when the call of sex is new and strange; both these boys, at a time of seeking to adjust their young lives to the world, moved by the strongest feelings and passions that have ever moved men; both these boys, at the time boys grow insane, at the time crimes are committed. All of this is added to all the rest of the vagaries of their lives. Shall we charge them with full responsibility that we may have a hanging? That we may deck Chicago in a holiday garb and let the people have their fill of blood; that you may put stains upon the heart of every man, woman and child on that day, and that the dead walls of Chicago will tell the story of the shedding of their blood?

For God's sake, are we crazy? In the face of history, of every line of philosophy, against the teaching of every religionist and seer and prophet the world has ever given us, we are still doing what our barbaric ancestors did when they came out of the caves and the woods.

From the age of fifteen to the age of twenty or twenty-one, the child has the burden of adolescence, of puberty and sex thrust upon him. Girls are kept at home and carefully watched. Boys without instruction are left to work the period out for themselves. It may lead to excess. It may lead to disgrace. It may lead to perversion. Who is to blame? Who did it? Did Dickie Loeb do it?

Your Honor, I am almost ashamed to talk about it. I can hardly imagine that we are in the twentieth century. And yet there are men who seriously say that for what nature has done, for what life has done, for what training has done, you should hang these boys.

Now, there is no mystery about this case, Your Honor. I seem to be criticizing their parents. They had parents who were kind and good and wise in their way. But I say to you seriously that the parents are more responsible than these boys. And yet few boys had better parents.

Your Honor, it is the easiest thing in the world to be a parent. We talk of motherhood, and yet every woman can be a mother. We talk of fatherhood, and yet every man can be a father. Nature takes care of that. It is easy to be a parent. But to be wise and farseeing enough to understand the boy is another thing; only a very few are so wise and so farseeing as that. When I think of the light way nature has of picking our parents and populating the earth, having them born and die, I cannot hold human beings to the same degree of responsibility that young lawyers hold them when they are enthusiastic in a prosecution. I know what it means.

I know there are no better citizens in Chicago than the fathers of these poor boys. I know there were no better women than their mothers. But I am going to be honest with this court, if it is at the expense of both. I know that one of two things happened to Richard Loeb: that this terrible crime was inherent in his organism, and came from some ancestor; or that it came through his education and his training after he was born. Do I need to prove it? Judge Crowe said at one point in this case, when some witness spoke about their wealth, that "probably that was responsible."

To believe that any boy is responsible for himself or his early training is an absurdity that no lawyer or judge should be guilty of today. Somewhere this came to the boy. If his failing came from his heredity, I do not know where or how. None of us are bred perfect and pure; and the color of our hair, the color of our eyes, our stature, the weight and fineness of our brain, and everything about us could, with full knowledge, be traced with absolute certainty to somewhere. If we had the pedigree it could be traced just the same in a boy as it could in a dog, a horse or a cow.

I do not know what remote ancestors have sent down the seed that corrupted him, and I do not know through how many ancestors it may have passed until it reached Dickie Loeb.

All I know is that it is true, and there is not a biologist in the world who will not say that I am right.

If it did not come that way, then I know that if he was normal, if he had been understood, if he had been trained as he should have been it would not have happened. Not that anybody may not slip, but I know it and Your Honor knows it, and every schoolhouse and every church in the land is an evidence of it. Else why build them?

Every effort to protect society is an effort toward training the youth to keep the path. Every bit of training in the world proves it, and it likewise proves that it sometimes fails. I know that if this boy had been understood and properly trained—properly for him—and the training that he got might have been the very best for someone; but if it had been the proper training for him he would not be in this courtoom today with the noose above his head. If there is responsibility anywhere, it is back of him; somewhere in the infinite number of his ancestors, or in his surroundings, or in both. And I submit, Your Honor, that under every principle of natural justice, under every principle of conscience, of right, and of law, he should not be made responsible for the acts of someone else.

[2]

Freedom and Necessity

A. J. Ayer

When I am said to have done something of my own free will it is implied that I could have acted otherwise; and it is only when it is believed that I could have acted otherwise that I am held to be morally responsible for what I have done. For a man is not thought to be morally responsible for an action that it was not in his power to avoid. But if human behavior is entirely governed by causal laws, it is not clear how any action that is done could ever have been avoided. It may be said of the agent that he would have acted otherwise if the causes of his action had been different, but they being what they were, it seems to follow that he was bound to act as he did. Now it is commonly assumed both that men are capable of acting freely, in the sense that is required to make them morally responsible, and that human behavior is entirely governed by causal laws: and it is the apparent conflict between these two assumptions that gives rise to the philosophical problem of the freedom of the will.

Confronted with this problem, many people will be inclined to agree with Dr. Johnson: "Sir, we *know* our will is free, and *there's* an end on't.' " But, while this does very well for those who accept Dr. Johnson's premise, it would hardly convince anyone who denied the freedom of the will. Certainly, if we do know that our wills are free, it follows that they are so. But the logical reply to this might be that since our wills are not free, it follows that no one can know that they are: so

Reprinted from *Philosophical Essays* (1954) by A. J. Ayer, by permission of Macmillan & Co. Ltd., London; The Macmillan Company of Canada Limited; and St. Martin's Press, Inc.

Sir Alfred Ayer (b. 1910) was Wykeham Professor of Logic at the University of Oxford.

that if anyone claims, like Dr. Johnson, to know that they are, he must be mistaken. What is evident, indeed, is that people often believe themselves to be acting freely; and it is to this "feeling" of freedom that some philosophers appeal when they wish, in the supposed interests of morality, to prove that not all human action is causally determined. But if these philosophers are right in their assumption that a man cannot be acting freely if his action is causally determined, then the fact that someone feels free to do, or not to do, a certain action does not prove that he really is so. It may prove that the agent does not himself know what it is that makes him act in one way rather than another: but from the fact that a man is unaware of the causes of his action, it does not follow that no such causes exist.

So much may be allowed to the determinist; but his belief that all human actions are subservient to causal laws still remains to be justified. If, indeed, it is necessary that every event should have a cause, then the rule must apply to human behavior as much as to anything else. But why should it be supposed that every event must have a cause? The contrary is not unthinkable. Nor is the law of universal causation a necessary presupposition of scientific thought. The scientist may try to discover causal laws, and in many cases he succeeds; but sometimes he has to be content with statistical laws, and sometimes he comes upon events which, in the present state of his knowledge, he is not able to subsume under any law at all. In the case of these events, he assumes that if he knew more he would be able to discover some law, whether causal or statistical, which would enable him to account for them. And this assumption cannot be disproved. For however far he may have carried his investigation, it is always open to him to carry it further; and it is always conceivable that if he carried it further he would discover the connection which had hitherto escaped him. Nevertheless, it is also conceivable that the events with which he is concerned are not systematically connected with any others: so that the reason why he does not discover the sort of laws that he requires is simply that they do not obtain.

Now in the case of human conduct the search for explanations has not in fact been altogether fruitless. Certain scientific laws have been established; and with the help of these laws we do make a number of successful predictions about the ways in which different people will behave. But these predictions do not always cover every detail. We may be able to predict that in certain circumstances a particular man will be angry, without being able to prescribe the precise form that the expression of his anger will take. We may be reasonably sure that he will shout, but not sure how loud his shout will be, or exactly what words he will use. And it is only a small proportion of human actions that we are able to forecast even so precisely as this. But that, it may be said, is because we have not carried our investigations very far. The science of psychology is still in its infancy and, as it is developed, not only will more human actions be explained, but the explanations will go into greater detail. The ideal of complete explanation may never in fact be attained; but it is theoretically attainable. Well, this may be so: and certainly it is impossible to show *a priori* that it is not so; but equally it cannot be shown that it is. This will not, however, discourage the scientist who, in the field of human behavior, as elsewhere, will continue to formulate theories and test them by the facts. And in this he is justified. For since he has no reason *a priori* to admit that there is a limit to what he can discover, the fact that he also cannot be sure that there is no limit does not make it unreasonable for him to devise theories, nor, having devised them, to try constantly to improve them.

But now suppose it to be claimed that, so far as men's actions are concerned, there is a limit; and that this limit is set by the fact of human freedom. An obvious objection is that in many cases in which a person feels himself to be free to do, or not to do, a certain action, we are even now able to explain, in causal terms, why it is that he acts as he does. But it might be argued that even if men are sometimes mistaken in believing that they act freely, it does not follow that they are always so mistaken. For it is not always the case that when a man believes that he has acted freely we are in fact able to account for his action in causal terms. A determinist would say that we should be able to account for it if we had more knowledge of the circumstances, and had been able to discover the appropriate natural laws. But until those discoveries have been made, this remains only a pious hope. And may it not be true that, in some cases at least, the reason why we can give no causal explanation is that no causal explanation is available; and that this is because the agent's choice was literally free, as he himself felt it to be?

The answer is that this may indeed be true, inasmuch as it is open to anyone to hold that no explanation is possible until some explanation is actually found. But even so it does not give the moralist what he wants. For he is anxious to show that men are capable of acting freely in order to infer that they can be morally responsible for what they do. But if it is a matter of pure chance that a man should act in one way rather than another, he may be free but he can hardly be responsible. And indeed when a man's actions seem to us quite unpredictable, when, as we say, there is no knowing what he will do, we do not look upon him as a moral agent. We look upon him rather as a lunatic.

To this it may be objected that we are not dealing fairly with the moralist. For when he makes it a condition of my being morally responsible that I should act freely, he does not wish to imply that it is purely a matter of chance that I act as I do. What he wishes to imply is that my actions are the result of my own free choice; and it is because they are the result of my own free choice that I am held to be morally responsible for them.

But now we must ask how it is that I come to make my choice. Either it is an accident that I choose to act as I do or it is not. If it is an accident, then it is merely a matter of chance that I did not choose otherwise; and if it is merely a matter of chance that I did not choose otherwise, it is surely irrational to hold me morally responsible for choosing as I did. But if it is not an accident that I choose to do one thing rather than another, then presumably there is some causal explanation of my choice; and in that case we are led back to determinism.

Again, the objection may be raised that we are not doing justice to the moralist's case. His view is not that it is a matter of chance that I choose to act as I do, but rather that my choice depends upon my character. Nevertheless he holds that I can still be free in the sense that he requires; for it is I who am responsible for my character. But in what way am I responsible for my character? Only, surely, in the sense that there is a causal connection between what I do now and what I have done in the past. It is only this that justifies the statement that I have made myself what I am; and even so this is an over-simplification, since it takes no account of the external influences to which I have been subjected. But, ignoring the external influences, let us assume that it is in fact the case that I have made myself what I am. Then it is still legitimate to ask how it is that I have come to make myself one sort of person rather than another. And if it be answered that it is a matter of my strength of will, we can put the same question in another form by asking how it is that my will has the strength that it has and not some other degree of strength. Once more, either it is an accident or it is not. If it is an accident, then by the same argument as before, I am not morally responsible, and if it is not an accident, we are led back to determinism.

Furthermore, to say that my actions proceed from my character or, more colloquially, that I act in character, is to say that my behavior is consistent and to that extent predictable; and since it is, above all, for the actions that I perform in character that I am held to be morally responsible, it looks as if the admission of moral responsibility, so far from being incompatible with determinism, tends rather to presuppose it. But how can this be so if it is a necessary condition of moral responsibility that the person who is held responsible should have acted freely? It seems that if we are to retain this idea of moral responsibility, we must either show that men can be held responsible for actions which they do not do freely, or else find some way of reconciling determinism with the freedom of the will.

It is no doubt with the object of effecting this reconciliation that some philosophers have defined freedom as the consciousness of necessity. And by so doing they are able to say not only that a man can be acting freely when his action is causally determined, but even that his action must be causally determined for it to be possible for him to be acting freely. Nevertheless, this definition has the serious disadvantage that it gives to the word "freedom" a meaning quite different from any that it ordinarily bears. It is indeed obvious that if we are allowed to give the word "freedom" any meaning that we please, we can find a meaning that will reconcile it with determinism; but this is no more a solution of our present problem than the fact that the word "horse" could be arbitrarily used to mean what is ordinarily meant by "sparrow" is a proof that horses have wings. For suppose that I am compelled by another person to do something "against my will." In that case, as the word "freedom" is ordinarily used, I should not be said to be acting freely; and the fact that I am fully aware of the constraint to which I am subjected makes no difference to the matter. I do not become free by becoming conscious that I am not. It may, indeed, be possible to show that my being aware that my action is causally determined is not incompatible with my acting freely; but it by no means follows that it is in this that my freedom consists. Moreover, I suspect that one of the reasons why people are inclined to define freedom as the consciousness of necessity is that they think that if one is conscious of necessity one may somehow be able to master it. But this is a fallacy. It is like someone's saying that he wishes he could see into the future, because if he did he would know what calamities lay in wait for him and so would be able to avoid them. But if he avoids the calamities, then they don't lie in the future and it is not true that he foresees them. And similarly, if I am able to master necessity, in the sense of escaping the operation of a necessary law, then the law in question is not necessary. And if the law is not necessary, then neither my freedom nor anything else can consist in my knowing that it is.

Let it be granted, then, that when we speak of reconciling freedom with determinism we are using the word "freedom" in an ordinary sense. It still remains for us to make this usage clear; and perhaps the best way to make it clear is to show what it is that freedom, in this sense, is contrasted with. Now we begin with the assumption that freedom is contrasted with causality; so that a man cannot be said to be acting freely if his action is causally determined. But this assumption has led us into difficulties and I now wish to suggest that it is mistaken. For it is not, I think, causality that freedom is to be contrasted with, but constraint. And while it is true that being constrained to do an action entails being caused to do it, I shall try to show that the converse does not hold. I shall try to show that from the fact that my action is causally determined, it does not necessarily follow that I am constrained to do it; and this is equivalent to saying that it does not necessarily follow that I am not free.

If I am constrained, I do not act freely. But in what circumstances can I legitimately be said to be constrained? An obvious instance is the case in which I am compelled by another person to do what he wants. In a case of this sort the compulsion need not be such as to deprive one of the power of choice. It is not required that the other person should have hypnotized me, or that he should make it physically impossible for me to go against his will. It is enough that he should induce me to do what he wants by making it clear to me that, if I do not, he will bring about some situation that I regard as even more undesirable than the consequences of the action that he wishes me to do. Thus, if the man points a pistol at my head, I may still choose to disobey him; but this does not prevent its being true that if I do fall in with his wishes he can legitimately be said to have compelled me. And if the circumstances are such that no reasonable person would be expected to choose the other alternative, then the action that I am made to do is not one for which I am held to be morally responsible.

A similar, but still somewhat different, case is that in which another person has obtained an habitual ascendancy over me. Where this is so, there may be no question of my being induced to act as the other person wishes by being confronted with a still more disagreeable alternative; for if I am sufficiently under his influence, this special stimulus will not be necessary. Nevertheless I do not act freely, for the reason that I have been deprived of the power of choice. And this means that I have acquired so strong a habit of obedience, that I no longer go through any process of deciding whether or not to do what the other person wants. About other matters I may still deliberate; but as regards the fulfillment of this other person's wishes, my own deliberations have ceased to be a causal factor in my behavior. And it is in this sense that I may be said to be constrained. It is not, however, necessary that such constraint should take the form of subservience to another person. A kleptomaniac is not a free agent, in respect to his stealing, because he does not go through any process of deciding whether or not to steal. Or rather, if he does go through such a process, it is irrelevant to his behavior. Whatever he resolved to do, he would steal all the same. And it is this that distinguishes him from the ordinary thief.

But now it may be asked whether there is any essential difference between these cases and those in which the agent is commonly thought to be free. No doubt the ordinary thief does go through a process of deciding whether or not to steal, and no doubt it does affect his behavior. If he resolved to refrain from stealing, he could carry his resolution out. But if it be allowed that his making or not making this resolution is causally determined, then how can he be any more free than the kleptomaniac? It may be true that unlike the kleptomaniac, he could refrain from stealing if he chose; but if there is a cause, or set of causes, which necessitate his choosing as he does, how can he be said to have the power of choice? Again, it may be true that no one now compels me to get up and walk across the room; but if my doing so can be causally explained in terms of my history or my environment, or whatever it may be, then how am I any more free than if some other person had compelled me? I do not have the feeling of constraint that I have when a pistol is manifestly pointed at my head but the chains of causation by which I am bound are no less effective for being invisible.

The answer to this is that the cases I have mentioned as examples of constraint do differ from the others; and they differ just in the ways that I have tried to bring out. If I suffered from a compulsion neurosis, so that I got up and walked across the room, whether I wanted to or not, or if I did so because somebody else compelled me, then I should not be acting freely. But if I do it now, I shall be acting freely, just because these conditions do not obtain; and the fact that my action may nevertheless have a cause is, from this point of view, irrelevant. For it is not when my action has any cause at all, but only when it has a special sort of cause, that it is reckoned not to be free.

But here it may be objected that, even if this distinction corresponds to ordinary usage, it is still very irrational. For why should we distinguish, with regard to a person's freedom, between the operations of one sort of cause and those of another? Do not all causes equally necessitate? And is it not therefore arbitrary to say that a person is free when he is necessitated in one fashion, but not when he is necessitated in another?

That all causes equally necessitate is indeed a tautology, if the word "necessitate" is taken merely as equivalent to "cause"; but if, as the objection requires, it is taken as equivalent to "constrain" or "compel," then I do not think that this proposition is true. For all that is needed for one event to be the cause of another is that, in the given circumstances, the event which is said to be the effect would not have occurred if it had not been for the occurrence of the event which is said to be the cause, or *vice versa,* according as causes are interpreted as necessary, or sufficient, conditions; and this fact is usually deducible from some causal law which states that whenever an event of the one kind occurs then, given suitable conditions, an event of the other kind will occur in a certain temporal or spatio-temporal relationship to it. In short, there is an invariable concomitance between the two classes of events; but there is no compulsion in any but a metaphorical sense. Suppose, for example, that a psychoanalyst is able to account for some aspect of my behavior by referring it to some lesion that I suffered in my childhood. In that case, it may be said that my childhood experience, together with certain other events, necessitates my behaving as I do. But all that this involves is that it is found to be true in general that when people have had certain experiences as children, they subsequently behave in certain specifiable ways; and my case is just another instance of this general law. It is in this way indeed that my behavior is explained. But from the fact that my behavior is capable of being explained, in the sense that it can be subsumed under some natural law, it does not follow that I am acting under constraint.

If this is correct, to say that I could have acted otherwise is to say, first, that I should have acted otherwise if I had so chosen; secondly, that my action was voluntary in the sense in which the actions, say, of the kleptomaniac are not; and thirdly, that nobody compelled me to choose as I did; and these three conditions may very well be fulfilled. When they are fulfilled, I may be said to have acted freely. But this is not to say that it was a matter of chance that I acted as I did, or, in other words, that my action could not be explained. And that my action should be capable of being explained is all that is required by the postulate of determinism.

If more than this seems to be required it is, I think, because the use of the very word "determinism" is in some degree misleading. For it tends to suggest that one event is somehow in the power of another, whereas the truth is merely that they are factually correlated. And the same applies to the use, in this context, of the word "necessity" and even of the word "cause" itself. Moreover, there are various reasons for this. One is the tendency to confuse causal with logical necessitation, and so to infer mistakenly that the effect is contained in the cause. Another is the uncritical use of a concept of force which is derived from primitive experiences of pushing and striking. A third is the survival of an animistic conception of causality, in which all causal relationships are modeled on the example of one person's exercising authority over another. As a result we tend to form an imaginative picture of an unhappy effect trying vainly to escape from the clutches of an overmastering cause. But, I repeat, the fact is simply that when an event of one type occurs, an event of another type occurs also, in a certain temporal or spatio-temporal relation to the first. The rest is only metaphor. And it is because of the metaphor, and not because of the fact, that we come to think that there is an antithesis between causality and freedom.

Nevertheless, it may be said, if the postulate of determinism is valid, then the future can be explained in terms of the past: and this means that if one knew enough about the past one would be able to predict the future. But in that case what will happen in the future is already decided. And how then can I be said to be free? What is going to happen is going to happen and nothing that I do can prevent it. If the determinist is right, I am the helpless prisoner of fate.

But what is meant by saying that the future course of events is already decided? If the implication is that some person has arranged it, then the proposition is false. But if all that is meant is that it is possible, in principle, to deduce it from a set of particular facts about the past, together with the appropriate general laws, then, even if this is true, it does not in the least entail that I am the helpless prisoner of fate. It does not even entail that my actions make no difference to the future: for they are causes as well as effects; so that if they were different their consequences would be different also. What it does entail is that my behavior can be predicted; but to say that my behavior can be predicted is not to say that I am acting under constraint. It is indeed true that I cannot escape my destiny if this is taken to mean no more than that I shall do what I shall do. But this is a tautology, just as it is a tautology that what is going to happen is going to happen. And such tautologies as these prove nothing whatsoever about the freedom of the will.

[3]

Free Will

C. A. Campbell

1. It is something of a truism that in philosophic enquiry the exact formulation of a problem often takes one a long way on the road to its solution. In the case of the Free Will problem I think there is a rather special need of careful formulation. For there are many sorts of human freedom; and it can easily happen that one wastes a great deal of labor in proving or disproving a freedom which has almost nothing to do with the freedom which is at issue in the traditional problem of Free Will. The abortiveness of so much of the argument for and against Free Will in contemporary philosophical literature seems to me due in the main to insufficient pains being taken over the preliminary definition of the problem. There is, indeed, one outstanding exception, Professor Broad's brilliant inaugural lecture entitled "Determinism, Indeterminism, and Libertarianism,"[1] in which forty-three pages are devoted to setting out the problem, as against seven to its solution! I confess that the solution does not seem to myself to follow upon the formulation quite as easily as all that;[2] but Professor Broad's eminent example fortifies me in my decision to give here what may seem at first sight a disproportionate amount of time to the business of determining the essential characteristics of the kind of freedom with which the traditional problem is concerned.

Fortunately we can at least make a beginning with a certain amount of confidence. It is not seriously disputable that the kind of freedom in question is the freedom which is commonly recognized to be in some

Reprinted from *On Selfhood and Godhood* (London: George Allen & Unwin Ltd., 1957), by permission of the publisher.

C. A. Campbell (b. 1897) is Professor Emeritus at The University of Glasgow.

115

sense, a precondition of moral responsibility. Clearly, it is on account
of this integral connection with moral responsibility that such exceptional importance has always been felt to attach to the Free Will problem. But in what precise sense is free will a precondition of moral responsibility, and thus a postulate of the moral life in general? This is
an exceedingly troublesome question: but until we have satisfied ourselves
about the answer to it, we are not in a position to state, let alone decide,
the question whether "Free Will" in its traditional, ethical, significance
is a reality.

Our first business, then, is to ask, exactly what kind of freedom
is it which is required for moral responsibility? And as to method of
procedure in this inquiry, there seems to me to be no real choice. I know
of only one method that carries with it any hope of success; viz., the
critical comparison of those acts for which, on due reflection, we deem
it proper to attribute moral praise or blame to the agents, with those
acts for which, on due reflection, we deem such judgments to be improper.
The ultimate touchstone, as I see it, can only be our moral consciousness
as it manifests itself in our more critical and considered moral judgments. The "linguistic" approach by way of the analysis of moral
sentences seems to me, despite its present popularity, to be an almost
infallible method for reaching wrong results in the moral field, but I
must reserve what I have to say about this for the next lecture.

2. The first point to note is that the freedom at issue (as indeed the
very name "Free *Will* Problem" indicates) pertains primarily not to overt
acts but to inner acts. The nature of things has decreed that, save in
the case of one's self, it is only overt acts which one can directly observe.
But a very little reflection serves to show that in our moral judgments
upon others their overt acts are regarded as significant only in so far
as they are the expression of inner acts. We do not consider the acts
of a robot to be morally responsible acts; nor do we consider the acts
of a man to be so save insofar as they are distinguishable from those
of a robot by reflecting an inner life of choice. Similarly, from the other
side, if we are satisfied (as we may on occasion be, at least in the case
of ourselves) that a person has definitely elected to follow a course which
he believes to be wrong, but has been prevented by external circumstances from translating his inner choice into an overt act, we still regard him as morally blameworthy. Moral freedom, then, pertains to *inner* acts.

The next point seems at first sight equally obvious and uncontro-
versial; but, as we shall see, it has awkward implications if we are in
real earnest with it (as almost nobody is). It is the simple point that
the act must be one of which the person judged can be regarded as
the *sole* author. It seems plain enough that if there are any *other*

determinants of the act, external to the self, to that extent the act is not an act which the *self* determines, and to that extent not an act for which the self can be held morally responsible. The self is only part-author of the act, and his moral responsibility can logically extend only to those elements within the act (assuming for the moment that these can be isolated) of which he is the *sole* author.

The awkward implications of this apparent truism will be readily appreciated. For, if we are mindful of the influences exerted by heredity and environment, we may well feel some doubt whether there is any act of will at all of which one can truly say that the self is sole author, sole determinant. No man has a voice in determining the raw material of impulses and capacities that constitute his hereditary endowment, and no man has more than a very partial control of the material and social environment in which he is destined to live his life. Yet it would be manifestly absurd to deny that these two factors do constantly and profoundly affect the nature of a man's choices. That this is so we all of us recognize in our moral judgments when we "make allowances," as we say, for a bad heredity or a vicious environment, and acknowledge in the victim of them a diminished moral responsibility for evil courses. Evidently we do *try*, in our moral judgments, however crudely, to praise or blame a man only in respect of that of which we can regard him as *wholly* the author. And evidently we do recognize that, for a man to be the author of an act in the full sense required for moral responsibility, it is not enough merely that he "wills" or "chooses" the act; since even the most unfortunate victim of heredity or environment does, as a rule, "will" what he does. It is significant, however, that the ordinary man, though well enough aware of the influence upon choices of heredity and environment, does not feel obliged thereby to give up his assumption that moral predicates *are* somehow applicable. Plainly he still believes that there is *something* for which a man is morally responsible, something of which we can fairly say that he is the sole author. *What is this something?* To that question common-sense is not ready with an explicit answer—though an answer is, I think, implicit in the line which its moral judgments take. I shall do what I can to give an explicit answer later in this lecture. Meantime, it must suffice to observe that, if we are to be true to the deliverances of our moral consciousness, it is very difficult to deny that *sole* authorship is a necessary condition of the morally responsible act.

Thirdly, we come to a point over which much recent controversy has raged. We may approach it by raising the following question. Granted an act of which the agent is sole author, does this "sole authorship" suffice to make the act a morally free act? We may be inclined to think that it does, until we contemplate the possibility that an act of which the agent is sole author might conceivably occur as a necessary expression of the agent's nature; the way in which, e.g. some philosophers have supposed the Divine act of creation to occur. This consideration excites a legitimate doubt; for it is far from easy to see how a person can be regarded as a proper subject for moral praise or blame in respect of an act which he *cannot help* performing—even if it be his own "nature" which necessitates it. Must we not recognize it as a condition of the morally free act that the agent "could have acted otherwise" than he in fact did? It is true, indeed, that we sometimes praise or blame a man for an act about which we are prepared to say, in the light of our knowledge of his established character, that he "could no other." But I think a little reflection shows that in such cases we are not praising or blaming the man strictly for what he does *now* (or at any rate we ought not to be), but rather for those past acts of his which have generated the firm habit of mind from which his *present* act follows "necessarily." In other words, our praise and blame, so far as justified, are really retrospective, being directed not to the agent *qua* performing *this* act, but to the agent *qua* performing those past acts which have built up his present character, and in respect to which we presume that he *could* have acted otherwise, that there really *were* open possibilities before him. These cases, therefore, seem to me to constitute no valid exception to what I must take to be the rule, viz., that a man can be morally praised or blamed for an act only if he could have acted otherwise.

Now philosophers today are fairly well agreed that it is a postulate of the morally responsible act that the agent "could have acted otherwise" in *some* sense of that phrase. But sharp differences of opinion have arisen over the way in which the phrase ought to be interpreted. There is a strong disposition to water down its apparent meaning by insisting that it is not (as a postulate of moral responsibility) to be understood as a straightforward categorical proposition, but rather as a disguised hypothetical proposition. All that we really require to be assured of, in order to justify our holding X morally responsible for an act, is, we are told, that X could have acted otherwise *if* he had *chosen* otherwise or perhaps that X could have acted otherwise *if* he had had a different character, or *if* he had been placed in different circumstances.

I think it is easy to understand, and even, in a measure, to sympathize with, the motives which induce philosophers to offer these counterinterpretations. It is not just the fact that "X could have acted otherwise," as a bald categorical statement, is incompatible with the universal sway of casual law—though this is, to some philosophers, a serious stone of stumbling. The more widespread objection is that it at least looks as though it were compatible with that causal continuity of an agent's character with his conduct which is implied when we believe (surely with justice) that we can often tell the sort of thing a man will do from our knowledge of the sort of man he is.

We shall have to make our accounts with that particular difficulty later. At this stage I wish merely to show that neither of the hypothetical propositions suggested—and I think the same could be shown for *any* hypothetical alternative—is an acceptable substitute for the categorical proposition "X could have acted otherwise" as the presupposition of moral responsibility.

Let us look first at the earlier suggestion—"X could have acted otherwise *if* he had chosen otherwise." Now clearly there are a great many acts with regard to which we are entirely satisfied that the agent is thus situated. We are often perfectly sure that—for this is all it amounts to— if X had chosen otherwise, the circumstances presented no external obstacle to the translation of that choice into action. For example, we often have no doubt at all that X, who in point of fact told a lie, could have told the truth *if* he had so chosen. But does our confidence on this score allay all legitimate doubts about whether X is really blameworthy? Does it entail that X is free in the sense required for moral responsibility? Surely not. The obvious question immediately arises: "But *could* X have *chosen* otherwise than he did?" It is doubt about the true answer to *that* question which leads most people to doubt the reality of moral responsibility. Yet on this crucial question the hypothetical proposition which is offered as a sufficient statement of the condition justifying the ascription of moral responsibility gives us no information whatsoever.

Indeed this hypothetical substitute for the categorical "X could have acted otherwise" seems to me to lack all plausibility unless one contrives to forget why it is, after all, that we ever come to feel fundamental doubts about man's moral responsibility. Such doubts are born, surely, when one becomes aware of certain reputable world-views in religion or philosophy, or of certain reputable scientific beliefs, which in their several ways imply that man's actions are necessitated, and thus could not be otherwise than they in fact are. But clearly a doubt so based is not even touched by the recognition that a man would very often act otherwise *if* he so chose. That proposition is entirely compatible with the necessitarian theories which generate our doubt: indeed it is this very compatibility that has recommended it to some philosophers, who are reluctant to give up either moral responsibility or Determinism. The proposition which we *must* be able to affirm if moral praise or blame of X is to be justified is the categorical proposition that X could have acted otherwise because—not if—he could have chosen otherwise; or, since it is essentially the inner side of the act that matters, the proposition simply that X could have chosen otherwise.

For the second of the alternative formulae suggested, we cannot spare more than a few moments. But its inability to meet the demands it is required to meet is almost transparent. "X could have acted otherwise," as a statement of a precondition of X's moral responsibility, really means (we are told) "X could have acted otherwise *if* he were differently constituted, or *if* he had been placed in different circumstances." It seems a sufficient reply to this to point out that the person whose moral responsibility is at issue is X; a specific individual, in a specific set of circumstances. It is totally irrelevant to X's moral responsibility that we should be able to say that some person differently constituted from X, or X in a different set of circumstances, could have done something different from what X did.

3. Let me, then, briefly sum up the answer at which we have arrived to our question about the kind of freedom required to justify moral responsibility. It is that a man can be said to exercise free will in a morally significant sense only in so far as his chosen act is one of which he is the sole cause or author, and only if—in the straightforward, categorical sense of the phrase—he "could have chosen otherwise."

I confess that this answer is in some ways a disconcerting one, disconcerting, because most of us, however objective we are in the actual conduct of our thinking, would *like* to be able to believe that moral responsibility is real; whereas the freedom required for moral responsibility, on the analysis we have given, is certainly far more difficult to establish than the freedom required on the analysis we found ourselves obliged to reject. If, e.g., moral freedom entails only that I could have acted otherwise *if* I had chosen otherwise, there is no real "problem" about it at all. I am "free" in the normal case where there is no external obstacle to prevent my translating the alternative choice into action, and not free in other cases. Still less is there a problem if all that moral freedom entails is that I could have acted otherwise *if* I had been a differently constituted person, or been in different circumstances. Clearly, I am *always* free in *this* sense of freedom. But, as I have argued, these so-called "freedoms" fail to give us the pre-conditions of moral responsibility, and hence leave the freedom of the traditional free-will problem, the freedom that people are really concerned about, precisely where it was.

4. Another interpretation of freedom which I am bound to reject on the same general ground, i.e. that it is just not the kind of freedom that is relevant to moral responsibility, is the old idealist view which identifies the *free* will with the *rational* will; the rational will in its turn being identified with the will which wills the moral law in whole-hearted, single-minded obedience to it. This view is still worth at least a passing mention, if only because it has recently been resurrected in an interesting work by Professor A. E. Teale.[3] Moreover, I cannot but feel

Free Will   121

a certain nostalgic tenderness for a view in which I myself was (so to speak) philosophically cradled. The almost apostolic fervor with which my revered nursing-mother, the late Sir Henry Jones, was wont to impart it to his charges, and, hardly less, his ill-concealed scorn for ignoble natures (like my own), which still hankered after a free will in the old "vulgar" sense, are vividly recalled for me in Professor Teale's stirring pages.

The true interpretation of free will, according to Professor Teale, the interpretation to which Kant, despite occasional back-slidings, adhered in his better moments, is that "the will is free in the degree that it is informed and disciplined by the moral principle."[4]

Now this is a perfectly intelligible sense of the word "free"—or at any rate it can be made so with a little explanatory comment, which Professor Teale well supplies but for which there is here no space. But clearly it is a very different sort of freedom from that which is at issue in the traditional problem of free will. This idealist "freedom" sponsored by Teale belongs, on his own showing, only to the self in respect of its *good* willing. The freedom with which the traditional problem is concerned, inasmuch as it is the freedom presupposed by moral responsibility, must belong to the self in respect of its *bad*, no less than its *good*, willing. It is, in fact, the freedom to decide between genuinely open alternatives of good and bad willing.

Professor Teale, of course, is not unaware that the freedom he favors differs from freedom as traditionally understood. He recognizes the traditional concept under its Kantian title of "elective" freedom. But he leaves the reader in no kind of doubt about his disbelief in both the reality and the value of this elective freedom to do, or forbear from doing, one's duty.

The question of the reality of elective freedom I shall be dealing with shortly; and it will occupy us to the end of the lecture. At the moment, I am concerned only with its value, and with the rival view that all that matters for the moral life is the "rational" freedom which a man has in the degree that his will is "informed and disciplined by the moral principle." I confess that to myself the verdict on the rival view seems plain and inescapable. No amount of verbal ingenuity or argumentative convolutions can obscure the fact that it is in flat contradiction to the implications of moral responsibility. The point at issue is really perfectly straightforward. If, as this idealist theory maintains, my acting in defiance of what I deem to be my duty is not a "free" act in *any* sense, let alone in the sense that "I could have acted otherwise," then I cannot be morally blameworthy, and that is all there is to it. Nor, for that matter, is the idealist entitled to say that I am morally praiseworthy if I act dutifully; for although that act *is* a "free" act in the idealist sense, it is on his own avowal not free in the sense that "I could have acted otherwise."

It seems to me idle, therefore, to pretend that if one has to give up freedom in the traditional elective sense one is not giving up anything important. What we are giving up is, quite simply, the reality of the moral life. I recognize that to a certain type of religious nature (as well as, by an odd meeting of extremes, to a certain type of secular nature) that does not appear to matter so very much; but, for myself, I still think it sufficiently important to make it well worth while inquiring seriously into the possibility that the elective freedom upon which it rests may be real after all.

5. That brings me to the second, and more constructive, part of this lecture. From now on I shall be considering whether it is reasonable to believe that man does in fact possess a free will of the kind specified in the first part of the lecture. If so, just how and where within the complex fabric of the volitional life are we to locate it?—for although free will must presumably belong (if anywhere) to the volitional side of human experience, it is pretty clear from the way in which we have been forced to define it that it does not pertain simply to volition as such, not even to all volitions that are commonly dignified with the name of "choices." It has been, I think, one of the more serious impediments to profitable discussion of the Free Will problem that Libertarians and Determinists alike have so often failed to appreciate the comparatively narrow area within which the free will that is necessary to "save" morality is required to operate. It goes without saying that this failure has been gravely prejudicial to the case for Libertarianism. I attach a good deal of importance, therefore, to the problem of locating free will correctly within the volitional orbit. Its solution forestalls and annuls, I believe, some of the more tiresome clichés of Determinist criticism.

We saw earlier that Common Sense's practice of "making allowances" in its moral judgments for the influence of heredity and environment indicates Common Sense's conviction, both that a just moral judgment must discount determinants of choice over which the agent has no control, and also (since it still accepts moral judgments as legitimate) that *something* of moral relevance survives which can be regarded as genuinely self-originated. We are now to try to discover what this "something" is. And I think we may still usefully take Common Sense as our guide. Suppose one asks the ordinary intelligent citizen *why* he deems it proper to make allowances for X, whose heredity and/or environment are unfortunate. He will tend to reply, I think, in some such terms as these: that X has more and stronger temptations to deviate from what is right than Y or Z, who are normally circumstanced, so that he must put forth a *stronger moral effort* if he is to achieve the same level of external conduct. The intended implication seems to be that X is just as morally praiseworthy as Y or Z *if* he exerts an equivalent moral effort, even though he may not thereby achieve an equal success in conforming his will to the "concrete" demands of duty. And this implies, again, Common Sense's belief that *in moral effort* we have something for which a man is responsible *without qualification,* something that is *not* affected by heredity and environment but depends *solely* upon the self itself.

Now, in my opinion, Common Sense has here, in principle, hit upon the one and only defensible answer. Here, and here alone, so far as I can see, in the act of deciding whether to put forth or withhold the moral effort required to resist temptation and rise to duty, is to be found an act which is free in the sense required for moral responsibility; an act of which the self is sole author, and of which it is true to say that "it could be" (or, after the event, "could have been") "otherwise." Such is the thesis which we shall now try to establish.

6. The species of argument appropriate to the establishment of a thesis of this sort should fall, I think, into two phases. First, there should be a consideration of the evidence of the moral agent's own inner experience. What *is* the act of moral decision, and what does it imply, from the standpoint of the actual participant? Since there is no way of knowing the act of moral decision—or for that matter any other form of activity—except by actual participation in it, the evidence of the subject, or agent, is on an issue of this kind of palmary importance. It can hardly, however, be taken as in itself conclusive. For even if that evidence should be overwhelmingly to the effect that moral decision does have the characteristics required by moral freedom, the question is bound to be raised—and in view of considerations from other quarters pointing in contrary direction is *rightly* raised—Can we *trust* the evidence of inner experience? That brings us to what will be the second phase of the argument. We shall have to go on to show, if we are to make good our case, that the extraneous considerations so often supposed to be fatal to the belief in moral freedom are in fact innocuous to it.

In the light of what was said in the last lecture about the self's experience of moral decision as a *creative* activity, we may perhaps be absolved from developing the first phase of the argument at any great length. The appeal is throughout to one's own experience in the actual taking of the moral decision in the situation of moral temptation. "Is it possible," we must ask, "for anyone so circumstanced to *dis*believe that he could be deciding otherwise?" The answer is surely not in doubt. When we decide to exert moral effort to resist a temptation, we feel quite certain that we *could* withhold the effort; just as, if we decide to withhold the effort and yield to our desires, we feel quite certain that we *could* exert it—otherwise we should not blame ourselves afterwards for having succumbed. It may be, indeed, that this conviction is mere self-delusion. But that is not at the moment our concern. It is enough at present to establish that the act of deciding to exert or to withhold moral effort, as we know it from the inside in actual moral living, belongs to the category of acts which "could have been otherwise."

Mutatis mutandis, the same reply is forthcoming if we ask, "Is it possible for the moral agent in the taking of his decision to *dis*believe that he is the *sole* author of that decision?" Clearly he cannot disbelieve that it is *he* who takes the decision. That, however, is not in itself sufficient to enable him, on reflection, to regard himself as *solely* responsible for the act. For his "character" as so far formed might conceivably be a factor in determining it, and no one can suppose that the constitution of his "character" is uninfluenced by circumstances of heredity and environment with which *he* has nothing to do. But as we pointed out in the last lecture, the very essence of the moral decision as it is experienced is that it is a decision whether or not to *combat* our strongest desire, and our strongest desire *is* the expression in the situation of our character as so far formed. Now clearly our character cannot be a factor in determining the decision whether or not to *oppose* our character. I think we are entitled to say, therefore, that the act of moral decision is one in which the self is for itself not merely "author" but "sole author."

7. We may pass on, then, to the second phase of our constructive argument; and this will demand more elaborate treatment. Even if a moral agent *qua* making a moral decision in the situation of "temptation" cannot help believing that he has free will in the sense at issue—a moral freedom between real alternatives, between genuinely open possibilities—are there, nevertheless, objections to a freedom of this kind so cogent that we are bound to distrust the evidence of "inner experience"?

I begin by drawing attention to a simple point whose significance tends, I think, to be underestimated. If the phenomenological analysis we have offered is substantially correct, no one, while functioning as a moral agent, can help believing that he enjoys free will. Theoretically he may be completely convinced by Determinist arguments, but when actually confronted with a personal situation of conflict between duty and desire he is quite certain that it lies with him here and now whether or not he will rise to duty. It follows that if Determinists could produce convincing theoretical arguments against a free will of this kind, the awkward predicament would ensure that man has to deny as a theoretical being what he has to assert as a practical being. Now I think the Determinist ought to be a good deal more worried about this then he usually is. He seems to imagine that a strong case on general theoretical grounds is enough to prove that the "practical" belief in free will, even if inescapable for us as practical beings, is mere illusion. But in fact it proves nothing of the sort. There is no reason whatever why a belief that we find ourselves obligated to hold *qua* practical beings should be required to give way before a belief which we find ourselves obliged to hold *qua* theoretical beings; or, for that matter, *vice versa*. All that the theoretical arguments of Determinism can prove, unless they are reinforced by a refutation of the phenomenological analysis that supports Libertarianism, is that there is a radical conflict between the theoretical and the practical sides of man's nature, an antimony at the very heart of the self. And this is a state of affairs with which no one can easily rest satisified. I think therefore that the Determinist ought to concern himself a great deal more than he does with phenomenological analysis, in order to show, if he can, that the assurance of free will is not really an inexpugnable element in man's practical consciousness. There is just as much obligation upon him, convinced though he may be of the soundness of his theoretical arguments, to expose the errors of the Libertarian's phenomenological analysis, as there is upon us, convinced though we may be of the soundness of the Libertarian's phenomenological analysis, to expose the errors of the Determinist's theoretical arguments.

8. However, we must at once begin the discharge of our own obligation. The rest of this lecture will be devoted to trying to show that the arguments which seem to carry most weight with Determinists are, to say the least of it, very far from compulsive.

Fortunately, a good many of the arguments which at an earlier time in the history of philosophy would have been strongly urged against us make almost no appeal to the bulk of philosophers today, and we may here pass them by. That applies to any criticism of "open possibilities" based on a metaphysical theory about the nature of the universe as a whole. Nobody today *has* a metaphysical theory about the nature of the universe as a whole! It applies also, with almost equal force, to criticisms based upon the universality of causal law as a supposed postulate of science. There have always been, in my opinion, sound philosophic reasons for doubting the validity, as distinct from the convenience, of the causal postulate in its universal form, but at the present time, when scientists themselves are deeply divided about the need for postulating causality even within their own special field, we shall do better to concentrate our attention upon criticisms which are more confidently advanced. I propose to ignore also, on different grounds, the type of criticism of free will that is sometimes advanced from the side of religion, based upon religious postulates of Divine Omnipotence and Omniscience. So far as I can see, a postulate of human freedom is every bit as necessary to meet certain religious demands (e.g. to make sense of the "conviction of sin"), as postulates of Divine Omniscience and Omnipotence are to meet certain other religious demands. If so, then it can hardly be argued that religious experience as such tells more strongly against than for the position we are defending; and we may be satisfied, in the present context, to leave the matter there. It will be more profitable to discuss certain arguments which contemporary philosophers do think important, and which recur with a somewhat monotonous regularity in the literature of anti-Libertarianism.

These arguments can, I think, be reduced in principle to no more than two: first, the argument from "predictability"; second, the argument from the alleged meaninglessness of an act supposed to be the self's act and yet not an expression of the self's character. Contemporary criticism of free will seems to me to consist almost exclusively of variations on these two themes. I shall deal with each in turn.

9. On the first we touched in passing at an earlier stage. Surely it is beyond the question (the critic urges) that when we know a person intimately we can foretell with a high degree of accuracy how he will respond to at least a large number of practical situations. One feels safe in predicting that one's dog-loving friend will not use his boot to repel the little mongrel that comes yapping at his heels; or again that one's wife will not pass with incurious eyes (or indeed pass at all) the new hat-shop in the city. So to behave would not be (as we say) "in character." But, so the criticism runs, you with your doctrine of "genuinely open possibilities," of free will by which the self can diverge from its own character, remove all rational basis from such prediction. You require us to make the absurd supposition that the success of countless predictions of the sort in the past has been mere matter of chance. If you *really* believed in your theory, you would not be surprised if tomorrow your friend with the notorious horror of strong drink should suddenly exhibit a passion for whiskey and soda, or if your friend whose taste for reading has hitherto been satisfied with the sporting columns of the newspapers should be discovered on a fine Saturday afternoon poring over the works of Hegel. But of course you *would* be surprised. Social life would be sheer chaos if there were not well-grounded social expectations; and social life is not sheer chaos. Your theory is hopelessly wrecked upon obvious facts.

Now whether or not this criticism holds good against some versions of Libertarian theory, I need not here discuss. It is sufficient if I can make it clear that against the version advanced in this lecture, according to which free will is localized in a relatively narrow field of operation, the criticism has no relevance whatsoever.

Let us remind ourselves briefly of the setting within which, on our view, free will functions. There is X, the course which we believe we ought to follow, and Y, the course towards which we feel our desire is strongest. The freedom which we ascribe to the agent is the freedom to put forth or refrain from putting forth the moral effort required to resist the pressure of desire and do what he thinks he ought to do.

But then there is surely an immense range of practical situations—covering by far the greater part of life—in which there is no question of a conflict within the self between what he most desires to do and what he thinks he ought to do? Indeed such conflict is a comparatively rare phenomenon for the majority of men. Yet over that whole vast range there is nothing whatever in our version of Libertarianism to prevent our agreeing that character determines conduct. In the absence, real or supposed, of any "moral" issue, what a man chooses will be simply that course which, after such reflection as seems called for, he deems most likely to bring him what he most strongly desires; and that is the same as to say the course to which his present character inclines him.

Over by far the greater area of human choices, then, our theory offers no more barrier to successful prediction on the basis of character than any other theory. For where there is no clash of strongest desire with duty, the free will we are defending has no business. There is just nothing for it to do.

But what about the situations—rare enough though they may be—in which there *is* this clash and in which free will does therefore operate? Does our theory entail that there at any rate, as the critic seems to suppose, "anything may happen"?

Not by any manner of means. In the first place, and by the very nature of the case, the range of the agent's possible choices is bounded by what he thinks he ought to do on the one hand, and what he most strongly desires on the other. The freedom claimed for him is a freedom of decision to make or withhold the effort required to do what he thinks he ought to do. There is no question of a freedom to act in some "wild" fashion, out of all relation to his characteristic beliefs and desires. This so-called "freedom of caprice," so often charged against the Libertarian is, to put it bluntly, a sheer figment of the critic's imagination, with no *habitat* in serious Libertarian theory. Even in situations where free will does come into play, it is perfectly possible, on a view like ours, given the appropriate knowledge of a man's character, to predict within certain limits how he will respond.

But "probable" prediction in such situations can, I think, go further than this. It is obvious that where desire and duty are at odds, the felt "gap" (as it were) between the two may vary enormously in breadth in different cases. The moderate drinker and the chronic tippler may each want another glass, and each deem it his duty to abstain, but the felt gap between desire and duty in the case of the former is trivial beside the great gulf which is felt to separate them in the case of the latter. Hence it will take a far harder moral effort for the tippler than for the moderate drinker to achieve the same external result of abstention. So much is matter of common agreement. And we are entitled, I think, to take it into account in prediction, on the simple principle that the harder the moral effort required to resist desire the less likely it is to occur. Thus in the example taken, most people would predict that the tippler will very probably succumb to his desires, whereas there is a reasonable likelihood that the moderate drinker will make the comparatively slight effort needed to resist them. So long as the prediction does not pretend to more than a measure of probability, there is nothing in our theory which would disallow it.

I claim, therefore, that the view of free will I have been putting forward is consistent with predictability of conduct on the basis of character over a very wide field indeed. And I make the further claim that that field will cover all the situations in life concerning which there is any empirical evidence that successful prediction is possible.

10. Let us pass on to consider the second main line of criticism. This is, I think, much the more illuminating of the two, if only because it compels the Libertarian to make explicit certain concepts which are indispensable to him, but which, being desperately hard to state clearly, are apt not to be stated at all. The critic's fundamental point might be stated somewhat as follows:

"Free will as you describe it is completely unintelligible. On your own showing no *reason* can be given, because there just *is* no reason, why a man decides to exert rather than to withhold moral effort, or *vice versa*. But such an act—or more properly, such an 'occurrence'— it is nonsense to speak of as an act of a *self*. If there is nothing in the self's character to which it is, even in principle, in any way traceable, the self has nothing to do with it. Your so-called 'freedom,' therefore, so far from supporting the self's moral responsibility, destroys it as surely as the crudest Determinism could do."

If we are to discuss this criticism usefully, it is important, I think, to begin by getting clear about two different senses of the word "intelligible."

If, in the first place, we mean by an "intelligible" act one whose occurrence is in principle capable of being inferred, since it follows necessarily from something (though we may not know in fact from what), then it is certainly true that the Libertarian's free will is unintelligible. But that is only saying, is it not, that the Libertarian's "free" act is not an act which follows necessarily from something! This can hardly rank as a *criticism* of Libertarianism. It is just a description of it. That there can be nothing unintelligible in *this* sense is precisely what the Determinist has got to *prove*.

Yet it is surprising how often the critic of Libertarianism involves himself in this circular mode of argument. Repeatedly it is urged against the Libertarian, with a great air of triumph, that on his view he can't say *why* I now decide to rise to duty, or now decide to follow my strongest desire in defiance of duty. Of course he can't. If he could he wouldn't *be* a Libertarian. To "account for" a "free" act is a contradiction in terms. A free will is *ex hypothesi* the sort of thing of which the request for an *explanation* is absurd. The assumption that an explanation must be in principle possible for the act of moral decision deserves to rank as a classic example of the ancient fallacy of "begging the question."

But the critic usually has in mind another sense of the word "unintelligible." He is apt to take it for granted that an act which is unintelligble in the *above* sense (as the morally free act of the Libertarian undoubtedly is) is unintelligible in the *further* sense that we can attach no meaning to it. And this is an altogether more serious matter. If it could really be shown that the Libertarian's "free will" were unintelligible in this sense of being meaningless, that, for myself at any rate, would be the end of the affair. Libertarianism would have been conclusively refuted.

But it seems to me manifest that this can *not* be shown. The critic has allowed himself, I submit, to become the victim of a widely accepted but fundamentally vicious assumption. He has assumed that whatever is meaningful must exhibit its meaningfulness to those who view it from the standpoint of external observation. Now if one chooses thus to limit one's self to the role of external observer, it is, I think, perfectly true that one can attach no meaning to an act which is the act of something we call a "self" and yet follows from nothing in that self's character. But then *why should we* so limit ourselves, when what is under consideration is a subjective activity? For the apprehension of subjective acts there is *another* standpoint available, that of *inner experience,* of the practical consciousness in its actual functioning. If our free will should turn out to be something to which we can attach a meaning from *this* standpoint, no more is required. And no more ought to be expected. For I must repeat that only from the inner standpoint of living experience *could* anything of the nature of "activity" be directly grasped. Observation from without is in the nature of the case impotent to apprehend the active *qua* active. We can from without observe sequences of states. If into these we read activity (as we sometimes do), this can only be on the basis of what we discern in ourselves from the inner standpoint. It follows that if anyone insists upon taking his criterion of the meaningful simply from the standpoint of external observation, he is really deciding in advance of the evidence that the notion of activity, and *a fortiori* the notion of a free will, is "meaningless." He looks for the free act through a medium which is in the nature of the case incapable of revealing it, and then, because inevitably he doesn't find it, he declares that it doesn't exist!

But if, as we surely ought in this context, we adopt the inner standpoint, then (I am suggesting) things appear in a totally different light. From the inner standpoint, it seems to me plain, there is no difficulty whatever in attaching meaning to an act which is the self's act and which nevertheless does not follow from the self's character. So much I claim has been established by the phenomenological analysis, in this and the previous lecture, of the act of moral decision in face of moral temptation. It is thrown into particularly clear relief where the moral decision is to make the moral effort required to rise to duty. For the very function of moral effort, as it appears to the agent engaged in the act, is to enable the self to act against the line of least resistance, against the line to which his character as so far formed most strongly inclines him. But if the self is thus conscious here of *combating* his formed character, he surely cannot possibly suppose that the act, although his own act, *issues from* his formed character? I submit, therefore, that the self knows very well indeed—from the inner standpoint—what is meant by an act which is the *self's* act and which nevertheless does not follow from the self's *character*.

What this implies—and it seems to me to be an implication of cardinal importance for any theory of the self that aims at being more than superficial—is that the nature of the self is for itself something more than just its character as so far formed. The "nature" of the self and what we commonly call the "character" of the self are by no means the same thing, and it is utterly vital that they should not be confused. The "nature" of the self comprehends, but is not without remainder reducible.to, its "character"; it must, if we are to be true to the testimony of our experience of it, be taken as including *also* the authentic creative power of fashioning and re-fashioning "character."

The misguided, and as a rule quite uncritical, belittlement, of the evidence offered by inner experience has, I am convinced, been responsible for more bad argument by the opponents of Free Will than has any other single factor. How often, for example, do we find the Determinist critic saying, in effect, *"Either* the act follows necessarily upon precedent states, *or* it is a mere matter of chance and accordingly of no moral significance." The disjunction is invalid, for it does not exhaust the possible alternatives. It seems to the critic to do so only because he *will* limit himself to the standpoint which is proper, and indeed alone possible, in dealing with the physical world, the standpoint of the external observer. If only he would allow himself to assume the standpoint which is not merely proper for, but necessary to, the apprehension of subjective activity, the inner standpoint of the practical consciousness in its actual functioning, he would find himself obliged to recognize the falsity of his disjunction. Reflection upon the act of moral decision as apprehended from the inner standpoint would force him to recognize a *third* possibility, as remote from chance as from necessity, that, namely, of *creative activity,* in which (as I have ventured to express it) nothing determines the act save the agent's doing of it.

11. There we must leave the matter. But as this lecture has been, I know, somewhat densely packed, it may be helpful if I conclude by reminding you, in bald summary, of the main things I have been trying to say. Let me set them out in so many successive theses.

1. The freedom which is at issue in the traditional Free Will problem is the freedom which is presupposed in moral responsibility.

2. Critical reflection upon carefully considered attributions of moral responsibility reveals that the only freedom that will do is a freedom which pertains to inner acts of choice, and that these acts must be acts (*a*) of which the self is *sole* author, and (*b*) which the self could have performed otherwise.

3. From phenomenological analysis of the situation of moral temptation, we find that the self as engaged in this situation is inescapably convinced that it possesses a freedom of precisely the specified kind, located in the decision to exert or withhold the moral effort needed to rise to duty where the pressure of its desiring nature is felt to urge it in a contrary direction.

   Passing to the question of the *reality* of this moral freedom which the moral agent believes himself to possess, we argued:

4. Of the two types of Determinist criticism which seem to have most influence today, that based on the predictability of much human behavior fails to touch a Libertarianism which confines the area of free will as above indicated. Libertarianism so understood is compatible with all the predictability that the empirical facts warrant. And:

5. The second main type of criticism, which alleges the "meaninglessness" of an act which is the self's act and which is yet not determined by the self's character, is based on a failure to appreciate that the standpoint of inner experience is not only legitimate but indispensable where what is at issue is the reality and nature of a subjective activity. The creative act of moral decision is inevitably meaningless to the mere external observer; but from the inner standpoint is as real, and as significant, as anything in human experience.

NOTES

1. Reprinted in *Ethics and the History of Philosophy, Selected Essays.*
2. I have explained the grounds for my dissent from Broad's final conclusions on pp. 27 ff. of *In Defense of Free Will* (Jackson Son & Co., 1938).
3. *Kantian Ethics.*
4. Ibid., p. 261.

[4]

The Ontological Argument

Saint Anselm

THAT GOD TRULY EXISTS

Therefore, Lord, You Who give understanding to faith, give to me: insofar as You know it to be advantageous, let me understand that You exist, as we believe, and also that You are that which we believe You to be. And indeed, we believe You to be something than which nothing greater could be conceived. Or is there thus not something of such a nature, since the fool has said in his heart—there is no God [Psalm 14:1, 53:1]. But surely this same fool, when he hears this very thing that I speak—"something than which nothing greater can be conceived"— understands that which he hears, and that which he understands is in his understanding, even if he does not understand it to exist. For it is one thing for a thing to be in the understanding, and another to understand a thing to exist. For when a painter conceives before hand that which he is to make, he certainly has it in the understanding, but he does not yet understand to exist that which he has not yet made. However, when he has painted it, he both has it in the understanding and understands that that which he has now made exists. Therefore, even the fool is convinced that something than which nothing greater can be conceived is at least in the understanding, since when he hears this, he understands it, and whatever is understood is in the understanding. And surely that than which a greater cannot be conceived cannot be in the understanding alone. For if it is even in the understanding alone, it can be conceived to exist in reality also, which is greater. Thus if that

Reprinted from *Proslogion*, translated by William Mann. © William E. Mann.
Saint Anselm (1035–1109) was Archbishop of Canterbury.

than which a greater cannot be conceived is in the understanding alone, then that than which a greater cannot be conceived itself is that than which a greater can be conceived. But surely this cannot be. Therefore without doubt, something than which a greater cannot be conceived exists, both in the understanding and in reality.

THAT GOD CANNOT BE CONCEIVED NOT TO EXIST

And surely it exists so truly that it could not be conceived not to exist. For something can be conceived to exist which could not be conceived not to exist, which is greater than that which can be conceived not to exist. Thus if that than which a greater cannot be conceived can be conceived not to exist, then that than which a greater cannot be conceived itself is not that than which a greater cannot be conceived, which cannot be made consistent. Thus something than which a greater cannot be conceived exists so truly that it could not be conceived not to exist.

And this You are, Lord our God. Thus so truly do You exist, Lord my God, that You could not be conceived not to exist. And justly so. For if some mind could conceive of something better than You, the creature would rise above the creator and would judge the creator, which is exceedingly absurd. And indeed, whatever is distinct from You alone can be conceived not to exist. Therefore You alone are the truest of all things and thus You have existence as the greatest of all things, since anything else does not exist so truly, and for that reason has less existence. And so why has the fool said in his heart that there is no God, when to a rational mind it would be so obvious that You exist as the greatest of all things? Why, unless because he is stupid and a fool?

HOW THE FOOL HAS SAID IN HIS HEART
WHAT CANNOT BE CONCEIVED

Indeed, how has he said in his heart what he has not been able to conceive, or how has he not been able to conceive what he has said in his heart, when to say in the heart and to conceive are the same? If he truly—rather, *since* he truly—both has conceived (since he has spoken in his heart) and has not spoken in his heart (since he has not been able to conceive), then there is not only one way in which something is said in the heart or is conceived. For in one way a thing is conceived when a word signifying it is conceived; in another when that thing itself is understood. In the former way, thus, God can be conceived not to exist; in the latter, not at all. No one, in fact, understanding what God is, can conceive that God does not exist, although he may say these words in his heart, either without significance or with some extraneous significance. For God is that than which a greater cannot be conceived. He who understands this well certainly understands this very being to exist in such a way that it is not able not to exist in conception. Thus he who understands that God so exists, cannot conceive Him not to exist.

I give thanks to You, good Lord, I give thanks to You, because that which before I believed through Your giving to me, I now so understand through Your illuminating me that if I were unwilling to believe that You exist, I would not be able to understand that You exist.

[5]

The Cosmological Argument

Richard Taylor

An active, living, and religious belief in the gods has probably never arisen and been maintained on purely metaphysical grounds. Such beliefs are found in every civilized land and time and are often virtually universal in a particular culture, yet relatively few people have much of a conception of metaphysics. There are in fact entire cultures, such as that of ancient Israel, to whom metaphysics is quite foreign, though these cultures may nevertheless be religious.

Belief in the gods seems to have its roots in human desires and fears, particularly those associated with self-preservation. Like all other creatures, human beings have a profound will to live, which is what mainly gives one's existence a meaning from one sunrise to the next. Unlike other creatures, however, human beings are capable of the full and terrible realization of their own inevitable decay. A person can bring before his mind the image of his own grave, and with it the complete certainty of its ultimate reality, and against this his will naturally recoils. It can hardly seem to him less than an absolute catastrophe, the very end, so far as he is concerned, of everything, though he has no difficulty viewing death, as it touches others more or less remote from himself, as a perhaps puzzling, occasionally distressing, but nonetheless necessary aspect of nature. It is probably partly in response to this fear that human beings turn to the gods, as those beings of such power that they can overturn this verdict of nature.

Richard Taylor, *Metaphysics*, 3d. ed., © 1983. Reprinted by permission of Prentice-Hall, Inc., Englewood Cliffs, N.J.

Richard Taylor (b. 1919) was professor of philosophy at Brown University, Columbia University, and the University of Rochester.

The sources of religious belief are doubtless much more complex than this, but they seem to lie in the will rather than in speculative intelligence, nevertheless. Those who possess such a belief seldom permit any metaphysical considerations to wrest it from them, while those who lack it are seldom turned toward it by other metaphysical considerations. Still, in every land in which philosophy has flourished, there have been profound thinkers who have sought to discover some metaphysical basis for a rational belief in the existence of some supreme being or beings. Even though religion may properly be a matter of faith rather than reason, still, a philosophical person can hardly help wondering whether it might, at least in part, be also a matter of reason, and whether, in particular, the existence of God might be something that can be now merely believed but shown. It is this question that we want now to consider; that is, we want to see whether there are not strong metaphysical considerations from which the existence of some supreme being might reasonably be inferred.

THE PRINCIPLE OF SUFFICIENT REASON

Suppose you were strolling in the woods and, in addition to the sticks, stones, and other accustomed litter of the forest floor, you one day came upon some quite unaccustomed object, something not quite like what you had ever seen before and would never expect to find in such a place. Suppose, for example, that it is a large ball, about your own height, perfectly smooth and translucent. You would deem this puzzling and mysterious, certainly, but if one considers the matter, it is no more inherently mysterious that such a thing should exist than that anything else should exist. If you were quite accustomed to finding such objects of various sizes around you most of the time, but had never seen an ordinary rock, then upon finding a large rock in the woods one day you would be just as puzzled and mystified. This illustrates the fact that something that is mysterious ceases to seem so simply by its accustomed presence. It is strange indeed, for example, that a world such as ours should exist; yet few people are very often struck by this strangeness but simply take it for granted.

Suppose, then, that you have found this translucent ball and are mystified by it. Now whatever else you might wonder about it, there is one thing you would hardly question; namely, that it did not appear there all by itself, that it owes its existence to something. You might not have the remotest idea whence and how it came to be there, but you would hardly doubt that there was an explanation. The idea that it might have come from nothing at all, that it might exist without there being any explanation of its existence, is one that few people would consider worthy of entertaining.

This illustrates a metaphysical belief that seems to be almost a part of reason itself, even though few ever think upon it; the belief, namely, that there is some explanation for the existence of anything whatever, some reason why it should exist rather than not. The sheer nonexistence of anything, which is not to be confused with the passing out of existence of something, never requires a reason; but existence does. That there should never have been any such ball in the forest does not require any explanation or reason, but that there should ever be such a ball does. If one were to look upon a barren plain and ask why there is not and never has been any large translucent ball there, the natural response would be to ask why there should be; but if one finds such a ball, and wonders why it is there, it is not quite so natural to ask why it should *not* be—as though existence should simply be taken for granted. That anything should not exist, then, and that, for instance, no such ball should exist in the forest, or that there should be no forest for it to occupy, or no continent containing a forest, or no Earth, nor any world at all, do not seem to be things for which there needs to be any explanation or reason; but that such things should be *does* seem to require a reason.

The principle involved here has been called the principle of sufficient reason. Actually, it is a very general principle, and it is best expressed by saying that, in the case of any positive truth, there is some sufficient reason for it, something that, in this sense, makes it true—in short, that there is some sort of explanation, known or unknown, for everything.

Now, some truths depend on something else, and are accordingly called *contingent*, while others depend only upon themselves, that is, are true by their very natures and are accordingly called *necessary*. There is, for example, a reason why the stone on my window sill is warm; namely, that the sun is shining upon it. This happens to be true, but not by its very nature. Hence, it is contingent, and depends upon something other than itself. It is also true than all the points of a circle are equidistant from the center, but this truth depends upon nothing but itself. No matter what happens, nothing can make it false. Similarly, it is a truth, and a necessary one, that if the stone on my window sill is a body, as it is, then it has a form, because this fact depends upon nothing but itself for its confirmation. Untruths are also, of course, either contingent or necessary, it being contingently false, for example, that the stone on my window sill is cold, and necessarily false that it is both a body and formless, because this is by its very nature impossible.

The principle of sufficient reason can be illustrated in various ways, as we have done, and if one thinks about it, he is apt to find that he presupposes it in his thinking about reality, but it cannot be proved. It does not appear to be itself a necessary truth, and at the same time it would be most odd to say it is contingent. If one were to try proving it, he would sooner or later have to appeal to considerations that are less plausible than the principle itself. Indeed, it is hard to see how one could even make an argument for it without already assuming it. For this reason it might properly be called a presupposition of reason itself. One can deny that it is true, without embarrassment or fear of refutation, but one is then apt to find that what he is denying is not really what the principle asserts. We shall, then, treat it here as a datum— not something that is provably true, but as something that people, whether they ever reflect upon it or not, seem more or less to presuppose.

THE EXISTENCE OF A WORLD

It happens to be true that something exists, that there is, for example, a world, and although no one ever seriously supposes that this might not be so, that there might exist nothing at all, there still seems to be nothing the least necessary in this, considering it just by itself. That no world should ever exist at all is perfectly comprehensible and seems to express not the slightest absurdity. Considering any particular item in the world it seems not at all necessary that the totality of these things, or any totality of things, should ever exist.

From the principle of sufficient reason it follows, of course, that there must be a reason not only for the existence of everything in the world but for the world itself, meaning by "the world" simply everything that ever does exist, except God, in case there is a god. This principle does not imply that there must be some purpose or goal for everything, or for the totality of all things; for explanations need not be, and in fact seldom are, teleological or purposeful. All the principle requires is that there be some sort of reason for everything. And it would certainly be odd to maintain that everything in the world owes its existence to something, that nothing in the world is either purely accidental, or such that it just bestows its own being upon itself, and then to deny this of the world itself. One can indeed *say* that the world is in some sense a pure accident, that there simply is no reason at all why this or any world should exist, and one can equally say that the world exists by its very nature, or is an inherently necessary being. But it is at least very odd and arbitrary to deny of this existing world the need for any sufficient reason, whether independent of itself or not, while presupposing that there is a reason for every other thing that ever exists.

Consider again the strange ball that we imagine has been found in the forest. Now, we can hardly doubt that there must be an explanation for the existence of such a thing, though we may have no notion what that explanation is. It is not, moreover, the fact of its having been found in the forest rather than elsewhere that renders an explanation necessary. It matters not in the least where it happens to be, for our question is not how it happens to be *there* but how it happens to be at all. If we in our imagination annihilate the forest, leaving only this ball in an open field, our conviction that it is a contingent thing and owes its existence to something other than itself is not reduced in the least. If we now imagine the field to be annihilated, and in fact everything else as well to vanish into nothingness, leaving only this ball to constitute the entire physical universe, then we cannot for a moment suppose that its existence has thereby been explained, or the need for any explanation eliminated, or that its existence is suddenly rendered self-explanatory. If we now carry this thought one step further and suppose that no other reality ever has existed or ever will exist, that this ball forever constitutes the entire physical universe, then we must still insist on there being some reason independent of itself why it should exist rather than not. If there must be a reason for the existence of any particular thing, then the necessity of such a reason is not eliminated by the mere supposition that certain other things do *not* exist. And again, it matters not at all what the thing in question is, whether it be large and complex, such as the world we actually find ourselves in, or whether it be something small, simple, and insignificant, such as a ball, a bacterium, or the merest grain of sand. We do not avoid the necessity of a reason for the existence of something merely by describing it in this way or that. And it would, in any event, seem quite plainly absurd to say that if the world were composed entirely of a single ball about six feet in diameter, or of a single grain of sand, then it would be contingent and there would have to be some explanation other than itself why such a thing exists, but that, since the actual world is vastly more complex than this, there is no need for an explanation of its existence, independent of itself.

BEGINNINGLESS EXISTENCE

It should now be noted that it is no answer to the question, why a thing exists, to state *how long* it has existed. A geologist does not suppose that she has explained why there should be rivers and mountains merely by pointing out that they are old. Similarly, if one were to ask, concerning the ball of which we have spoken, for some sufficient reason for its being, he would not receive any answer upon being told that it had been there since yesterday. Nor would it be any better answer to say that it had existed since before anyone could remember, or even that it had always existed; for the question was not one concerning its age but its existence. If, to be sure, one were to ask where a given thing came from, or how it came into being, then upon learning that it had always existed, he would learn that it never really *came* into being at all; but he could still reasonably wonder why it should exist at all. If, accordingly, the world—that is, the totality of all things excepting God, in case there is a god—had really no beginning at all, but has always existed in some form or other, then there is clearly no answer to the question, where it came from and when; it did not, on this supposition, *come* from anything at all, at any time. But still, it can be asked why there is a world, why indeed there is a beginningless world, why there should have perhaps always been something rather than nothing. And, if the principle of sufficient reason is a good principle, there must be an answer to that question, an answer that is by no means supplied by giving the world an age, or even an infinite age.

CREATION

This brings out an important point with respect to the concept of creation that is often misunderstood, particularly by those whose thinking has been influenced by Christian ideas. People tend to think that creation—for example, the creation of the world by God—*means* creation *in time*, from which it of course logically follows that if the world had no beginning in time, then it cannot be the creation of God. This, however, is erroneous, for creation means essentially *dependence*, even in Christian theology. If one thing is the creation of another, then it depends for its existence on that other, and this is perfectly consistent with saying that both are eternal, that neither ever came into being, and hence, that neither was ever created at any point of time. Perhaps an analogy will help convey this point. Consider, then, a flame that is casting beams of light. Now, there seems to be a clear sense in which the beams of light are dependent for their existence upon the flame, which is their source, while the flame, on the other hand, is not similarly dependent for its existence upon them. The beams of light arise from the flame, but the flame does not arise from them. In this sense, they are the creation of the flame; they derive their existence from it. And none of this has any reference to time; the relationship of dependence in such a case would not be altered in the slightest if we supposed that the flame, and with it the beams of light, had always existed, that neither had ever *come* into being.

Now if the world is the creation of God, its relationship to God should be thought of in this fashion; namely, that the world depends for its existence upon God, and could not exist independently of God. If God is eternal, as those who believe in God generally assume, then the world may (though it need not) be eternal too, without that altering in the least its dependence upon God for its existence, and hence without altering its being the creation of God. The supposition of God's eternality, on the other hand, does not by itself imply that the world is eternal too; for there is not the least reason why something of finite duration might not depend for its existence upon something of infinite duration—though the reverse is, of course, impossible.

GOD

If we think of God as "the creator of heaven and earth," and if we consider heaven and earth to include everything that exists except God, then we appear to have, in the foregoing considerations, fairly strong reasons for asserting that God, as so conceived, exists. Now of course most people have much more in mind than this when they think of God, for religions have ascribed to God ever so many attributes that are not at all implied by describing him merely as the creator of the world; but that is not relevant here. Most religious persons do, in any case, think of God as being at least the creator, as that being upon which everything ultimately depends, no matter what else they may say about him in addition. It is, in fact, the first item in the creeds of Christianity that God is the "creator of heaven and earth." And, it seems, there are good metaphysical reasons, as distinguished from the persuasions of faith, for thinking that such a creative being exists.

If, as seems clearly implied by the principle of sufficient reason, there must be a reason for the existence of heaven and earth—i.e., for the world—then that reason must be found either in the world itself, or outside it, in something that is literally supranatural, or outside heaven and earth. Now if we suppose that the world—i.e., the totality of all things except God—contains within itself the reason for its existence, we are supposing that it exists by its very nature, that is, that it is a necessary being. In that case there would, of course, be no reason for saying that it must depend upon God or anything else for its existence; for if it exists by its very nature, then it depends upon nothing but itself, much as the sun depends upon nothing but itself for its heat. This, however, is implausible, for we find nothing about the world or anything in it to suggest that it exists by its own nature, and we do find, on the contrary, ever so many things to suggest that it does not. For in the first place, anything that exists by its very nature must necessarily be eternal and indestructible. It would be a self-contradiction to say of anything that it exists by its own nature, or is a necessarily existing thing, and at the same time to say that it comes into being or passes away, or that it ever could come into being or pass away. Nothing about the world seems at all like this, for concerning anything in the world, we can perfectly easily think of it as being annihilated, or as never having existed in the first place, without there being the slightest hint of any absurdity in such a supposition. Some of the things in the universe are, to be sure, very old; the moon, for example, or the stars and the planets. It is even possible to imagine that they have always existed. Yet it seems quite impossible to suppose that they owe their existence to nothing but themselves, that they bestow existence upon themselves by their very natures, or that they are in themselves things of such nature that it would be impossible for them not to exist. Even if we suppose that something, such as the sun, for instance, has existed forever, and will never cease, still we cannot conclude just from this that it exists by its own nature. If, as is of course very doubtful, the sun has existed forever and will never cease, then it is possible that its heat and light have also existed forever and will never cease; but that would not show that the heat and light of the sun exist by their own natures. They are obviously contingent and depend on the sun for their existence, whether they are beginningless and everlasting or not.

There seems to be nothing in the world, then, concerning which it is at all plausible to suppose that it exists by its own nature, or contains within itself the reason for its existence. In fact, everything in the world appears to be quite plainly the opposite, namely, something that not only need not exist, but at some time or other, past or future or both, does not in fact exist. Everything in the world seems to have a finite duration, whether long or short. Most things, such as ourselves, exist only for a short while; they come into being, then soon cease. Other things, like the heavenly bodies, last longer, but they are still corruptible, and from all that we can gather about them, they too seem destined eventually to perish. We arrive at the conclusion, then, that although the world may contain some things that have always existed and are destined never to perish, it is nevertheless doubtful that it contains any such thing, and, in any case, everything in the world is capable of perishing, and nothing in it, however long it may already have existed and however long it may yet remain, exists by its own nature but depends instead upon something else.

Although this might be true of everything in the world, is it necessarily true of the world itself? That is, if we grant, as we seem forced to, that nothing in the world exists by its own nature, that everything in the world is contingent and perishable, must we also say that the world itself, or the totality of all these perishable things, is also contingent and perishable? Logically, we are not forced to, for it is logically possible that the totality of all perishable things might itself be imperishable, and hence, that the world might exist by its own nature, even though it is composed exclusively of things that are contingent. It is not logically necessary that a totality should share the defects of its members. For example, even though every person is mortal, it does not follow from this that the human race, or the totality of all people, is also mortal; for it is possible that there will always be human beings, even though there are no human beings who will always exist. Similarly, it is possible that the world is in itself a necessary thing, even though it is composed entirely of things that are contingent.

This is logically possible, but it is not plausible. For we find nothing whatever about the world, any more than in its parts, to suggest that it exists by its own nature. Concerning anything in the world, we have not the slightest difficulty in supposing that it should perish, or even that it should never have existed in the first place. We have almost as little difficulty in supposing this of the world itself. It might be somewhat hard to think of everything as utterly perishing and leaving no trace whatever of its ever having been, but there seems to be not the slightest difficulty in imagining that the world should never have existed in the first place. We can, for instance, perfectly easily suppose that nothing in the world had ever existed except, let us suppose, a single grain of sand, and we can thus suppose that this grain of sand has forever constituted the whole universe. Now if we consider just this grain of sand, it is quite impossible for us to suppose that it exists by its very nature and could never have failed to exist. It clearly depends for its existence upon something other than itself, if it depends on anything at all. The same will be true if we consider the world to consist not of one grain of sand but of two, or of a million, or, as we in fact find, of a vast number of stars and planets and all their minute parts.

It would seem, then, that the world, in case it happens to exist at all—and this is quite beyond doubt—is contingent and thus dependent upon something other than itself for its existence, if it depends upon anything at all. And it must depend upon something, for otherwise there could be no reason why it exists in the first place. Now, that upon which the world depends must be something that either exists by its own nature or does not. If it does not exist by its own nature, then it, in turn depends for its existence upon something else, and so on. Now then, we can say either of two things; namely, (1) that the world depends for its existence upon something else, which in turn depends on still another thing, this depending upon still another, *ad infinitum*; or (2) that the world derives its existence from something that exists by its own nature and that is accordingly eternal and imperishable, and is the creator of heaven and earth. The first of these alternatives, however, is impossible, for it does not render a sufficient reason why anything should exist in the first place. Instead of supplying a reason why any world should exist, it repeatedly begs off giving a reason. It explains what is dependent and perishable in terms of what is itself dependent and perishable, leaving us still without a reason why perishable things should exist at all, which is what we are seeking. Ultimately, then, it would seem that the world, or the totality of contingent or perishable things, in case it exists at all, must depend upon something that is necessary and imperishable, and that accordingly exists, not in dependence upon something else, but by its own nature.

"SELF-CAUSED"

What has been said thus far gives some intimation of what meaning should be attached to the concept of a self-caused being, a concept that is quite generally misunderstood, sometimes even by scholars. To say that something—God, for example—is self-caused, or is the cause of its own existence, does not mean that this being brings itself into existence, which is a perfectly absurd idea. Nothing can *bring* itself into existence. To say that something is self-caused (*causa sui*) means only that it exists, not contingently or in dependence upon something else but by its own nature, which is only to say that it is a being which is such that it can neither come into being nor perish. Now, whether in fact such a being exists or not, there is in any case no absurdity in the idea. We have found, in fact, that the principle of sufficient reason seems to point to the existence of such a being, as that upon which the world, with everything in it, must ultimately depend for its existence.

"NECESSARY BEING"

A being that depends for its existence upon nothing but itself and is in this sense self-caused, can equally be described as a necessary being; that is to say, a being that is not contingent, and hence not perishable. For in the case of anything that exists by its own nature and is dependent upon nothing else, it is impossible that it should not exist, which is equivalent to saying that it is necessary. Many persons have professed to find the gravest difficulties in this concept, too, but that is partly because it has been confused with other notions. If it makes sense to speak of anything as an *impossible* being, or something that by its very nature does not exist, then it is hard to see why the idea of a necessary being, or something that in its very nature exists, should not be just as comprehensible. And of course, we have not the slightest difficulty in speaking of something, such as a square circle or a formless body, as an impossible being. And if it makes sense to speak of something as being perishable, contingent, and dependent upon something other than itself for its existence, as it surely does, then there seems to be no difficulty in thinking of something as imperishable and dependent upon nothing other than itself for its existence.

"FIRST CAUSE"

From these considerations we can see also what is properly meant by a first cause, an appellative that has often been applied to God by theologians and that many persons have deemed an absurdity. It is a common criticism of this notion to say that there need not be any first cause, because the series of causes and effects that constitute the history of the universe might be infinite or beginningless and must, in fact, be infinite in case the universe itself had no beginning in time. This criticism, however, reflects a total misconception of what is meant by a first cause. *First* here does not mean first in time, and when God is spoken of as a first cause He is not being described as a being that, at some time in the remote past, *started* everything. To describe God as a first cause is only to say that He is literally a *primary* rather than a secondary cause, an *ultimate* rather than a derived cause, or a being upon which all other things, heaven and earth, ultimately depend for their existence. It is, in short, only to say that God is the creator, in the sense of creation previously explained. Now this, of course, is perfectly consistent with saying that the world is eternal or beginningless. As we have seen, one gives no reason for the existence of a world merely by giving it an age, even if it is supposed to have an infinite age. To use a helpful analogy, we can say that the sun is the first cause of daylight and, for that matter, of the moonlight of the night as well, which means only that daylight and moonlight ultimately depend upon the sun for their existence. The moon, on the other hand, is only a secondary or derivative cause of its light. This light would be no less dependent upon the sun if we affirmed that it had no beginning, for an ageless and beginningless light requires a source no less than an ephemeral one. If we supposed that the sun has always existed, and with it its light, then we would have to say that the sun has always been the first—i.e., the primary or ultimate—cause of its light. Such is precisely the manner in which God should be thought of, and is by theologians often thought of, as the first cause of heaven and earth.

[6]

The Teleological Argument

David Hume

Not to lose any time in circumlocutions, said Cleanthes, addressing himself to Demea, much less in replying to the pious declamations of Philo,[1] I shall briefly explain how I conceive this matter. Look round the world: Contemplate the whole and every part of it: You will find it to be nothing but one great machine, subdivided into an infinite number of lesser machines, which again admit of subdivisions to a degree beyond what human senses and faculties can trace and explain. All these various machines, and even their most minute parts, are adjusted to each other with an accuracy which ravishes into admiration all men who have ever contemplated them. The curious adapting of means to ends, throughout all nature, resembles exactly, though it much exceeds, the productions of human contrivance—of human design, thought, wisdom, and intelligence. Since therefore the effects resemble each other, we are led to infer, by all the rules of analogy, that the causes also resemble, and that the Author of Nature is somewhat similar to the mind of man, though possessed of much larger faculties, proportioned to the grandeur of the work which he has executed. By this argument *a posteriori,* and by this argument alone, do we prove at once the existence of a Deity and his similarity to human mind and intelligence. . . .

Philo, after a short pause, proceeded in the following manner.

That all inferences, Cleanthes, concerning fact are founded on experience, and that all experimental reasonings are founded on the supposition that similar causes prove similar effects, and similar effects

From *Dialogues Concerning Natural Religion* (1779).

David Hume (1711-1776), Scottish philosopher and historian, played a central role in the development of modern philosophy.

similar causes, I shall not at present much dispute with you. But observe, I entreat you, with what extreme caution all just reasoners proceed in the transferring of experiments to similar cases. Unless the cases be exactly similar, they repose no perfect confidence in applying their past observation to any particular phenomenon. Every alteration of circumstances occasions a doubt concerning the event; and it requires new experiments to prove certainly that the new circumstances are of no moment or importance. A change in bulk, situation, arrangement, age, disposition of the air, or surrounding bodies—any of these particulars may be attended with the most unexpected consequences. And unless the objects be quite familiar to us, it is the highest temerity to expect with assurance, after any of these changes, an event similar to that which before fell under our observation. The slow and deliberate steps of philosophers here, if anywhere, are distinguished from the precipitate march of the vulgar, who, hurried on by the smallest similitude, are incapable of all discernment or consideration.

But can you think, Cleanthes, that your usual phlegm and philosophy have been preserved in so wide a step as you have taken when you compared to the universe houses, ships, furniture, machines; and, from their similarity in some circumstances, inferred a similarity in their causes? Thought, design, intelligence, such as we discover in men and other animals, is no more than one of the springs and principles of the universe, as well as heat or cold, attraction or repulsion, and a hundred others which fall under daily observation. It is an active cause by which some particular parts of nature, we find, produce alterations on other parts. But can a conclusion, with any propriety, be transferred from parts to the whole? Does not the great disproportion bar all comparison and inference? From observing the growth of a hair, can we learn anything concerning the generation of a man? Would the manner of a leaf's blowing, even though perfectly known, afford us any instruction concerning the vegetation of a tree?

But allowing that we were to take the *operations* of one part of nature upon another for the foundation of our judgment concerning the *origin* of the whole (which never can be admitted), yet why select so minute, so weak, so bounded a principle as the reason and design of animals is found to be upon this planet? What peculiar privilege has this little agitation of the brain which we call *thought*, that we must thus make it the model of the whole universe? Our partiality in our own favor does indeed present it on all occasions, but sound philosophy ought carefully to guard against so natural an illusion.

So far from admitting, continued Philo, that the operations of a part can afford us any just conclusion concerning the origin of the whole, I will not allow any one part to form a rule for another part if the latter be very remote from the former. Is there any reasonable ground to conclude that the inhabitants of other planets possess thought, intelligence, reason, or anything similar to these faculties in men? When nature has so extremely diversified her manner of operation in this small globe, can we imagine that she incessantly copies herself throughout so immense a universe? And if thought, as we may well suppose, be confined merely to this narrow corner and has even there so limited a sphere of action, with what propriety can we assign it for the original cause of all things? The narrow views of a peasant who makes his domestic economy the rule for the government of kingdoms is in comparison a pardonable sophism.

But were we ever so much assured that a thought and reason resembling the human were to be found throughout the whole universe, and were its activity elsewhere vastly greater and more commanding than it appears in this globe; yet I cannot see why the operations of a world constituted, arranged, adjusted, can with any propriety be extended to a world which is in its embryo-state, and is advancing toward that constitution and arrangement. By observation we know somewhat of the economy, action, and nourishment of a finished animal; but we must transfer with great caution that observation to the growth of a fetus in the womb, and still more to the formation of an animalcule in the loins of its male parent. Nature, we find, even from our limited experience, possesses an infinite number of springs and principles which incessantly discover themselves on every change of her position and situation. And what new and unknown principles would actuate her in so new and unknown a situation as that of the formation of a universe, we cannot, without the utmost temerity, pretend to determine.

A very small part of this great system, during a very short time, is very imperfectly discovered to us; and do we thence pronounce decisively concerning the origin of the whole?

Admirable conclusion! Stone, wood, brick, iron, brass, have not, at this time, in this minute globe of earth, an order or arrangement without human art and contrivance; therefore, the universe could not originally attain its order and arrangement without something similar to human art. But is a part of nature a rule for another part very wide of the former? Is it a rule for the whole? Is a very small part a rule for the universe? Is nature in one situation a certain rule for nature in another situation vastly different from the former? . . .

But to show you still more inconveniences, continued Philo, in your anthropomorphism, please to take a new survey of your principles. *Like effects prove like causes.* This is the experimental argument; and this, you say too, is the sole theological argument. Now it is certain that the liker the effects are which are seen and the liker the causes which are inferred, the stronger is the argument. Every departure on either side diminishes the probability and renders the experiment less conclusive. You cannot doubt of the principle; neither ought you to reject its consequences. . . .

Now, Cleanthes, said Philo, with an air of alacrity and triumph, mark the consequences. *First,* by this method of reasoning you renounce all claim to infinity in any of the attributes of the Deity. For, as the cause ought only to be proportioned to the effect, and the effect, so far as it falls under our cognizance, is not infinite, what pretensions have we, upon your suppositions, to ascribe that attribute to the divine Being? You will still insist that, by removing him so much from all similarity to human creatures, we give in to the most arbitrary hypothesis, and at the same time weaken all proofs of his existence.

Secondly, you have no reason, on your theory, for ascribing perfection to the Deity, even in his finite capacity; or for supposing him free from every error, mistake, or incoherence, in his undertakings. There are many inexplicable difficulties in the works of nature which, if we allow a perfect author to be proved *a priori,* are easily solved, and become only seeming difficulties from the narrow capacity of man, who cannot trace infinite relations. But according to your method of reasoning, these difficulties become all real; and perhaps, will be insisted on as new instances of likeness to human art and contrivance. At least, you must acknowledge that it is impossible for us to tell, from our limited views, whether this system contains any great faults or deserves any considerable praise if compared to other possible and even real systems. Could a peasant, if the *Aeneid* were read to him, pronounce that poem to be absolutely faultless, or even assign to it its proper rank among the productions of human wit, he who had never seen any other production?

But were this world ever so perfect a production, it must still remain uncertain whether all the excellences of the work can justly be ascribed to the workman. If we survey a ship, what an exalted idea must we form of the ingenuity of the carpenter who framed so complicated, useful, and beautiful a machine? And what surprise must we feel when we find him a stupid mechanic who imitated others, and copied an art which, through a long succession of ages, after multiplied trials, mistakes, corrections, deliberations, and controversies, had been gradually improving? Many worlds might have been botched and bungled, throughout an eternity, ere this system was struck out; much labor lost; many fruitless trials made; and a slow but continued improvement carried on during infinite ages in the art of world-making. In such subjects, who can determine where the truth, nay, who can conjecture where the probability lies, amidst a great number of hypotheses which may be proposed, and a still greater which may be imagined?

And what shadow of an argument, continued Philo, can you produce from your hypothesis to prove the unity of the Deity? A great number of men join in building a house or ship, in rearing a city, in framing a commonwealth; why may not several deities combine in contriving and framing a world? This is only so much greater similarity to human affairs. By sharing the work among several, we may so much further limit the attributes of each, and get rid of that extensive power and knowledge which must be supposed in one deity, and which, according to you, can only serve to weaken the proof of his existence. And if such foolish, such vicious creatures as man can yet often unite in framing and executing one plan, how much more those deities or demons, whom we may suppose several degrees more perfect?

To multiply causes without necessity is indeed contrary to true philosophy, but this principle applies not to the present case. Were one deity antecedently proved by your theory who were possessed of every attribute requisite to the production of the universe, it would be needless, I own (though not absurd), to suppose any other deity existent. But while it is still a question whether all these attributes are united in one subject or dispersed among several independent beings; by what phenomena in nature can we pretend to decide the controversy? Where we see a body raised in a scale, we are sure that there is in the opposite scale, however concealed from sight, some counterpoising weight equal to it; but it is still allowed to doubt whether that weight be an aggregate of several distinct bodies or one uniform united mass. And if the weight requisite very much exceeds anything which we have ever seen conjoined in any single body, the former supposition becomes still more probable and natural. An intelligent being of such vast power and capacity as is necessary to produce the universe—or, to speak in the language of ancient philosophy, so prodigious an animal—exceeds all analogy and even comprehension.

But further, Cleanthes, men are mortal, and renew their species by generation; and this is common to all living creatures. The two great sexes of male and female, says Milton, animate the world. Why must this circumstance, so universal, so essential, be excluded from those numerous and limited deities? Behold, them, the theogeny of ancient times brought back upon us.

And why not become a perfect anthropomorphite? Why not assert the deity or deities to be corporeal, and to have eyes, a nose, mouth, ears, etc.? Epicurus maintained that no man had ever seen reason but in a human figure; therefore, the gods must have a human figure. And this argument, which is deservedly so much ridiculed by Cicero, becomes, according to you, solid and philosophical.

In a word, Cleanthes, a man who follows your hypothesis is able, perhaps, to assert or conjecture that the universe sometime arose from something like design; but beyond that position he cannot ascertain one single circumstance, and is left afterwards to fix every point of his theology by the utmost license of fancy and hypothesis. This world, for aught he knows, is very faulty and imperfect, compared to a superior standard; and was only the first rude essay of some infant deity who afterwards abandoned it, ashamed of his lame performance; it is the work only of some dependent, inferior deity, and is the object of derision to his superiors; it is the production of old age and dotage in some superannuated deity; and ever since his death has run on at adventures, from the first impulse and active force which it received from him. You justly give signs of horror, Demea, at these strange suppositions; but these, and a thousand more of the same kind, are Cleanthes' suppositions, not mine. From the moment the attributes of the Deity are supposed finite, all these have place. And I cannot, for my part, think that so wild and unsettled a system of theology is, in any respect, preferable to none at all.

These suppositions I absolutely disown, cried Cleanthes; they strike me, however, with no horror, especially when proposed in that rambling way in which they drop from you. On the contrary, they give me pleasure when I see that, by the utmost indulgence of your imagination, you never get rid of the hypothesis of design in the universe, but are obliged at every turn to have recourse to it. To this concession I adhere steadily; and this I regard as a sufficient foundation for religion.

It must be a slight fabric, indeed, said Demea, which can be erected on so tottering a foundation. While we are uncertain whether there is one deity or many, whether the deity or deities, to whom we owe our existence, be perfect or imperfect, subordinate or supreme, dead or alive, what trust or confidence can we repose in them? What devotion or worship address to them? What veneration or obedience pay them? To all the purposes of life the theory of religion becomes altogether useless; and even with regard to speculative consequences its uncertainty, according to you, must render it totally precarious and unsatisfactory.

To render it still more unsatisfactory, said Philo, there occurs to me another hypothesis which must acquire an air of probability from the method of reasoning so much insisted on by Cleanthes. That like effects arise from like causes—this principle he supposes the foundation of all religion. But there is another principle of the same kind, no less certain and derived from the same source of experience, that, where several known circumstances are observed to be similar, the unknown will also be found similar. Thus, if we see the limbs of a human body, we conclude that it is also attended with a human head, though hid from us. Thus, if we see, through a chink in a wall, a small part of the sun, we conclude that were the wall removed we would see the whole body. In short, this method of reasoning is so obvious and familiar that no scruple can ever be made with regard to its solidity.

Now, if we survey the universe, so far as it falls under our knowledge, it bears a great resemblance to an animal or organized body, and seems actuated with a like principle of life and motion. A continual circulation of matter in it produces no disorder; a continual waste in every part is incessantly repaired; the closest sympathy is perceived throughout the entire system; and each part or member, in performing its proper offices, operates both to its own preservation and to that of the whole. The world, therefore, I infer, is an animal; and the Deity is the *soul* of the world, actuating it, and actuated by it.

You have too much learning, Cleanthes, to be at all surprised at this opinion which, you know, was maintained by almost all the theists of antiquity, and chiefly prevails in their discourses and reasonings. For though sometimes the ancient philosophers reason from final causes, as if they thought the world the workmanship of God, yet it appears rather their favorite notion to consider it as his body whose organization renders it subservient to him. And it must be confessed that, as the universe resembles more a human body than it does the works of human art and contrivance, if our limited analogy could ever, with any propriety, be extended to the whole of nature, the inference seems juster in favor of the ancient than the modern theory.

There are many other advantages, too, in the former theory which recommended it to the ancient theologians. Nothing more repugnant to all their notions—because nothing more repugnant to common experience—than mind without body; a mere spiritual substance which fell not under their senses nor comprehension, and of which they had not observed one single instance throughout all nature. Mind and body they knew because they felt both; and order, arrangement, organization, or internal machinery, in both they likewise knew, after the same manner; and it could not but seem reasonable to transfer this experience to the universe, and to suppose the divine mind and body to be also coeval and to have, both of them, order and arrangement naturally inherent in them and inseparable from them.

Here, therefore, is a new species of *anthropomorphism,* Cleanthes, on which you may deliberate; and a theory which seems not liable to any considerable difficulties. You are too much superior, surely, to *systematical prejudices* to find any more difficulty in supposing an animal body to be, originally, of itself or from unknown causes, possessed of order and organization, than in supposing a similar order to belong to mind. But the *vulgar prejudice* that body and mind ought always to accompany each other ought not, one should think, to be entirely neglected; since it is founded on *vulgar experiences,* the only guide which you profess to follow in all these theological inquiries. And if you assert that our limited experience is an unequal standard by which to judge of the unlimited extent of nature, you entirely abandon your own hypothesis, and must thenceforward adopt our mysticism, as you call it, and admit of the absolute incomprehensibility of the Divine Nature.

This theory, I own, replied Cleanthes, has never before occurred to me, though a pretty natural one; and I cannot readily, upon so short an examination and reflection, deliver any opinion with regard to it. You are very scrupulous, indeed, said Philo; were I to examine any system of yours, I should not have acted with half that caution and reserve, in starting objections and difficulties to it. However, if anything occurs to you, you will oblige us by proposing it.

Why then, replied Cleanthes, it seems to me that, though the world does, in many circumstances, resemble an animal body, yet is the analogy also defective in many circumstances the most material: no organs of sense; no seat of thought or reason; no one precise origin of motion and action. In short, it seems to bear a stronger resemblance to a vegetable than to an animal, and your inference would be so far inconclusive in favor of the soul of the world. . . .

But here, continued Philo, in examining the ancient system of the soul of the world there strikes me, all on a sudden, a new idea which, if just, must go near to subvert all your reasoning, and destroy even your first inferences on which you repose such confidence. If the universe bears a greater likeness to animal bodies and to vegetables than to the works of human art, it is more probable that its cause resembles the cause of the former than that of the latter, and its origin ought rather to be ascribed to generation or vegetation than to reason or design. Your conclusion, even according to your own principles, is therefore lame and defective.

Pray open up this argument a little further, said Demea, for I do not rightly apprehend it in that concise manner in which you have expressed it.

Our friend Cleanthes, replied Philo, as you have heard, asserts that since no question of fact can be proved otherwise than by experience, the existence of a Deity admits not of proof from any other medium. The world, says he, resembles the works of human contrivance; therefore its cause must also resemble that of the other. Here we may remark that the operation of one very small part of nature, to wit, man, upon another very small part, to wit, that inanimate matter lying within his reach, is the rule by which Cleanthes judges of the origin of the whole; and he measures objects, so widely disproportioned, by the same individual standard. But to waive all objections drawn from this topic, I affirm that there are other parts of the universe (besides the machines of human invention) which bear still a greater resemblance to the fabric of the world, and which, therefore, afford a better conjecture concerning the universal origin of this system. These parts are animals and vegetables. The world plainly resembles more an animal or a vegetable than it does a watch or a knitting-loom. Its cause, therefore, it is more probable, resembles the cause of the former. The cause of the former is generation or vegetation. The cause, therefore, of the world we may infer to be something similar or analogous to generation or vegetation.

But how is it conceivable, said Demea, that the world can arise from anything similar to vegetation or generation?

Very easily, replied Philo. In like manner as a tree sheds its seed into the neighboring fields and produces other trees; so the great vegetable, the world, or this planetary system, produces within itself certain seeds which, being scattered into the surrounding chaos, vegetate into new worlds. A comet, for instance, is the seed of a world; and after it has been fully ripened, by passing from sun to sun, and star to star, it is at last tossed into the unformed elements which everywhere surround this universe, and immediately sprouts up into a new system.

Or if, for the sake of variety (for I see no other advantage) we should suppose this world to be an animal; a comet is the egg of this animal; and in like manner as an ostrich lays its egg in the sand, which, without any further care, hatches the egg and produces a new animal, so. . . . I understand you, says Demea: But what wild, arbitrary suppositions are these? What *data* have you for such extraordinary conclusions? And is the slight, imaginary resemblance of the world to a vegetable or an animal sufficient to establish the same inference with regard to both? Objects which are in general so widely different; ought they to be a standard for each other?

Right, cries Philo: This is the topic on which I have all along insisted. I have still asserted that we have no *data* to establish any system of cosmogony. Our experience, so imperfect in itself and so limited both in extent and duration, can afford us no probable conjecture concerning the whole of things. But if we must needs fix on some hypothesis, by what rule, pray, ought we to determine our choice? Is there any other rule than the great similarity of the objects compared? And does not a plant or an animal, which springs from vegetation or generation, bear a stronger resemblance to the world than does any artificial machine, which arises from reason and design? . . .

It is my opinion, I own, replied Demea, that each man feels, in a manner, the truth of religion within his own breast; and, from a consciousness of his imbecility and misery rather than from any reasoning, is led to seek protection from that Being on whom he and all nature are dependent. So anxious or so tedious are even the best scenes of life that futurity is still the object of all our hopes and fears. We incessantly look forward and endeavor, by prayers, adoration, and sacrifice, to appease those unknown powers whom we find, by experience, so able to afflict and oppress us. Wretched creatures that we are! What resource for us amidst the innumerable ills of life did not religion suggest some methods of atonement, and appease those terrors with which we are incessantly agitated and tormented?

I am indeed persuaded, said Philo, that the best and indeed the only method of bringing everyone to a due sense of religion is by just representations of the misery and wickedness of men. And for that purpose a talent of eloquence and strong imagery is more requisite than that of reasoning and argument. For is it necessary to prove what everyone feels within himself? It is only necessary to make us feel it, if possible, more intimately and sensibly.

The people, indeed, replied Demea, are sufficiently convinced of this great and melancholy truth. The miseries of life, the unhappiness of man, the general corruptions of our nature, the unsatisfactory enjoyment of pleasures, riches, honors—these phrases have become almost proverbial in all languages. And who can doubt of what all men declare from their own immediate feeling and experience?

In this point, said Philo, the learned are perfectly agreed with the vulgar; and in all letters, *sacred* and *profane,* the topic of human misery has been insisted on with the most pathetic eloquence that sorrow and melancholy could inspire. The poets, who speak from sentiment, without a system, and whose testimony has therefore the more authority, abound in images of this nature. From Homer down to Dr. Young, the whole inspired tribe have ever been sensible that no other representation of things would suit the feeling and observation of each individual.

As to authorities, replied Demea, you need not seek them. Look round this library of Cleanthes. I shall venture to affirm that, except authors of particular sciences, such as chemistry or botany, who have no occasion to treat of human life, there is scarce one of those innumerable writers from whom the sense of human misery has not, in some passage or other, extorted a complaint and confession of it. At least, the chance is entirely on that side; and no one author has ever, so far as I can recollect, been so extravagant as to deny it.

There you must excuse me, said Philo: Leibniz has denied it, and is perhaps the first who ventured upon so bold and paradoxical opinion; at least, the first who made it essential to his philosophical system.

And by being the first, replied Demea, might he not have been sensible of his error? For is this a subject in which philosophers can propose to make discoveries especially in so late an age? And can any man hope by a simple denial (for the subject scarcely admits of reasoning) to bear down the united testimony of mankind, founded on sense and consciousness?

And why should man, added he, pretend to an exemption from the lot of all other animals? The whole earth, believe me, Philo, is cursed and polluted. A perpetual war is kindled among all living creatures. Necessity, hunger, want stimulate the strong and courageous; fear, anxiety, terror agitate the weak and infirm. The first entrance into life gives anguish to the new-born infant and to its wretched parent; weakness, impotence, distress attend each stage of that life, and it is, at last, finished in agony and horror.

Observe, too, says Philo, the curious artifices of nature in order to embitter the life of every living being. The stronger prey upon the weaker and keep them in perpetual terror and anxiety. The weaker, too, in their turn, often prey upon the stronger, and vex and molest them without relaxation. Consider that innumerable race of insects, which either are bred on the body of each animal or, flying about, infix their stings in him. These insects have others still less than themselves which torment them. And thus on each hand, before and behind, above and below, every animal is surrounded with enemies which incessantly seek his misery and destruction.

Man alone, said Demea, seems to be, in part, an exception to this rule. For by combination in society he can easily master lions, tigers, and bears, whose greater strength and agility naturally enable them to prey upon him.

On the contrary, it is here chiefly, cried Philo, that the uniform and equal maxims of nature are most apparent. Man, it is true, can, by combination, surmount all his *real* enemies and become master of the whole animal creation; but does he not immediately raise up to himself *imaginary* enemies, the demons of his fancy, who haunt him with superstitious terrors and blast every enjoyment of life? His pleasure, as he imagines, becomes in their eyes a crime; his food and repose give them umbrage and offense; his very sleep and dreams furnish new materials to anxious fear; and even death, his refuge from every other ill, presents only the dread of endless and innumerable woes. Nor does the wolf molest more the timid flock than superstition does the anxious breast of wretched mortals.

Besides, consider, Demea: This very society by which we surmount those wild beasts, our natural enemies, what new enemies does it not raise to us? What woe and misery does it not occasion? Man is the greatest enemy of man. Oppression, injustice, contempt, contumely, violence, sedition, war, calumny, treachery, fraud—by these they mutually torment each other, and they would soon dissolve that society which they had formed were it not for the dread of still greater ills which must attend their separation.

But though these external insults, said Demea, from animals, from men, from all the elements, which assault us form a frightful catalogue of woes, they are nothing in comparison of those which arise within ourselves, from the distempered condition of our mind and body. How many lie under the lingering torment of diseases? Hear the pathetic enumeration of the great poet.

Intestine stone and ulcer, colic-pangs,
Demoniac frenzy, moping melancholy,
And moon-struck madness, pining atrophy,
Marasmus, and wide-wasting pestilence.
Dire was the tossing, deep the groans: *Despair*
Tended the sick, busiest from couch to couch.
And over them triumphant *Death* his dart
Shook: but delay'd to strike, though oft invok'd
With vows, as their chief good and final hope.[2]

The disorders of the mind, continued Demea, though more secret, are not perhaps less dismal and vexatious. Remorse, shame, anguish, rage, disappointment, anxiety, fear, dejection, despair—who has ever passed through life without cruel inroads from these tormentors? How many have scarcely ever felt any better sensations? Labor and poverty, so abhorred by everyone, are-the certain lot of the far greater number; and those few privileged persons who enjoy ease and opulence never reach contentment or true felicity. All the goods of life united would not make a very happy man, but all the ills united would make a wretch indeed; and any one of them almost (and who can be free from every one), nay, often the absence of one good (and who can possess all) is sufficient to render life ineligible.

Were a stranger to drop on a sudden into this world, I would show him, as a specimen of its ills, a hospital full of diseases, a prison crowded with malefactors and debtors, a field of battle strewed with carcases, a fleet foundering in the ocean, a nation languishing under tyranny, famine, or pestilence. To turn the gay side of life to him and give him a notion of its pleasures—whither should I conduct him? To a ball, to an opera, to court? He might justly think that I was only showing him a diversity of distress and sorrow.

There is no evading such striking instances, said Philo, but by apologies which still further aggravate the charge. Why have all men, I ask, in all ages, complained incessantly of the miseries of life? . . . They have no just reason, says one: These complaints proceed only from their discontented, repining, anxious disposition. . . . And can there possibly, I reply, be a more certain foundation of misery than such a wretched temper?

But if they were really as unhappy as they pretend, says my antagonist, why do they remain in life? . . .

Not satisfied with life, afraid of death.

This is the secret chain, say I, that holds us. We are terrified, not bribed to the continuance of our existence.

It is only a false delicacy, he may insist, which a few refined spirits indulge, and which has spread these complaints among the whole race of mankind. . . .And what is this delicacy, I ask, which you blame? Is it anything but a greater sensibility to all the pleasures and pains of life? And if the man of a delicate, refined temper, by being so much more alive than the rest of the world, is only so much more unhappy, what judgment must we form in general of human life?

Let men remain at rest, says our adversary, and they will be easy. They are willing artificers of their own misery . . . . No! reply I: An anxious languor follows their repose; disappointment, vexation, trouble, their activity and ambition.

I can observe something like what you mention in some others, replied Cleanthes; but I confess I feel little or nothing of it in myself, and hope that it is not so common as you represent it.

If you feel not human misery yourself, cried Demea, I congratulate you on so happy a singularity. Others, seemingly the most prosperous, have not been ashamed to vent their complaints in the most melancholy strains. Let us attend to the great, the fortunate emperor, Charles V, when, tired with human grandeur, he resigned all his extensive dominions into the hands of his son. In the last harangue, which he made on that memorable occasion, he publicly avowed *that the greatest prosperities which he had ever enjoyed had been mixed with so many adversities that he might truly say he had never enjoyed any satisfaction or contentment.* But did the retired life in which he sought for shelter afford him any greater happiness? If we may credit his son's account, his repentance commenced the very day of his resignation.

Cicero's fortune, from small beginnings, rose to the greatest luster and renown; yet what pathetic complaints of the ills of life do his familiar letters, as well as philosophical discourses, contain? And suitably to his own experience, he introduces Cato, the great, the fortunate Cato protesting in his old age that had he a new life in his offer he would reject the present.

Ask yourself, ask any of your acquaintance, whether they would live over again the last ten or twenty years of their life. No! but the next twenty, they say, will be better:

> And from the dregs of life, hope to receive
> What the first sprightly running could not give.[3]

Thus, at last, they find (such is the greatness of human misery, it reconciles even contradictions) that they complain at once of the shortness of life and of its vanity and sorrow.

And is it possible, Cleanthes, said Philo, that after all these reflections, and infinitely more which might be suggested, you can still persevere in your anthropomorphism, and assert the moral attributes of the Deity, his justice, benevolence, mercy, and rectitude, to be of the same nature with these virtues in human creatures? His power, we allow, is infinite; whatever he wills is executed; but neither man nor any other animal is happy; therefore, he does not will their happiness. His wisdom is infinite; he is never mistaken in choosing the means to any end; but the course of nature tends not to human or animal felicity; therefore, it is not established for that purpose. Through the whole compass of human knowledge there are no inferences more certain and infallible than these. In what respect, then, do his benevolence and mercy resemble the benevolence and mercy of men?

Epicurus' old questions are yet unanswered.

Is he willing to prevent evil, but not able? then is he impotent. Is he able, but not willing? then is he malevolent. Is he both able and willing? whence then is evil?

You ascribe, Cleanthes (and I believe justly), a purpose and intention to nature. But what, I beseech you, is the object of that curious artifice and machinery which she has displayed in all animals—the preservation alone of individuals, and propagation of the species? It seems enough for her purpose, if such a rank be barely upheld in the universe, without any care or concern for the happiness of the members that compose it. No resource for this purpose: no machinery in order merely to give pleasure or ease: no fund of pure joy and contentment: no indulgence without some want or necessity accompanying it. At least, the few phenomena of this nature are overbalanced by opposite phenomena of still greater importance.

Our sense of music, harmony, and indeed beauty of all kinds, gives satisfaction, without being absolutely necessary to the preservation and propagation of the species. But what racking pains, on the other hand, arise from gouts, gravels, megrims, toothaches, rheumatisms, where the injury to the animal machinery is either small or incurable? Mirth, laughter, play, frolic seem gratuitous satisfactions which have no further tendency; spleen, melancholy, discontent, superstition are pains of the same nature. How then does the divine benevolence display itself, in the sense of you anthropomorphites? None but we mystics, as you were pleased to call us, can account for this strange mixture of phenomena, by deriving it from attributes infinitely perfect but incomprehensible.

And have you, at last, said Cleanthes smiling, betrayed your intentions, Philo? Your long agreement with Demea did indeed a little surprise me, but I find you were all the while erecting a concealed battery against me. And I must confess that you have now fallen upon a subject worthy of your noble spirit of opposition and controversy. If you can make out the present point, and prove mankind to be unhappy or corrupted, there is an end at once of all religion. For to what purpose establish the natural attributes of the Deity, while the moral are still doubtful and uncertain?

You take umbrage very easily, replied Demea, at opinions the most innocent and the most generally received, even amongst the religious and devout themselves; and nothing can be more surprising than to find a topic like this—concerning the wickedness and misery of man—charged with no less than atheism and profaneness. Have not all pious divines and preachers who have indulged their rhetoric on so fertile a subject; have they not easily, I say, given a solution of any difficulties which may attend it? This world is but a point in comparison of the universe; this life but a moment in comparison of eternity. The present evil phenomena, therefore, are rectified in other regions, and in some future period of existence. And the eyes of men, being then opened to larger views of things, see the whole connection of general laws, and trace, with adoration, the benevolence and rectitude of the Deity through all the mazes and intricacies of his providence.

No! replied Cleanthes, no! These arbitrary suppositions can never be admitted, contrary to matter of fact, visible and uncontroverted. Whence can any cause be known but from its known effects? Whence can any hypothesis be proved but from the apparent phenomena? To establish one hypothesis upon another is building entirely in the air; and the utmost we ever attain by these conjectures and fictions is to ascertain the bare possibility of our opinion, but never can we, upon such terms, establish its reality.

The only method of supporting divine benevolence—and it is what I willingly embrace—is to deny absolutely the misery and wickedness of man. Your representations are exaggerated; your melancholy views mostly fictitious; your inferences contrary to fact and experience. Health is more common than sickness; pleasure than pain; happiness than misery. And for one vexation which we meet with, we attain, upon computation, a hundred enjoyments.

Admitting your position, replied Philo, which yet is extremely doubtful, you must at the same time allow that, if pain be less frequent than pleasure, it is infinitely more violent and durable. One hour of it is often able to outweigh a day, a week, a month of our common insipid enjoyments; and how many days, weeks, and months are passed by several in the most acute torments? Pleasure, scarcely in one instance, is ever able to reach ecstasy and rapture; and in no one instance can it continue for any time at its highest pitch altitude. The spirits evaporate, the nerves relax, the fabric is disordered, and the enjoyment quickly degenerates into fatigue and uneasiness. But pain often, good God, how often! rises to torture and agony; and the longer it continues, it becomes still more genuine agony and torture. Patience is exhausted, courage languishes, melancholy seizes us, and nothing terminates our misery but the removal of its cause or another event which is the sole cure of all evil, but which, from our natural folly, we regard with still greater horror and consternation.

But not to insist upon these topics, continued Philo, though most obvious, certain, and important, I must use the freedom to admonish you, Cleanthes, that you have put the controversy upon a most dangerous issue, and are unawares introducing a total skepticism into the most essential articles of natural and revealed theology. What! no method of fixing a just foundation for religion unless we allow the happiness of human life, and maintain a continued existence even in this world, with all our present pains, infirmities, vexations, and follies, to be eligible and desirable! But this is contrary to everyone's feeling and experience; it is contrary to an authority so established as nothing can subvert. No decisive proofs can ever be produced against this authority; nor is it possible for you to compute, estimate, and compare all the pains and all the pleasures in the lives of all men and of all animals; and thus, by your resting the the whole system of religion on a point which, from its very nature, must forever be uncertain, you tacitly confess that that system is equally uncertain.

But allowing you what never will be believed, at least, what you never possibly can prove, that animal or, at least, human happiness in this life exceeds its misery, you have yet done nothing; for this is not, by any means, what we expect from infinite power, infinite wisdom, and infinite goodness. Why is there any misery at all in the world? Not by chance, surely. From some cause then. Is it from the intention of the Deity? But he is perfectly benevolent. Is it contrary to his intention? But he is almighty. Nothing can shake the solidity of this reasoning, so short, so clear, so decisive, except we assert that these subjects exceed all human capacity, and that our common measures of truth and falsehood are not applicable to them—a topic which I have all along insisted on, but which you have, from the beginning, rejected with scorn and indignation.

But I will be contented to retire still from this intrenchment, for I deny that you can ever force me in it. I will allow that pain or misery in man is *compatible* with infinite power and goodness in the Deity, even in your sense of these attributes: what are you advanced by all these concessions? A mere possible compatibility is not sufficient. You must *prove* these pure, unmixed and uncontrollable attributes from the present mixed and confused phenomena, and from these alone. A hopeful undertaking! Were the phenomena ever so pure and unmixed, yet, being finite, they would be insufficient for that purpose. How much more, where they are also so jarring and discordant!

Here, Cleanthes, I find myself at ease in my argument. Here I triumph. Formerly, when we argued concerning the natural attributes of intelligence and design, I needed all my skeptical and metaphysical subtlety to elude your grasp. In many views of the universe and of its parts, particularly the latter, the beauty and fitness of final causes strike us with such irresistible force that all objections appear (what I believe they really are) mere cavils and sophisms; nor can we then imagine how it was ever possible for us to repose any weight on them. But there is no view of human life or of the condition of mankind from which, without the greatest violence, we can infer the moral attributes or learn that infinite benevolence, conjoined with infinite power and infinite wisdom, which we must discover by the eyes of faith alone. It is your turn now to tug the laboring oar, and to support your philosophical subtleties against the dictates of plain reason and experience.

NOTES

1. Cleanthes claims that empirical evidence demonstrates the truth of traditional Christian theology. Demea is committed to that theology but does not believe such evidence can provide any defense for his faith. Philo doubts that reason yields conclusive results in any field of inquiry and is especially critical of theological dogmatism.
2. Milton: *Paradise Lost*, BK. XI.
3. John Dryden, *Aureng-Zebe*, Act IV, sc.1.

[7]

The Problem of Evil

John H. Hick

To many, the most powerful positive objection to belief in God is the fact of evil. Probably for most agnostics it is the appalling depth and extent of human suffering, more than anything else, that makes the idea of a loving Creator seem so implausible and disposes them toward one or another of the various naturalistic theories of religion.

As a challenge to theism, the problem of evil has traditionally been posed in the form of a dilemma: if God is perfectly loving, he must wish to abolish evil; and if he is all-powerful, he must be able to abolish evil. But evil exists; therefore God cannot be both omnipotent and perfectly loving.

Certain solutions, which at once suggest themselves, have to be ruled out so far as the Judaic Christian faith is concerned.

To say, for example (with contemporary Christian Science), that evil is an illusion of the human mind, is impossible within a religion based upon the stark realism of the Bible. Its pages faithfully reflect the characteristic mixture of good and evil in human experience. They record every kind of sorrow and suffering, every mode of man's inhumanity to man and of his painfully insecure existence in the world. There is no attempt to regard evil as anything but dark, menacingly ugly, heartrending, and crushing. In the Christian scriptures, the climax of this history of evil is the crucifixion of Jesus, which is presented not only as a case of utterly unjust suffering, but as the violent and murderous rejection of God's Messiah. There can be no doubt, then, that for bibli-

John H. Hick, *Philosophy of Religion*, 2d ed. © 1973. Reprinted by permission of Prentice-Hall, Inc., Englewood Cliffs, N.J.

John H. Hick (b. 1922) is Professor of Philosophy at the Claremont Graduate School.

cal faith evil is unambiguously evil and stands in direct opposition to God's will.

Again, to solve the problem of evil by means of the theory (sponsored, for example, by the Boston "Personalist" School)[1] of a finite deity who does the best he can with a material, intractable and coeternal with himself, is to have abandoned the basic premise of Hebrew-Christian monotheism; for the theory amounts to rejecting belief in the infinity and sovereignty of God.

Indeed, any theory that would avoid the problem of the origin of evil by depicting it as an ultimate constituent of the universe, co-ordinate with good, has been repudiated in advance by the classic Christian teaching, first developed by Augustine, that evil represents the going wrong of something that in itself is good.[2] Augustine holds firmly to the Hebrew-Christian conviction that the universe is *good*—that is to say, it is the creation of a good God for a good purpose. He completely rejects the ancient prejudice that matter is evil. There are, according to Augustine, higher and lower, greater and lesser goods in immense abundance and variety; but everything that has being is good in its own way and degree, except in so far as it may have become spoiled or corrupted. Evil—whether it be an evil will, an instance of pain, or some disorder or decay in nature—has not been set there by God, but represents the distortion of something that is inherently valuable. Whatever exists is, as such, and in its proper place, good; evil is essentially parasitic upon good, being disorder and perversion in a fundamentally good creation. This understanding of evil as something negative means that it is not willed and created by God; but it does not mean (as some have supposed) that evil is unreal and can be disregarded. On the contrary, the first effect of this doctrine is to accentuate even more the question of the origin of evil.

Theodicy,[3] as many modern Christian thinkers see it, is a modest enterprise, negative rather than positive in its conclusions. It does not claim to explain, nor to explain away, every instance of evil in human experience, but only to point to certain considerations that prevent the fact of evil (largely incomprehensible though it remains) from constituting a final and insuperable bar to rational belief in God.

In indicating these considerations it will be useful to follow the traditional division of the subject. There is the problem of *moral evil* or wickedness: why does an all-good and all-powerful God permit this? And there is the problem of the *nonmoral evil* of suffering or pain, both physical and mental: why has an all-good and all-powerful God created a world in which this occurs?

Christian thought has always considered moral evil in its relation to human freedom and responsibility. To be a person is to be a finite center of freedom, a (relatively) free and self-directing agent responsible for one's own decisions. This involves being free to act wrongly as well as to act rightly. The idea of a person who can be infallibly guaranteed always to act rightly is self-contradictory. There can be no certainty in advance that a genuinely free moral agent will never choose amiss. Consequently, the possibility of wrongdoing or sin is logically inseparable from the creation of finite persons, and to say that God should not have created beings who might sin amounts to saying that he should not have created people.

This thesis has been challenged in some recent philosophical discussions of the problem of evil, in which it is claimed that no contradiction is involved in saying that God might have made people who would be genuinely free but who could at the same time be guaranteed always to act rightly. A quote from one of these discussions follows:

> If there is no logical impossiblity in a man's freely choosing the good on one, or on several occasions, there cannot be a logical imppossibility in his freely choosing the good on every occasion. God was not, then, faced with a choice between making innocent automata and making beings who, in acting freely, would sometimes go wrong: there was open to him the obviously better possibility of making beings who would act freely but always go right. Clearly, his failure to avail himself of this possibility is inconsistent with his being both omnipotent and wholly good.[4]

A reply to this argument is indirectly suggested in another recent contribution to the discussion.[5] If by a free action we mean an action that is not externally compelled but that flows from the nature of the agent as he reacts to the circumstances in which he finds himself, there is indeed no contradiction between our being free and our actions being "caused" (by our own nature) and therefore being in principle predictable. There is a contradiction, however, in saying that God is the cause of our acting as we do but that we are free beings *in relation to God*. There is, in other words, a contradiction in saying that God has made us so that we shall of necessity act in a certain way, and that we are genuinely independent persons in relation to him. If all our thoughts and actions are divinely predestined, however free and morally responsible we may seem to be to ourselves, we cannot be free and morally responsible in the sight of God but must instead be his helpless puppets. Such "freedom" is like that of a patient acting out a series of posthypnotic suggestions: he appears, even to himself, to be free, but his volitions have actually been predetermined by another will, that of the hypnotist, in relation to whom the patient is not a free agent.

A different objector might raise the question of whether or not we deny God's omnipotence if we admit that he is unable to create persons who are free from the risks inherent in personal freedom. The answer that has always been given is that to create such beings is logically impossible. It is no limitation upon God's power that he cannot accomplish the logically impossible, since there is nothing here to accomplish, but only a meaningless conjunction of words[6]—in this case "person who is not a person." God is able to create beings of any and every conceivable kind; but creatures who lack moral freedom, however superior they might be to human beings in other respects, would not be what we mean by persons. They would constitute a different form of life that God might have brought into existence instead of persons. When we ask why God did not create such beings in place of persons the traditional answer is that only persons could, in any meaningful sense, become "children of God," capable of entering into a personal relationship with their Creator by a free and uncompelled response to his love.

When we turn from the possibility of moral evil as a correlate of man's personal freedom to its actuality, we face something that must remain inexplicable even when it can be seen to be possible. For we can never provide a complete causal explanation of a free act; if we could, it would not be a free act. The origin of moral evil lies forever concealed within the mystery of human freedom.

The necessary connection between moral freedom and the possibility, now actualized, of sin throws light upon a great deal of the suffering that afflicts mankind. For an enormous amount of human pain arises either from the inhumanity or the culpable incompetence of mankind. This includes such major scourges as poverty, oppression and persecution, war, and all the injustice, indignity, and inequity that occur even in the most advanced societies. These evils are manifestations of human sin. Even disease is fostered to an extent, the limits of which have not yet been determined by psychosomatic medicine, by emotional and moral factors seated both in the individual and in his social environment. To the extent that all of these evils stem from human failures and wrong decisions, their possibility is inherent in the creation of free persons inhabiting a world that presents them with real choices followed by real consequences.

We may now turn more directly to the problem of suffering. Even though the major bulk of actual human pain is traceable to man's misused freedom as a sole or part cause, there remain other sources of pain that are entirely independent of the human will, for example, earthquake, hurricane, storm, flood, drought, and blight. In practice, it is often impossible to trace a boundary between the suffering that results from human wickedness and folly and that which falls upon mankind from without; both kinds of suffering are inextricably mingled together in human experience. For our present purpose, however, it is important to note that the latter category does exist and that it seems to be built into the very structure of our world. In response to it, theodicy, if it is wisely conducted, follows a negative path. It is not possible to show positively that each item of human pain serves a divine purpose of good; but, on the other hand, it does seem possible to show that the divine purpose as it is understood in Judaism and Christianity could not be forwarded in a world that was designed as a permanent hedonistic paradise.[7]

An essential premise of this argument concerns the nature of the divine purpose in creating the world. The skeptic's assumption is that man is to be viewed as a completed creation and that God's purpose in making the world was to provide a suitable dwelling-place for this fully formed creature. Since God is good and loving, the environment that he has created for human life to inhabit will naturally be as pleasant and comfortable as possible. The problem is essentially similar to that of a man who builds a cage for some pet animal. Since our world, in fact, contains sources of hardship, inconvenience and danger of innumerable kinds, the conclusion follows that this world cannot have been created by a perfectly benevolent and all-powerful deity.[8]

Christianity, however, has never supposed that God's purpose in the creation of the world was to construct a paradise whose inhabitants would experience a maximum of pleasure and a minimum of pain. The world is seen, instead, as a place of "soul making" or person making in which free beings, grappling with the tasks and challenges of their existence in a common environment, may become "children of God" and "heirs of eternal life." A way of thinking theologically of God's continuing creative purpose for man was suggested by some of the early Hellenistic Fathers of the Christian Church, especially Irenaeus. Following hints from Saint Paul, Irenaeus taught that man has been made as a person in the image of God but has not yet been brought as a free and responsible agent into the finite likeness of God, which is revealed in Christ.[9] Our world, with all its rough edges, is the sphere in which this second and harder stage of the creative process is taking place.

This conception of the world (whether or not set in Irenaeus's theological framework) can be supported by the method of negative theodicy. Suppose, contrary to fact, that this world were a paradise from which all possibility of pain and suffering where excluded. The consequences would be very far-reaching. For example, no one could ever injure anyone else: the murderer's knife would turn to paper or his bullets to thin air; the bank safe, robbed of a million dollars, would miraculously become filled with another million dollars (without this device, on however large a scale, proving inflationary); fraud, deceit, conspiracy, and treason would somehow always leave the fabric of society undamaged. Again, no one would ever be injured by accident: the mountain climber, steeplejack, or playing child falling from a height would float unharmed to the ground; the reckless driver would never meet with disaster. There would be no need to work, since no harm could result from avoiding work; there would be no call to be concerned for others in time of need or danger, for in such a world there could be no real needs or dangers.

To make possible this continual series of individual adjustments, nature would have to work by "special providences" instead of running according to general laws that men must learn to respect on penalty of pain or death. The laws of nature would have to be extremely flexible: sometimes gravity would operate, sometimes not; sometimes an object would be hard and solid, sometimes soft. There could be no science, for there would be no enduring world structure to investigate. In eliminating the problems and hardships of an objective environment, with its own laws, life would become like a dream in which, delightfully but aimlessly, we would float and drift at ease.[10]

One can at least begin to imagine such a world. It is evident that our present ethical concepts would have no meaning in it. If, for example, the notion of harming someone is an essential element in the concept of a wrong action, in our hedonistic paradise there could be no wrong actions—nor any right actions in distinction from wrong. Courage and fortitude would have no point in an environment in which there is, by definition, no danger or difficulty. Generosity, kindness, the *agape* aspect of love, prudence, unselfishness, and all other ethical notions which presuppose life in an objective environment could not even be formed. Consequently, such a world, however well it might promote pleasure, would be very ill adapted for the development of the moral qualities of human personality. In relation to this purpose it might be the worst of all possible worlds!

It would seem, then, that an environment intended to make possible the growth in free beings of the finest characteristics of personal life must have a good deal in common with our present world. It must operate according to general and dependable laws; and it must involve real dangers, difficulties, problems, obstacles, and possibilities of pain, failure, sorrow, frustration, and defeat. If it did not contain the particular trials and perils that—subtracting man's own very considerable contribution—our world contains, it would have to contain others instead.

To realize this is not, by any means, to be in possession of a detailed theodicy. It is to understand that this world, with all its "heartaches and the thousand natural shocks that flesh is heir to," an environment so manifestly not designed for the maximization of human pleasure and the minimization of human pain, may nevertheless be rather well adapted to the quite different purpose of "soul making."[11]

These considerations are related to theism as such. Specifically Christian theism goes further in the light of the death of Christ, which is seen paradoxically both (as the murder of the divine Son) as the worst thing that has ever happened and (as the occasion of man's salvation) as the best thing that has ever happened. As the supreme evil turned to supreme good, it provides the paradigm for the distinctively Christian reaction to evil. Viewed from the standpoint of Christian faith, evils do not cease to be evils; and certainly, in view of Christ's healing work, they cannot be said to have been sent by God. Yet, it has been the persistent claim of those seriously and wholeheartedly committed to Christian discipleship that tragedy, though truly tragic, may nevertheless be turned, through a man's reaction to it, from a cause of despair and alienation from God to a stage in the fulfillment of God's loving purpose for that individual. As the greatest of all evils, the crucifixion of Christ, was made the occasion of man's redemption, so good can be won from other evils. As Jesus saw his execution by the Romans as an experience which God desired him to accept, an experience which was to be brought within the sphere of the divine purpose and made to serve the divine ends, so the Christian response to calamity is to accept the adversities, pains, and afflictions which life brings, in order that they can be turned to a positive spiritual use.[12]

At this point, theodicy points forward in two ways to the subject of life after death, which is to be discussed in later chapters.

First, although there are many striking instances of good being triumphantly brought out of evil through a man's or a woman's reaction to it, there are many other cases in which the opposite has happened. Sometimes obstacles breed strength of character, dangers evoke courage and unselfishness, and calamities produce patience and moral steadfastness. But sometimes they lead, instead, to resentment, fear, grasping selfishness, and disintegration of character. Therefore, it would seem that any divine purpose of soul making that is at work in earthly history must continue beyond this life if it is ever to achieve more than a very partial and fragmentary success.[13]

Second, if we ask whether the business of soul making is worth all the toil and sorrow of human life, the Christian answer must be in terms of a future good great enough to justify all that has happened on the way to it.

NOTES

1. Edgar Brightman's *A Philosophy of Religion* (Englewood Cliffs, N.J.: Prentice-Hall, Inc., 1940), Chaps. 8–10, is a classic exposition of one form of this view.

2. See Augustine's *Confessions,* Book VII, Chap. 12; *City of God,* Book XII, Chap. 3; *Enchiridion,* Chap. 4.

3. The word "theodicy," from the Greek *theos* (God) and *dike* (righteous), means the justification of God's goodness in the face of the fact of evil.

4. J. L. Mackie, "Evil and Omnipotence," *Mind* (April, 1955), p. 209. A similar point is made by Antony Flew in "Divine Omnipotence and Human Freedom," *New Essays in Philosophical Theology.* An important critical comment on these arguments is offered by Ninian Smart in "Omnipotence, Evil, and Supermen," *Philosophy* (April, 1961), with replies by Flew (January, 1962) and Mackie (April, 1962).

5. Flew, in *New Essays in Philosophical Theology.*

6. As Aquinas said, ". . . nothing that implies a contradiction falls under the scope of God's omnipotence." *Summa Theologica,* Part I, Question 25, Art. 4.

7. From the Greek *hedone,* pleasure.

8. This is essentially David Hume's argument in his discussion of the problem of evil in his *Dialogues;* [see source #6—Ed.].

9. See Irenaeus's *Against Heresies,* Book IV, Chaps. 37 and 38.

10. Tennyson's poem, *The Lotus-Eaters,* well expresses the desire (analyzed by Freud as a wish to return to the peace of the womb) for such "dreamful ease."

11. This brief discussion has been confined to the problem of human suffering. The large and intractable problem of animal pain is not taken up here. For a discussion of it see, for example, Austin Farrer, *Love Almighty and Ills Unlimited* (Garden City, N.Y.: Doubleday & Company, Inc., 1961), Chap. 5, and John Hick, *Evil and the God of Love* (London: Collins, The Fontana Library, 1968), pp. 345-53.

12. This conception of providence is stated more fully in John Hick, *Faith and Knowledge,* 2nd ed. (Ithaca, N.Y.: Cornell University Press, 1966), Chap. 10, some sentences from which are incorporated in this paragraph.

13. The position presented above is developed more fully in the author's *Evil and the God of Love,* 1966 (London: Fontana paperback ed., 1968). For an important philosophical critique of theodicies see Edward H. Madden and Peter H. Hare, *Evil and the Concept of God* (Springfield, Ill.: Charles C. Thomas, Publishers, 1968). Some of the most important recent articles on the subject are collected in Nelson Pike, ed., *God and Evil* (Englewood Cliffs, N.J.: Prentice-Hall, Inc., 1964).

[8]

Theology and Falsification

Antony Flew

Let us begin with a parable. It is a parable developed from a tale told by John Wisdom in his haunting and revelatory article "Gods."[1] Once upon a time, two explorers came upon a clearing in the jungle. In the clearing were growing many flowers and many weeds. One explorer says, "Some gardener must tend this plot." The other disagrees, "There is no gardener." So they pitch their tents and set a watch. No gardener is ever seen. "But perhaps he is an invisible gardener." So they set up a barbed-wire fence. They electrify it. They patrol with bloodhounds. (For they remember how H. G. Wells's *The Invisible Man* could be both smelt and touched through he could not be seen.) But no shrieks ever suggest that some intruder has received a shock. No movements of the wire ever betray an invisible climber. The bloodhounds never give cry. Yet still the Believer is not convinced. "But there is a gardener, invisible, intangible, insensible to electric shocks, a gardener who has no scent and makes no sound, a gardener who comes secretly to look after the garden which he loves." At last the Skeptic despairs, "But what remains of your original assertion? Just how does what you call an invisible, intangible, eternally elusive gardener differ from an imaginary gardener or even from no gardener at all?"

In this parable we can see how what starts as an assertion, that something exists or that there is some analogy between certain complexes of phenomena, may be reduced step by step to an altogether dif-

---

Reprinted with permission of The Macmillan Company (New York) and the Student Christian Movement Press Limited (London) from *New Essays in Philosophical Theology* by Antony Flew and Alasdair MacIntyre, eds. First published in 1955.

Antony Flew (b. 1923) is Professor Emeritus of Philosophy at the University of Reading in England.

ferent status, to an expression perhaps of a "picture preference."[2] The Skeptic says there is no gardener. The Believer says there is a gardener (but invisible, etc.). One man talks about sexual behavior. Another man prefers to talk of Aphrodite (but knows that there is not really a superhuman person additional to, and somehow responsible for, all sexual phenomena). The process of qualification may be checked at any point before the original assertion is completely withdrawn and something of that first assertion will remain (Tautology). Mr. Wells's invisible man could not, admittedly, be seen, but in all other respects he was a man like the rest of us. But though the process of qualification may be, and of course usually is, checked in time, it is not always judiciously so halted. Someone may dissipate his assertion completely without noticing that he has done so. A fine brash hypothesis may thus be killed by inches, the death by a thousand qualifications.

And in this, it seems to me, lies the peculiar danger, the endemic evil, of theological utterance. Take such utterances as "God has a plan," "God created the world," "God loves us as a father loves his children." They look at first sight very much like assertions, vast cosmological assertions. Of course, this is no sure sign that they either are, or are intended to be, assertions. But let us confine ourselves to the cases where those who utter such sentences intend them to express assertions. (Merely remarking parenthetically that those who intend or interpret such utterances as crypto-commands, expressions of wishes, disguised ejaculations, concealed ethics, or as anything else but assertions, are unlikely to succeed in making them either properly orthodox or practically effective.)

Now to assert that such and such is the case is necessarily equivalent to denying that such and such is not the case. Suppose then that we are in doubt as to what someone who gives vent to an utterance is asserting, or suppose that, more radically, we are skeptical as to whether he is really asserting anything at all, one way of trying to understand (or perhaps it will be to expose) his utterance is to attempt to find what he would regard as counting against, or as being incompatible with, its truth. For if the utterance is indeed an assertion, it will necessarily be equivalent to a denial of the negation of that assertion. And anything which would count against the assertion, or which would induce the speaker to withdraw it and to admit that it had been mistaken, must be part of (or the whole of) the meaning of the negation of that assertion. And to know the meaning of the negation of an assertion, is as near as makes not matter, to know the meaning of that assertion. And if there is nothing which a putative assertion denies then there is nothing which it asserts either: and so it is not really an assertion. When the Skeptic in the parable asked the Believer, "Just how does what you call an invisible, intangible, eternally elusive gardener differ from an imaginary gardener or even from no gardener at all?" he was suggesting that the Believer's earlier statement had been so eroded by qualification that it was no longer an assertion at all.

Now it often seems to people who are not religious as if there was no conceivable event or series of events the occurrence of which would be admitted by sophisticated religious people to be a sufficient reason for conceding "There wasn't a God after all" or "God does not really love us then." Someone tells us that God loves us as a father loves his children. We are reassured. But then we see a child dying of inoperable cancer of the throat. His earthly father is driven frantic in his efforts to help, but his Heavenly Father reveals no obvious sign of concern. Some qualification is made—God's love is "not a merely human love" or it is "an inscrutable love," perhaps—and we realize that such sufferings are quite compatible with the truth of the assertion that "God loves us as a father (but, of course, . . .)." We are reassured again. But then perhaps we ask: what is this assurance of God's (appropriately qualified) love worth, what is this apparent guarantee really a guarantee against? Just what would have to happen not merely (morally and wrongly) to tempt but also (logically and rightly) to entitle us to say "God does not love us" or even "God does not exist"? I therefore put to the succeeding symposiasts the simple central questions, "What would have to occur or to have occurred to constitute for you a disproof of the love of, or of the existence of, God?"

NOTES

1. P. A. S., 1944-5, reprinted as Chap. X of *Logic and Language,* Vol. 1 (Blackwell, 1951), and in his *Philosophy and Psychoanalysis* (Blackwell, 1953).

2. See J. Wisdom, "Other Minds," *Mind,* 1940; reprinted in his *Other Minds* (Blackwell, 1952).

[9]

God and Morality

Plato

EUTHYPHRO: What's new, Socrates, to make you leave your usual haunts in the Lyceum and spend your time here by the king-Archon's court? Surely you are not prosecuting anyone before the king Archon as I am?

SOCRATES: The Athenians do not call this a prosecution but an indictment, Euthyphro.

E: What is this you say? Someone must have indicted you, for you are not going to tell me that you have indicted someone else.

S: No indeed.

E: But someone else has indicted you?

S: Quite so.

E: Who is he?

S: I do not really know him myself, Euthyphro. He is apparently young and unknown. They call him Meletus, I believe. He belongs to the Pitthean deme, if you know anyone from that deme called Meletus, with long hair, not much of a beard, and a rather aquiline nose.

E: I don't know him, Socrates. What charge does he bring against you?

S: What charge? A not ignoble one I think, for it is no small thing for a young man to have knowledge of such an important subject. He says he knows how our young men are corrupted and who corrupts them. He is likely to be wise, and when he sees my ignorance corrupting his contemporaries, he proceeds to accuse me to the city

Reprinted from *The Trial and Death of Socrates*, translated by G. M. A. Grube (1975), by permission of Hackett Publishing Company, Inc., Indianapolis, Indiana.

Plato (ca, 427-347 B.C.), the Athenian philosopher, wrote a series of dialogues which are among the foundations of Western thought.

as to their mother. I think he is the only one of our public men to start out the right way, for it is right to care first that the young should be as good as possible, just as a good farmer is likely to take care of the young plants first, and of the others later. So, too, Meletus first gets rid of us who corrupt the growth of the young, as he says, and then afterwards he will obviously take care of the older and become a source of great blessings for the city, as seems likely to happen to one who started out this way.

E: I could wish this were true, Socrates, but I fear the opposite may happen. He seems to me to start out by harming the very heart of the city by attempting to wrong you. Tell me, what does he say you do to corrupt the young?

S: Strange things, to hear him tell it, for he says that I am a maker of gods, that I create new gods while not believing in the old gods, and he has indicted me for this very reason, as he puts it.

E: I understand, Socrates. This is because you say that the divine sign keeps coming to you. So he has written this indictment against you as one who makes innovations in religious matters, and he comes to court to slander you, knowing that such things are easily misrepresented to the crowd. The same is true in my case. Whenever I speak of divine matters in the assembly and foretell the future, they laugh me down as if I were crazy; and yet I have foretold nothing that did not happen. Nevertheless, they envy all of us who do this. One need not give them any thought, but carry on just the same.

S: My dear Euthyphro, to be laughed at does not matter perhaps, for the Athenians do not mind anyone they think clever, as long as he does not teach his own wisdom, but if they think that he makes others to be like himself they get angry, whether through envy, as you say, or for some other reason.

E: I have certainly no desire to test their feelings toward me in this matter.

S: Perhaps you seem to make yourself but rarely available, and not to be willing to teach your own wisdom, but my liking for people makes them think that I pour out to anybody anything I have to say, not only without charging a fee but appearing glad to reward anyone who is willing to listen. If then they were intending to laugh at me, as you say they laugh at you, there would be nothing unpleasant in their spending their time in court laughing and jesting, but if they are going to be serious, the outcome is not clear except to you prophets.

E: Perhaps it will come to nothing, Socrates, and you will fight your case as you think best, as I think I will mine.

S: What is your case, Euthyphro? Are you the defendant or the prosecutor?

E: The prosecutor.

S: Whom do you prosecute?

E: One whom I am thought crazy to prosecute.

S: Are you pursuing someone who will easily escape you?

E: Far from it, for he is quite old.

S: Who is it?

E: My father.

S: My dear sir! Your own father?

E: Certainly.

S: What is the charge? What is the case about?

E: Murder, Socrates.

S: Good heavens! Certainly, Euthyphro, most men would not know how they could do this and be right. It is not the part of anyone to do this, but of one who is far advanced in wisdom.

E: Yes by Zeus, Socrates, that is so.

S: Is then the man your father killed one of your relatives? Or is that obvious, for you would not prosecute your father for the murder of a stranger.

E: It is ridiculous, Socrates, for you think that it makes any difference whether the victim is a stranger or a relative. One should only watch whether the killer acted justly or not; if he acted justly, let him go, but if not, one should prosecute, even if the killer shares your hearth and table. The pollution is the same if you knowingly keep company with such a man and do not cleanse yourself and him by bringing him to justice. The victim was a dependent of mine, and when we were farming in Naxos he was a servant of ours. He killed one of our household slaves in drunken anger, so my father bound him hand and foot and threw him in a ditch, then sent a man here to inquire from the priest what should be done. During that time he gave no thought or care to the bound man, as being a killer, and it was no matter if he died, which he did. Hunger and cold and his bonds caused his death before the messenger came back from the seer. Both my father and my other relatives are angry that I am prosecuting my father for murder on behalf of a murderer, as he did not even kill him. They say that such a victim does not deserve a thought and that it is impious for a son to prosecute his father for murder. But their ideas of the divine attitude to piety and impiety are wrong, Socrates.

S: Whereas, by Zeus, Euthyphro, you think that your knowledge of the divine, and of piety and impiety, is so accurate that, when those things happened as you say, you have no fear of having acted impiously in bringing your father to trial?

E: I should be of no use, Socrates, and Euthyphro would not be superior to the majority of men, if I did not have accurate knowledge of all such things.

S: It is indeed most important, my admirable Euthyphro, that I should become your pupil, and as regards this indictment challenge Meletus about these very things and say to him: that in the past too I considered knowledge about the divine to be most important, and that now that he says that I improvise and innovate about the gods I have become your pupil. I would say to him: "If, Meletus, you agree that Euthyphro is wise in these matters, consider me, too, to have the right beliefs and do not bring me to trial. If you do not think so, then prosecute that teacher of mine for corrupting the older men, me and his own father, by teaching me and by exhorting and punishing him. If he is not convinced, does not discharge me, or indicts you instead of me, I shall repeat the same challenge in court.

E: Yes by Zeus, Socrates, and, if he should try to indict me, I think I would find his weak spots and the talk in court would be about him rather than about me.

S: It is because I realize this that I am eager to become your pupil, my dear friend. I know that other people as well as this Meletus do not even seem to notice you, whereas he sees me so sharply and clearly that he indicts me for ungodliness. So tell me now, by Zeus, what you just now maintained you clearly knew: what kind of thing do you say that godliness and ungodliness are, both as regards murder and other things; or is the pious not the same and alike in every action, and the impious the opposite of all that is pious and like itself, and everything that is to be impious presents us with one form or appearance in so far as it is impious.

E: Most certainly, Socrates.

S: Tell me then, what is the pious, and what the impious, do you say?

E: I say that the pious is to do what I am doing now, to prosecute the wrongdoer, be it about murder or temple robbery or anything else, whether the wrongdoer is your father or your mother or anyone else; not to prosecute is impious. And observe, Socrates, that I can quote the law as a great proof that this is so. I have already said to others that such actions are right, not to favor the ungodly, whoever they are. These people themselves believe that Zeus is the best and most just of the gods, yet they agree that he bound his father because he unjustly swallowed his sons, and that he in turn castrated his father for similar reasons. But they are angry with me because I am prosecuting my father for his wrongdoing. They contradict themselves in what they say about the gods and about me.

S: Indeed, Euthyphro, this is the reason why I am a defendant in the case, because I find it hard to accept things like that being said about the gods, and it is likely to be the reason why I shall be told I do wrong. Now, however, if you, who have full knowledge of such things, share their opinions, then we must agree with them too, it would seem. For what are we to say, we who agree that we ourselves have no knowledge? Tell me, by the god of friendship, do you really believe these things are true?

E: Yes, Socrates, and so are even more surprising things, of which the majority has no knowledge.

S: And do you believe that there really is war among the gods, and terrible enmities and battles, and other such things as are told by the poets, and other sacred stories such as are embroidered by good writers and by representations of which the robe of the goddess is adorned when it is carried up to the Acropolis. Are we to say these things are true, Euthyphro?

E: Not only these, Socrates, but, as I was saying just now, I will, if you wish, relate many other things about the gods which I know will amaze you.

S: I should not be surprised, but you will tell me these at leisure some other time. For now, try to tell me more clearly what I was asking just now, for, my friend, you did not teach me adequately when I asked you what the pious was, but you told me that what you are doing now, to prosecute your father for murder, is pious.

E: And I told the truth, Socrates.

S: Perhaps. You agree, however, that there are many other pious actions.

E: There are.

S: Bear in mind then that I did not bid you tell me one or two of the many pious actions but that form itself that makes all pious actions pious, for you agreed that all impious actions are impious and all pious actions pious through one form, or don't you remember?

E: I do.

S: Tell me then what form itself is, so that I may look upon it, and using it as a model, say that any acting of yours or another's that is of that kind is pious, and if it is not that it is not.

E: If that is how you want it, Socrates, that is how I will tell you.

S: That is what I want.

E: Well then, what is dear to the gods is pious, what is not is impious.

S: Splendid, Euthyphro! You have now answered in the way I wanted. Whether your answer is true I do not know yet, but you will obviously show me that what you say is true.

E: Certainly.

S: Come then, let us examine what we mean. An action or a man dear to the gods is pious, but an action or a man hated by the gods is impious. They are not the same, but opposites, the pious and impious. Is that not so?

E: It is indeed.

S: And that seems to be a good statement?

E: I think so, Socrates.

S: We have also stated that the gods are in a state of discord, that they are at odds with each other, Euthyphro, and that they are enmity with each other. That too has been said.

E: It has.

S: What are the subjects of difference that cause hatred and anger? Let us look at it this way. If you and I were to differ about numbers as to which is the greater, would this difference make us enemies and angry with each other, or would we proceed to count and soon resolve our difference about this?

E: We would certainly do so.

S: Again, if we differed about the larger and the smaller, we would turn to measurement and soon cease to differ.

E: That is so.

S: And about the heavier and the lighter, we would resort to weighing and be reconciled.

E: Of course.

S: What subject of difference would make us angry and hostile to each other if we were unable to come to a decision? Perhaps you do not have an answer ready, but examine as I tell you whether these subjects are the just and the unjust, the beautiful and the ugly, the good and the bad. Are these not the subjects of difference about which, when we are unable to come to a satisfactory decision, you and I and other men become hostile to each other whenever we do.

E: That is the difference, Socrates, about those subjects.

S: What about the gods, Euthyphro? If indeed they have differences, will it not be about these same subjects?

E: It certainly must be so.

S: Then according to your argument, my good Euthyphro, different gods consider different things to be just, beautiful, ugly, good and bad, for they would not be at odds with one another unless they differed about these subjects, would they?

E: You are right.

S: And they like what each of them considers beautiful, good, and just, and hate the opposites of these?

E: Certainly.

S: But you say that the same things are considered just by some gods and unjust by others, and as they dispute about these things they are at odds and at war with each other. Is that not so?

E: It is.

S: The same things then are loved by the gods and hated by the gods, both god-loved and god-hated.

E: It seems likely.

S: And the same things would be both pious and impious, according to this argument?

E: I'm afraid so.

S: So you did not answer my question, you surprising man. I did not ask you what same thing is both pious and impious, and it appears that what is loved by the gods is also hated by them. So it is in no way surprising if your present action, namely punishing your father, may be pleasing to Zeus but displeasing to Kronos and Ouranos, pleasing to Hephaestus but displeasing to Hera, and so with any other gods who differ from each other on this subject.

E: I think, Socrates, that on this subject no gods would differ from one another, that whoever has killed anyone unjustly should pay the penalty.

S: Well now, Euthyphro, have you ever heard any man maintaining that one who has killed or done anything else unjustly should not pay the penalty?

E: They never cease to dispute on this subject, both elsewhere and in the courts, for when they have committed many wrongs they do and say anything to avoid the penalty.

S: Do they agree they have done wrong, Euthyphro, and in spite of so agreeing do they nevertheless say they should not be punished?

E: No, they do not agree on that point.

S: So they do not say or do anything. For they do not venture to say this, or dispute that they must not pay the penalty if they have done wrong, but I think they deny doing wrong. Is that not so?

E: That is true.

S: Then they do not dispute that the wrongdoer must be punished, but they may disagree as to who the wrongdoer is, what he did and when.

E: You are right.

S: Do not the gods have the same experience, if indeed they are at odds with each other about the just and the unjust, as your argument maintains? Some assert that they wrong one another, while others deny it, but no one among gods or men ventures to say that the wrongdoer must not be punished.

E: Yes, that is true, Socrates, as to the main point.

S: And those who disagree, whether men or gods, dispute about each action, if indeed the gods disagree. Some say it is done justly, others unjustly. Is that not so?

E: Yes indeed.

S: Come now, my dear Euthyphro, tell me, too, that I may become wiser, what proof you have that all the gods consider that man to have been killed unjustly who became a murderer while in your service, was bound by the master of his victim, and died in his bonds be-

fore the one who bound him found out from the seers what was to
be done with him, and that it is right for a son to denounce and
to prosecute his father on behalf of such a man. Come, try to show
me a clear sign that all the gods definitely believe this action to be
right. If you can give me adequate proof of this, I shall never cease
to extol your wisdom.

E: This is perhaps no light task, Socrates, though I could show you
very clearly.

S: I understand that you think me more dull-witted than the jury, as
you will obviously show them that these actions were unjust and
that all the gods hate such actions.

E: I will show it to them clearly, Socrates, if only they will listen to me.

S: They will listen if they think you show them well. But this thought
came to me as I was speaking, and I am examining it, saying to
myself: "If Euthyphro shows me conclusively that all the gods consider such a death unjust, to what greater extent have I learned from
him the nature of piety and impiety? This action would then, it seems,
be hated by the gods, but the pious and the impious were not thereby now defined, for what is hated by the gods has also been shown
to be loved by them." So I will not insist on this point; let us assume, if you wish, that all the gods consider this unjust and that
they all hate it. However, is this the correction we are making in
our discussion, that what all the gods hate is impious, and what they
all love is pious, and that what some gods love and others hate is
neither or both? Is that how you now wish us to define piety and
impiety?

E: What prevents us from doing so, Socrates?

S: For my part nothing, Euthyphro, but you look whether on your part
this proposal will enable you to teach me most easily what you
promised.

E: I would certainly say that the pious is what all the gods love, and
the opposite, which all the gods hate, is the impious.

S: Then let us again examine whether that is a sound statement, or
do we let it pass, and if one of us, or someone else, merely says that
this is so, do we accept that it is so? Or should we examine what
the speaker means?

E: We must examine it, but I certainly think that this is now a fine
statement.

S: We shall soon know better whether it is. Consider this: Is the pious
loved by the gods because it is pious, or is it pious because it is loved
by the gods?

E: I don't know what you mean, Socrates.

S: I shall try to explain more clearly; we speak of something being carried
and something carrying, of something being led and something lead-

ing, of something being seen and something seeing, and you understand that these things are all different from one another and how they differ?

E: I think I do.

S: So there is something being loved and something loving, and the loving is a different thing.

E: Of course.

S: Tell me then whether that which is (said to be) being carried is being carried because someone carries it or for some other reason.

E: No, that is the reason.

S: And that which is being led is so because someone leads it, and that which is being seen because someone sees it?

E: Certainly.

S: It is not seen by someone because it is being seen but on the contrary it is being seen because someone sees it, nor is it because it is being led that someone leads it but because someone leads it that it is being led; it is not because it is being seen that somone sees it, but it is being seen because someone sees it; nor does someone carry an object because it is being carried, but it is being carried because someone carries it. Is what I want to say clear, Euthyphro? I want to say this, namely, that if anything comes to be, or is affected, it does not come to be because it is coming to be, but it is coming to be because it comes to be; nor is it affected because it is being affected but because something affects it. Or do you not agree?

E: I do.

S: What is being loved is either something that comes to be or something that is affected by something?

E: Certainly.

S: So it is in the same case as the things just mentioned; it is not loved by those who love it because it is being loved, but it is being loved because they love it?

E: Necessarily.

S: What then do we say about the pious, Euthyphro? Surely that it is loved by all the gods, according to what you say?

E: Yes.

S: Is it loved because it is pious, or for some other reason?

E: For no other reason.

S: It is loved then because it is pious, but it is not pious because it is loved?

E: Apparently.

S: And because it is loved by the gods it is being loved and is dear to the gods?

E: Of course.

S: The god-beloved is then not the same as the pious, Euthyphro, nor the pious the same as the god-beloved, as you say it is, but one differs from the other.

E: How so, Socrates?

S: Because we agree that the pious is beloved for the reason that it is pious, but it is not pious because it is loved. Is that not so?

E: Yes.

S: And that the god-beloved, on the other hand, is so because it is loved by the gods, by the very fact of being loved, but it is not loved because it is god-beloved.

E: True.

S: But if the god-beloved and the pious were the same, my dear Euthyphro, and the pious were loved because it was pious, then the god-beloved would be loved because it was god-beloved, and if the god-beloved was god-beloved because it was loved by the gods, then the pious would also be pious because it was loved by the gods; but now you see that they are in opposite cases as being altogether different from each other: the one is of a nature to be loved because it is loved, the other is loved because it is of a nature to be loved. I'm afraid, Euthyphro, that when you were asked what piety is, you did not wish to make its nature clear to me, but you told me an affect or quality of it, that the pious has the quality of being loved by all the gods, but you have not yet told me what the pious is. Now if you will, do not hide things from me but tell me again from the beginning what piety is, whether loved by the gods or having some other quality—we shall not quarrel about that—but be keen to tell me what the pious and the impious are.

E: But Socrates, I have no way of telling you what I have in mind, for whatever proposition we put forward goes around and refuses to stay put where we establish it.

S: Your statements, Euthyphro, seem to belong to my ancestor, Daedalus. If I were stating them and putting them forward, you would perhaps be making fun of me and say that because of my kinship with him my conclusions in discussion run away and will not stay where one puts them. As these propositions are yours, however, we need some other jest, for they will not stay put for you, as you say yourself.

E: I think the same jest will do for our discussion, Socrates, for I am not the one who makes them go round and not remain in the same place; it is you who are the Daedalus; for as far as I am concerned they would remain as they were.

S: It looks as if I was cleverer than Daedalus in using my skill, my friend, in so far as he could only cause to move the things he made himself, but I can make other people's move as well as my own. And the smartest part of my skill is that I am clever without wanting to be, for I would rather have my arguments remain unmoved than possess the wealth of Tantalus as well as the cleverness of Daedalus. But enough of this. Since I think you are making unnecessary difficulties, I am as eager as you are to find a way to teach me about piety, and do not give up before you do. See whether you think all that is pious is of necessity just.

E: I think so.

S: And is then all that is just pious? Or is all that is pious just, but not all that is just pious, but some of it is and some is not?

E: I do not follow what you are saying, Socrates.

S: Yet you are younger than I by as much as you are wiser. As I say, you are making difficulties because of your wealth of wisdom. Pull yourself together, my dear sir, what I am saying is not difficult to grasp. I am saying the opposite of what the poet said who wrote:

You do not wish to name Zeus, who had done it, and who made all things grow, for where there is fear there is also shame.

I disagree with the poet. Shall I tell you why?

E: Please do.

S: I do not think that "where there is fear there is also shame," for I think that many people who fear disease and poverty and many other such things feel fear, but are not ashamed of the things they fear. Do you not think so?

E: I do indeed.

S: But where there is shame there is also fear. Does anyone feel shame at something who is not also afraid at the same time of a reputation for wickedness?

E: He is certainly afraid.

S: It is then not right to say "where there is fear there is also shame," but that where there is shame there is also fear, for fear covers a larger area than shame. Shame is a part of fear just as odd is a part of number, with the result that it is not true where there is number there is also oddness, but that where there is oddness there is also number. Do you follow me?

E: Surely.

S: This is the kind of thing I was asking before, whether where there is piety there is also justice, but where there is justice there is not always piety, for the pious is a part of justice. Shall we say that, or do you think otherwise?

E: No, but like that, for what you say appears to be right.

S: See what comes next; if the pious is a part of the just, we must, it seems, find out what part of the just it is. Now if you asked me something of what we mentioned just now, such as what part of number is the even, and what number that is, I would say it is the number that is divisible into two equal, not unequal, parts. Or do you not think so?

E: I do.

S: Try in this way to tell me what part of the just the pious is, in order to tell Meletus not to wrong us any more and not to indict me for ungodliness, since I have learned from you sufficiently what is godly and pious and what is not.

E: I think, Socrates, that the godly and pious is the part of the just that is concerned with the care of the gods, while that concerned with the care of men is the remaining part of justice.

S: You seem to me to put that very well, but I still need a bit of information. I do not know yet what you mean by care, for you do not mean it in the sense as the care of other things, as, for example, not everyone knows how to care for horses, but the horse breeder does.

E: Yes, I do mean it that way.

S: So horse breeding is the care of horses.

E: Yes.

S: Nor does everyone know how to care for dogs, but the hunter does.

E: That is so.

S: So hunting is the care of dogs.

E: Yes.

S: And cattle raising is the care of cattle.

E: Quite so.

S: While piety and godliness is the care of the gods, Euthyphro. Is that what you mean?

E: It is.

S: Now care in each case has the same effect; it aims at the good and the benefit of the object cared for, as you can see that horses cared for by horse breeders are benefited and become better. Or do you not think so?

E: I do.

S: So dogs are benefited by dog breeding, cattle by cattle raising, and so with all the others. Or do you think that care aims to harm the object of its care?

E: By Zeus, no.

S: It aims to benefit the object of its care.

E: Of course.

S: Is piety then, which is the care of the gods, also to benefit the gods and make them better? Would you agree that when you do something pious you make some one of the gods better?

E: By Zeus, no.

S: Nor do I think that this is what your mean—far from it—but that is why I asked you what you meant by the care of gods, because I did not believe you meant this kind of care.

E: Quite right, Socrates, that is not the kind of care I mean.

S: Very well, but what kind of care of the gods would piety be?

E: The kind of care, Socrates, that slaves take of their masters.

S: I understand. It is likely to be the service of the gods.

E: Quite so.

S: Could you tell me to the achievement of what goal service to doctors tends? Is it not, do you think to achieving health?

E: I think so.

S: What about service to shipbuilders? To what achievement is it directed?

E: Clearly, Socrates, to the building of a ship.

S: And service to housebuilders to the building of a house?

E: Yes.

S: Tell me then, my good sir, to the achievement of what aim does service to the gods tend? You obviously know since you say that you, of all men, have the best knowledge of the divine.

E: And I am telling the truth, Socrates.

S: Tell me then, by Zeus, what is that excellent aim that the gods achieve, using us as their servants?

E: Many fine things, Socrates.

S: So do generals, my friend. Nevertheless you could tell me their main concern, which is to achieve victory in war, is it not?

E: Of course.

S: The farmers too, I think, achieve many fine things, but the main point of their efforts is to produce food from the earth.

E: Quite so.

S: Well then, how would you sum up the many fine things that the gods achieve?

E: I told you a short while ago, Socrates, that it is a considerable task to acquire any precise knowledge of these things, but, to put it simply, I say that if a man knows how to say and do what is pleasing to the gods at prayer and sacrifice, those are pious actions such as preserve both private houses and public affairs of state. The opposite of these pleasing actions are impious and overturn and destroy everything.

S: You could tell me in far fewer words, if you were willing, the sum of what I asked, Euthyphro, but you are not keen to teach me, that is clear. You were on the point of doing so, but you turned away. If you had given that answer, I should now have acquired from you sufficient knowledge of the nature of piety. As it is, the lover of inquiry must follow it wherever it may lead him. Once more then, what do you say that piety and the pious are, and also impiety? Are they a knowledge of how to sacrifice and pray?

E: They are.

S: To sacrifice is to make a gift to the gods, whereas to pray is to beg from the gods?

E: Definitely, Socrates.

S: It would follow from this statement that piety would be a knowledge of how to give to, and beg from, the gods.

E: You understood what I said very well, Socrates.

S: That is because I am so desirous of your wisdom, and I concentrate my mind on it, so that no word of yours may fall to the ground. But tell me, what is this service to the gods? You say it is to beg from them and to give to them?

E: I do.

S: And to beg correctly would be to ask from them things that we need?

E: What else?

S: And to give correctly is to give them what they need from us, for it would not be skillful to bring gifts to anyone that are in no way needed.

E: True, Socrates.

S: Piety would then be a sort of trading skill between gods and men?

E: Trading yes, if you prefer to call it that.

S: I prefer nothing, unless it is true. But tell me, what benefit do the gods derive from the gifts they receive from us? What they give us is obvious to all. There is for us no good that we do not receive from them, but how are they benefited by what they receive from us? Or do we have such an advantage over them in the trade that we receive all our blessings from them and they receive nothing from us?

E: Do you suppose, Socrates, that the gods are benefited by what they receive from us?

S: What could those gifts from us to the gods be, Euthyphro?

E: What else, you think, than honor, reverence, and what I mentioned before, gratitude.

S: The pious is then, Euthyphro, pleasing to the gods, but not beneficial or dear to them?

E: I think it is of all things most dear to them.

S: So the pious is once again what is dear to the gods.

E: Most certainly.

S: When you say this, will you be surprised if your arguments seem to move about instead of staying put? And will you accuse me of being Daedalus who makes them move, though you are yourself much more skillful than Daedalus and make them go round in a circle? Or do you not realize that our argument has moved around and come again to the same place? You surely remember that earlier the pious and the god-beloved were shown not to be the same but different from each other. Or do you not remember?

E: I do.

S: Do you then not realize that when you say now that what is dear to the gods is the pious? Is this not the same as the god-beloved? Or is it not?

E: It certainly is.

S: Either we were wrong when we agreed before, or, if we were right then, we are wrong now.

E: That seems to be so.

S: So we must investigate again from the beginning what piety is, as I shall not willingly give up before I learn this. Do not think me unworthy, but concentrate your attention and tell the truth. For you know it, if any man does, and I must not let you go, like Proteus, before you tell me. If you had no clear knowledge of piety and impiety you would never have ventured to prosecute your old father for murder on behalf of a servant. For fear of the gods you would have been afraid to take the risk lest you should not be acting rightly, and would have been ashamed before men, but now I know well that believe you have clear knowledge of piety and impiety. So tell me, my good Euthyphro, and do not hide what you believe.

E: Some other time, Socrates, for I am in a hurry now, and it is time for me to go.

S: What a thing to do, my friend! By going you have cast me down from a great hope I had, that I would learn from you the nature of the pious and the impious and so escape Meletus' indictment by showing that I had acquired wisdom in divine matters from Euthyphro, and my ignorance would no longer cause me to be careless and inventive about such things, and that I would be better for the rest of my life.

[10]

Ethical Disagreement

Charles L. Stevenson

1

When people disagree about the value of something—one saying that it is good or right and another that it is bad or wrong—by what methods of argument or inquiry can their disagreement be resolved? Can it be resolved by the methods of science, or does it require methods of some other kind, or is it open to no rational solution at all?

The question must be clarified before it can be answered. And the word that is particularly in need of clarification, as we shall see, is the word "disagreement."

Let us begin by noting that "disagreement" has two broad senses: In the first sense it refers to what I shall call "disagreements in belief." This occurs when Mr. A believes p, when Mr. B believes not-p, or something incompatible with p, and when neither is content to let the belief of the other remain unchallenged. Thus doctors may disagree about the causes of an illness; and friends may disagree in belief about the exact date on which they last met.

In the second sense the word refers to what I shall call "disagreement in attitude." This occurs when Mr. A has a favorable attitude to something, when Mr. B has an unfavorable or less favorable attitude to it, and when neither is content to let the other's attitude remain unchanged. The term "attitude" is here used in much the same sense

Reprinted from *Facts and Values* (New Haven, Conn.: Yale University Press, 1963), by permission of the author's estate.

Charles L. Stevenson (1908-1979) was Professor of Philosophy at the University of Michigan.

that R. B. Perry uses "interest"; it designates any psychological disposition of being *for* or *against* something. Hence love and hate are relatively specific kinds of attitudes, as are approval and disapproval, and so on.

This second sense can be illustrated in this way: Two men are planning to have dinner together. One wants to eat at a restaurant that the other doesn't like. Temporarily, then, the men cannot "agree" on where to dine. Their argument may be trivial, and perhaps only half serious; but in any case it represents a disagreement *in attitude*. The men have divergent preferences and each is trying to redirect the preference of the other—though normally, of course, each is willing to revise his own preference in the light of what the other may say.

Further examples are readily found. Mrs. Smith wishes to cultivate only the four hundred; Mr. Smith is loyal to his old poker-playing friends. They accordingly disagree, in attitude, about whom to invite to their party. The progressive mayor wants modern school buildings and large parks; the older citizens are against these "new-fangled" ways; so they disagree on civic policy. These cases differ from the one about the restaurant only in that the clash of attitudes is more serious and may lead to more vigorous argument.

The difference between the two senses of "disagreement" is essentially this: the first involves an opposition of beliefs, both of which cannot be true, and the second involves an opposition of attitudes, both of which cannot be satisfied.

Let us apply this distinction to a case that will sharpen it. Mr. A believes that most voters will favor a proposed tax and Mr. B disagrees with him. The disagreement concerns attitudes—those of the voters—but note that A and B are *not* disagreeing in attitude. Their disagreement is *in belief about* attitudes. It is simply a special kind of disagreement in belief, differing from disagreement in belief about head colds only with regard to subject matter. It implies not an opposition of the actual attitudes of the speaker but only of their beliefs about certain attitudes. Disagreement *in* attitude, on the other hand, implies that the very attitudes of the speakers are opposed. A and B may have opposed beliefs about attitudes without having opposed attitudes, just as they may have opposed beliefs about head colds without having opposed head colds. Hence we must not, from the fact that an argument is concerned with attitudes, infer that it necessarily involves disagreement *in* attitude.

2

We may now turn more directly to disagreement about values, with particular reference to normative ethics. When people argue about what is good, do they disagree in belief, or do they disagree in attitude? A long tradition of ethical theorists strongly suggest, whether they always intend to or not, that the disagreement is one *in belief*. Naturalistic theorists, for instance, identify an ethical judgment with some sort of scientific statement, and so make normative ethics a branch of science. Now a scientific argument typically exemplifies disagreement in belief, and if an ethical argument is simply a scientific one, then it too exemplifies disagreement in belief. The usual naturalistic theories of ethics that stress attitudes—such as those of Hume, Westermarck, Perry, Richards, and so many others—stress disagreement in belief no less than the rest. They imply, of course, that disagreement about what is good is disagreement *in belief* about attitudes; but we have seen that that is simply one sort of disagreement in belief, and by no means the same as disagreement in attitude. Analyses that stress disagreement *in* attitude are extremely rare.

If ethical arguments, as we encounter them in everyday life, involved disagreement in belief exclusively—whether the beliefs were about attitudes or about something else—then I should have no quarrel with the ordinary sort of naturalistic analysis. Normative judgments could be taken as scientific statements and amenable to the usual scientific proof. But a moment's attention will readily show that disagreement in belief has not the exclusive role that theory has so repeatedly ascribed to it. It must be readily granted that ethical arguments usually involve disagreement in belief; but they *also* involve disagreement in attitude. And the conspicuous role of disagreement in attitude is what we usually take, whether we realize it or not, as the distinguishing feature of ethical arguments. For example:

Suppose that the representative of a union urges that the wage level in a given company ought to be higher—that it is only right that the workers receive more pay. The company representative urges in reply that the workers ought to receive no more than they get. Such an argument clearly represents a disagreement in attitude. The union is *for* higher wages; the company is *against* them, and neither is content to let the other's attitude remain unchanged. *In addition* to this disagreement in attitude, of course, the argument may represent no little disagreement in belief. Perhaps the parties disagree about how much the cost of living has risen and how much the workers are suffering under the present wage scale. Or perhaps they disagree about the company's earnings and the extent to which the company could raise wages and still operate at a profit. Like any typical ethical argument, then, this argument involves both disagreement in attitude and disagreement in belief.

It is easy to see, however, that the disagreement in attitude plays a unifying and predominating role in the argument. This is so in two ways:

In the first place, disagreement in attitude determines what beliefs are *relevant* to the argument. Suppose that the company affirms that the wage scale of fifty years ago was far lower than it in now. The union will immediately urge that this contention, even though true, is irrelevant. And it is irrelevant simply because information about the wage level of fifty years ago, maintained under totally different circumstances, is not likely to affect the present attitudes of either party. To be relevant, any belief that is introduced into the argument must be one that is likely to lead one side or the other to have a different attitude, and so reconcile disagreement in attitude. Attitudes are often functions of beliefs. We often change our attitudes to something when we change our beliefs about it; just as a child ceases to *want* to touch a live coal when he comes to *believe* that it will burn him. Thus in the present argument any beliefs that are at all likely to alter attitudes, such as those about the increasing cost of living or the financial state of the company, will be considered by both sides to be relevant to the argument. Agreement in belief on these matters may lead to agreement in attitude toward the wage scale. But beliefs that are likely to alter the attitudes of neither side will be declared irrelevant. They will have no bearing on the disagreement in attitude, with which both parties are primarily concerned.

In the second place, ethical argument usually terminates when disagreement in attitude terminates, even though a certain amount of disagreement in belief remains. Suppose, for instance, that the company and the union continue to disagree in belief about the increasing cost of living, but that the company, even so, ends by favoring the higher wage scale. The union will then be content to end the argument and will cease to press its point about living costs. It may bring up that point again, in some future argument of the same sort, or in urging the righteousness of its victory to the newspaper columnists; but for the moment the fact that the company has agreed in attitude is sufficient to terminate the argument. On the other hand: suppose that both parties agreed on all beliefs that were introduced into the argument, but even so continued to disagree in attitude. In that case neither party would feel that their dispute had been successfully terminated. They might look for other beliefs that could be introduced into the argument. They might use words to play on each other's emotion. They might agree (in attitude) to submit the case to arbitration, both feeling that a decision, even if strongly adverse to one party or the other, would be preferable to a continued impasse. Or, perhaps, they might abandon hope of settling their dispute by any peaceable means.

In many other cases, of course, men discuss ethical topics without having the strong, uncompromising attitudes that the present example has illustrated. They are often as much concerned with redirecting their own attitudes, in the light of greater knowledge, as with redirecting the attitudes of others. And the attitudes involved are often altruistic rather than selfish. Yet the above example will serve, so long as that is understood, to suggest the nature of ethical disagreement. Both disagreement in attitude and disagreement in belief are involved, but the former predominates in that (1) it determines what sort of disagreement in belief is relevantly disputed in a given ethical argument, and (2) it determines by its continued presence or its resolution whether or not the argument has been settled. We may see further how intimately the two sorts of disagreement are related: since attitudes are often functions of beliefs, an agreement in belief may lead people, as a matter of psychological fact, to agree in attitude.

3

Having discussed disagreement, we may turn to the broad question that was first mentioned, namely: By what methods of argument or inquiry may disagreement about matters of value be resolved?

It will be obvious that to whatever extent an argument involves disagreement in belief, it is open to the usual methods of the sciences. If these methods are the *only* rational methods for supporting beliefs—as I believe to be so, but cannot now take time to discuss—then scientific methods are the only rational methods for resolving the disagreement in *belief* that arguments about values may include.

But if science is granted an undisputed sway in reconciling beliefs, it does not thereby acquire, without qualification, an undisputed sway in reconciling attitudes. We have seen that arguments about values include disagreement in attitude, no less than disagreement in belief, and that in certain ways the disagreement in attitude predominates. By what methods shall the latter sort of disagreement be resolved?

The methods of science are still available for that purpose, but only in an indirect way. Initially, these methods have only to do with establishing agreement in belief. If they serve further to establish agreement in attitude, that will be due simply to the psychological fact that altered beliefs may cause altered attitudes. Hence scientific methods are conclusive in ending arguments about values only to the extent that their success in obtaining agreement in belief will in turn lead to agreement in attitude.

In other words: the extent to which scientific method can bring about agreement on values depends on the extent to which a commonly accepted body of scientific beliefs would cause us to have a commonly accepted set of attitudes.

How much is the development of science likely to achieve, then, with regard to values? To what extent *would* common beliefs lead to common attitudes? It is, perhaps, a pardonable enthusiasm to *hope* that science will do everything—to hope that in some rosy future, when all men know the consequences of their acts, they will all have common aspirations and live peaceably in complete moral accord. But if we speak not from our enthusiastic hopes but from our present knowledge, the answer must be far less exciting. We usually *do not know,* at the beginning of any argument about values, whether an agreement in belief, scientifically established, will lead to an agreement in attitude or not. It is logically possible, at least, that two men should continue to disagree in attitude even though they had all their beliefs in common, and even though neither had made any logical or inductive error, or omitted any relevant evidence. Differences in temperament, or in early training, or in social status, might make the men retain different attitudes even though both were possessed of the complete scientific truth. Whether this logical possibility is an empirical likelihood I shall not presume to say; but it is unquestionably a possibility that must not be left out of account.

To say that science can always settle arguments about value, we have seen, is to make this assumption: Agreement in attitude will always be consequent upon complete agreement in belief, and science can always bring about the latter. Taken as purely heuristic, this assumption has its usefulness. It leads people to discover the discrepancies in their beliefs and to prolong enlightening argument that *may* lead, as a matter of fact, from commonly accepted beliefs to commonly accepted attitudes. It leads people to reconcile their attitudes in a rational, permanent way, rather than by rhapsody or exhortation. But the assumption is *nothing more,* for present knowledge, than a heuristic maxim. It is wholly without any proper foundation of probability. I conclude, therefore, that scientific methods cannot be guaranteed the definite role in the so-called normative sciences that they may have in the natural sciences. Apart from a heuristic assumption to the contrary, it is possible that the growth of scientific knowledge may leave many disputes about values permanently unsolved. Should these disputes persist, there are nonrational methods for dealing with them, of course, such as impassioned, moving oratory. But the purely intellectual methods of science, and indeed *all* methods of reasoning, may be insufficient to settle disputes about values even though they may greatly help to do so.

For the same reasons I conclude that normative ethics is not a branch of any science. It deliberately deals with a type of disagreement that science deliberately avoids. Ethics is not psychology, for instance; for although psychologists may, of course, agree or disagree in belief about attitudes, they need not, as psychologists, be concerned with whether they agree or disagree with one another *in* attitude. Insofar as normative ethics draws from the sciences, in order to change attitudes *via* changing people's beliefs, it *draws* from *all* the sciences; but a moralist's peculiar aim—that of *redirecting* attitudes—is a type of activity, rather than knowledge, and falls within no science. Science may study that activity and may help indirectly to forward it; but is not *identical* with that activity.

4

I can take only a brief space to explain why the ethical terms, such as "good," "wrong," "ought," and so on, are so habitually used to deal with disagreement in attitude. On account of their repeated occurrence in emotional situations they have acquired a strong emotive meaning. This emotive meaning makes them serviceable in initiating changes in a hearer's attitudes. Sheer emotive impact is not likely, under many circumstances, to change attitudes in any permanent way; but it *begins* a process that can then be supported by other means.

There is no occasion for saying that the meaning of ethical terms is *purely* emotive, like that of "alas" or "hurrah." We have seen that ethical *arguments* include many expressions of *belief,* and the rough rules of ordinary language permit us to say that some of these beliefs are expressed by an ethical judgment itself. But the beliefs so expressed are by no means always the same. Ethical terms are notable for their ambiguity, and opponents in an argument may use them in different senses. Sometimes this leads to artificial issues, but it usually does not. So long as one person says "this is good" with emotive praise, and another says "no, it is bad," with emotive condemnation, a disagreement in attitude is manifest. Whether or not the beliefs that these statements express are logically incompatible may not be discovered until later in the argument; but even if they are actually compatible, disagreement in attitude will be preserved by emotive meaning; and this disagreement, so central to ethics, may lead to an argument that is certainly not artificial in its issues so long as it is taken for what it is.

The many theorists who have refused to identify ethical statements with scientific ones have much to be said in their favor. They have seen that ethical judgments mold or alter attitudes, rather than describe them, and they have seen that ethical judgments can be guaranteed no definitive scientific support. But one need not on that account provide ethics with any extra mundane, sui generis *subject matter.* The distinguishing features of an ethical judgment can be preserved by a recognition of emotive meaning and disagreement in attitude, rather than by some nonnatural quality—and with far greater intelligibility. If a unique subject matter is *postulated,* as it usually is, to preserve the important distinction between normative ethics and science, it serves no purpose that is not served by the very simple analysis I have here suggested. Unless nonnatural qualities can be defended by positive arguments, rather than as an "only resort" from the acknowledged weakness of ordinary forms of naturalism, they would seem nothing more than the invisible shadows cast by emotive meaning.

[11]

The Categorical Imperative

Immanuel Kant

Everything in nature works according to laws. Rational beings alone have the faculty of acting according *to the conception* of laws, that is according to principles, *i.e.,* have a *will.* Since the deduction of actions from principles requires *reason,* the will is nothing but practical reason. If reason infallibly determines the will, then the actions of such a being which are recognized as objectively necessary are subjectively necessary also, *i.e.,* the will is a faculty to choose *that only* which reason independent on inclination recognizes as practically necessary, *i.e.,* as good. But if reason of itself does not sufficiently determine the will, if the latter is subject also to subjective conditions (particular impulses) which do not always coincide with the objective conditions; in a word, if the will does not *in itself* completely accord with reason (which is actually the case with men), then the actions which objectively are recognized as necessary are subjectively contingent, and the determination of such a will according to objective laws is *obligation,* that is to say, the relation of the objective laws to a will that is not thoroughly good is conceived as the determination of the will of a rational being by principles of reason, but which the will from its nature does not of necessity follow.

The conception of an objective principle, in so far as it is obligatory for a will, is called a command (of reason), and the formula of the command is called an Imperative. . . .

From *Fundamental Principles of the Metaphysic of Morals,* translated by T. K. Abbott.

Immanuel Kant (1724-1804), Professor of Logic and Metaphysics at the University of Königsberg, was a major figure in the history of modern philosophy.

Now all *imperatives* command either *hypothetically* or *categorically.* The former represent the practical necessity of a possible action as means to something else that is willed (or at least which one might possibly will). The categorical imperative would be that which represented an action as necessary of itself without reference to another end. . . .

If now the action is good only as a means *to something else,* then the imperative is *hypothetical;* if it is conceived as good *in itself* and consequently as being necessarily the principle of a will which of itself conforms to reason, then it is *categorical.* . . .

When I conceive a hypothetical imperative in general I do not know beforehand what it will contain until I am given the condition. But when I conceive a categorical imperative I know at once what it contains. For as the imperative contains besides the law only the necessity that the maxims shall conform to this law, while the law contains no conditions restricting it, there remains nothing but the general statement that the maxim of the action should conform to a universal law, and it is this conformity alone that the imperative properly represents as necessary.

There is therefore but one categorical imperative, namely this: *Act only on that maxim whereby thou canst at the same time will that it should become a universal law.*

Now if all imperatives of duty can be deduced from this one imperative as from their principle, then, although it should remain undecided whether what is called duty is not merely a vain notion, yet at least we shall be able to show what we understand by it and what this notion means.

Since the universality of the law according to which effects are produced constitutes what is properly called *nature* in the most general sense (as to form), that is the existence of things so far as it is determined by general laws, the imperative of duty may be expressed thus: *Act as if the maxim of thy action were to become by thy will a Universal Law of Nature.*

We will now enumerate a few duties, adopting the usual division of them into duties to ourselves and to others . . .

1. A man reduced to despair by a series of misfortunes feels wearied of life, but is still so far in possession of his reason that he can ask himself whether it would not be contrary to his duty to himself to take his own life. Now he inquires whether the maxim of his action could become a universal law of nature. His maxim is: From self-love I adopt it as a principle to shorten my life when its longer duration is likely to bring more evil than satisfaction. It is asked then simply whether this principle founded on self-love can become a universal law of nature. Now we see at once that a system of nature of which it should be a law to destroy life by means of the very feeling whose special nature

it is to impel to the improvement of life would contradict itself, and therefore could not exist as a system of nature; hence that maxim cannot possibly exist as a universal law of nature, and consequently would be wholly inconsistent with the supreme principle of all duty.

2. Another finds himself forced by necessity to borrow money. He knows that he will not be able to repay it, but sees also that nothing will be lent to him, unless he promises stoutly to repay it in a definite time. He desires to make this promise, but he has still so much conscience as to ask himself: Is it not unlawful and inconsistent with duty to get out of a difficulty in this way? Suppose, however, that he resolves to do so, then the maxim if his action would be expressed thus: When I think myself in want of money, I will borrow money and promise to repay it, although I know that I never can do so. Now this principle of self-love or of one's own advantage may perhaps be consistent with my whole future welfare; but the question now is, Is it right? I change then the suggestion of self-love into a universal law, and state the question thus: How would it be if my maxim were a universal law? Then I see at once that it could never hold as a universal law of nature, but would necessarily contradict itself. For supposing it to be a universal law that everyone when he thinks himself in a difficulty should be able to promise whatever he pleases, with the purpose of not keeping his promise, the promise itself would become impossible, as well as the end that one might have in view in it, since no one would consider that anything was promised to him, but would ridicule all such statements as vain pretenses.

3. A third finds in himself a talent which with the help of some culture might make him a useful man in many respects. But he finds himself in comfortable circumstance, and prefers to indulge in pleasure rather than to take pains in enlarging and improving his happy natural capacities. He asks, however, whether his maxim of neglect of his natural gifts, besides agreeing with his inclination to indulgence, agrees also with what is called duty. He sees then that a system of nature could indeed subsist with such a universal law although men (like the South Sea islanders) should let their talents rust, and resolve to devote their lives merely to idleness, amusement, and propagation of their species—in a word, to enjoyment; but he cannot possibly *will* that this should be a universal law of nature, or be implanted in us as such by a natural instinct. For, as a rational being, he necessarily wills that his faculties be developed, since they serve him, and have been given him, for all sorts of possible purposes.

4. A fourth, who is in prosperity, while he sees that others have to contend with great wretchedness and that he could help them, thinks: What concern is it of mine? Let everyone be as happy as heaven pleases, or as he can make himself; I will take nothing from him nor even envy

him, only I do not wish to contribute anything to his welfare or to his assistance in distress! Now no doubt if such a mode of thinking were a universal law, the human race might very well subsist, and doubtless even better than in a state in which everyone talks of sympathy and good-will, or even takes care occasionally to put it into practice, but on the other side, also cheats when he can, betrays the rights of men, or otherwise violates them. But although it is possible that a universal law of nature might exist in accordance with that maxim, it is impossible to *will* that such a principle should have the universal validity of a law of nature. For a will which resolved this would contradict itself, inasmuch as many cases might occur in which one would have need of the love and sympathy of others, and in which, by such a law of nature, sprung from his own will, he would deprive himself of all hope of the aid he desires.

These are a few of the many actual duties, or at least what we regard as such, which obviously fall into two classes on the one principle that we have laid down. We must be *able to will* that a maxim of our action should be a universal law. This is the canon of the moral appreciation of the action generally. Some actions are of such a character that their maxim cannot without contradiction be even *conceived* as a universal law of nature, far from it being possible that we should *will* that it *should* be so. In others this intrinsic impossibility is not found, but still it is impossible to *will that* their maxim should be raised to the universality of a law of nature, since such a will would contradict itself. It is easily seen that the former violate strict or rigorous (inflexible) duty; the latter only laxer (meritorious) duty. Thus it has been completely shown by these examples how all duties depend as regards the nature of the obligation (not the object of the action) on the same principle.

If now we attend to ourselves on occasion of any transgression of duty, we shall find that we in fact do not will that our maxim should be universal law, for that is impossible for us; on the contrary we will that the opposite should remain a universal law, only we assume the liberty of making an *exception* in our own favor of (just for this time only) in favor of our inclination. Consequently if we considered all cases from one and the same point of view, namely, that of reason, we should find a contradiction in our own will, namely, that a certain principle should be objectively necessary as a universal law, and yet subjectively should not be universal, but admit of exceptions. As however we at one moment regard our action from the point of view of a will wholly conformed to reason, and then again look at the same action from the point of view of a will affected by inclination, there is not really any contradiction, but an antagonism of inclination to the precept of reason, whereby the universality of the principle is changed into a mere generality, so that the practical principle of reason shall meet the maxim half way.

Now, although this cannot be justified in our own impartial judgment, yet it proves that we do really recognize the validity of the categorical imperative and (with all respect for it) only allow ourselves a few exceptions, which we think unimportant and forced from us. . . .

The will is conceived as a faculty of determining oneself to action *in accordance with the conception of certain laws.* And such a faculty can be found only in rational beings. Now that which serves the will as the objective ground of its self-determination is the *end,* and if this is assigned by reason alone, it must hold for all rational beings. On the other hand, that which merely contains the ground of possibility of the action of which the effect is the end, this is called the *means.* The subjective ground of the desire is the *spring,* the objective ground of the volition is the *motive;* hence the distinction between subjective ends which rest on springs and objective ends which depend on motives valid for every rational being. Practical principles are *formal* when they abstract from all subjective ends, they are *material* when they assume these, and therefore particular springs of action. The ends which a rational being proposes to himself at pleasure as *effects* of his actions (material ends) are all only relative, for it is only their relation to the particular desires of the subject that gives them their worth, which therefore cannot furnish principles universal and necessary for all rational beings and for every volition, that is to say practical laws. Hence all these relative ends can give rise only to hypothetical imperatives.

Supposing, however, that there were something *whose existence* has *in itself* an absolute worth, something which, being *an end in itself,* could be a source of definite laws, then in this and this alone would lie the source of a possible categorical imperative, *i.e.,* a practical law.

Now I say: man and generally any rational being *exists* as end in himself, *not merely as a means* to be arbitrarily used by this or that will, but in all his actions, whether they concern himself or other rational beings, must be always regarded at the same time as an end. All objects of the inclinations have only a conditional worth, for if the inclinations and the wants founded on them did not exist, then their object would be without value. But the inclinations themselves being sources of want, are so far from having an absolute worth for which they should be desired, that on the contrary it must be the universal wish of every rational being to be wholly free from them. Thus the worth of any object which is *to be acquired* by our action is always conditional. Beings whose existence depends not on our will but on nature's, have nevertheless, if they are irrational beings, only a relative value as means, and are therefore called *things;* rational beings, on the contrary, are called *persons,* because their very nature points them out as ends in themselves, that is as something which must not be used merely as means, and so far therefore restricts freedom of action (and is an object of respect). These, therefore, are not merely subjective ends whose existence has a worth *for us* as an effect of our action but *objective ends,* that is things whose existence is an end in itself: an end moreover for which no other can be substituted, which they should subserve *merely* as means, for otherwise nothing whatever would possess *absolute worth;* but if all worth were conditioned and therefore contingent, then there would be no supreme practical principle of reason whatever.

If then there is a supreme practical principle or, in respect of the human will, a categorical imperative, it must be one which, being drawn from the conception of that which is necessarily an end for every one because it is *an end in itself,* constitutes an *objective* principle of will, and can therefore serves as a universal practical law. The foundation of this principle is: *rational nature exists as an end in itself.* Man necessarily conceives his own existence as being so; so far then this is a *subjective* principle of human actions. But every other rational being regards its existence similarly, just on the same rational principle that holds for me: so that it is at the same time an objective principle, from which as a supreme practical law all laws of the will must be capable of being deduced. Accordingly the practical imperative will be as follows: *So act as to treat humanity, whether in thine own person or in that of any other, in every case as an end withal, never as means only.* We will now inquire whether this can be practically carried out.

To abide by the previous examples:

Firstly, under the head of the necessary duty to oneself: He who contemplates suicide should ask himself whether his action can be consistent with the idea of humanity *as an end in itself.* If he destroys himself in order to escape from painful circumstances, he uses a person merely as *a means* to maintain a tolerable condition up to the end of life. But a man is not a thing, that is to say, something which can be used merely as a means, but must in all his actions be always considered as an end in himself. I cannot, therefore, dispose in any way of a man in my own person so as to mutilate him, to damage or kill him. (It belongs to ethics proper to define this principle more precisely so as to avoid all misunderstanding, *e.g.,* as to the amputation of the limbs in order to preserve myself; as to exposing my life to danger with a view to preserve it, &c. This question is therefore omitted here.)

Secondly, as regards necessary duties, or those of strict obligation, towards others; he who is thinking of making a lying promise to others will see at once that he would be using another man *merely as a means,* without the latter containing at the same time the end in himself. For he whom I propose by such a promise to use for my own purposes cannot possibly assent to my mode of action towards him, and therefore cannot himself contain the end of this action. This violation of the principle of humanity in other men is more obvious if we take in examples of attacks on the freedom and property of others. For then it is clear that he who transgresses the rights of men, intends to use the person of others merely as means, without considering that as rational beings they ought always to be esteemed also as ends, that is, as beings who must be capable of containing in themselves the end of the very same action.

Thirdly, as regards contingent (meritorious) duties to oneself; it is not enough that the action does not violate humanity in our own person as an end in itself, it must also *harmonize with* it. Now there are in humanity capacities of greater perfection which belong to the end that nature has in view in regard to humanity in ourselves as the subject: to neglect these might perhaps be consistent with the *maintenance* of humanity as an end in itself, but not with the *advancement* of this end.

Fourthly, as regards meritorious duties towards others: the natural end which all men have in their own happiness. Now humanity might indeed subsist, although no one should contribute anything to the happiness of others, provided he did not intentionally withdraw anything from it; but after all, this would only harmonize negatively not positively with *humanity as an end in itself,* if everyone does not also endeavor, as far as in him lies, to forward the ends of others. For the ends of any subject which is an end in himself, ought as far as possible to by *my* ends also, if that conception is to have its *full* effect with me.

[12]

Utilitarianism

John Stuart Mill

The creed which accepts as the foundation of morals "utility" or the "greatest happiness principle" holds that actions are right in proportion as they tend to promote happiness; wrong as they tend to produce the reverse of happiness. By happiness is intended pleasure and the absence of pain; by unhappiness, pain and the privation of pleasure. To give a clear view of the moral standard set up by the theory, much more requires to be said; in particular, what things it includes in the ideas of pain and pleasure, and to what extent this is left an open question. But these supplementary explanations do not affect the theory of life on which this theory of morality is grounded—namely, that pleasure and freedom from pain are the only things desirable as ends; and that all desirable things (which are as numerous in the utilitarian as in any other scheme) are desirable either for pleasure inherent in themselves or as means to the promotion of pleasure and the prevention of pain.

Now such a theory of life excites in many minds, and among them in some of the most estimable in feeling and purpose, inveterate dislike. To suppose that life has (as they express it) no higher end than pleasure—no better and nobler object of desire and pursuit—they designate as utterly mean and groveling, as a doctrine worthy only of swine, to whom the followers of Epicurus were, at a very early period, contemptuously likened; and modern holders of the doctrine are occasionally made the subject of equally polite comparisons by its German, French, and English assailants.

Reprinted from *Utilitarianism* (1863).

John Stuart Mill (1806–1873) was a philosopher, economist, and member of the House of Commons.

When thus attacked, the Epicureans have always answered that it is not they, but their accusers, who represent human nature in a degrading light, since the accusation supposes human beings to be capable of no pleasure except those of which swine are capable. If this supposition were true, the charge could not be gainsaid, but would then be no longer an imputation; for if the sources of pleasure were precisely the same to human beings and to swine, the rule of life which is good enough for the one would be good enough for the other. The comparison of the Epicurean life to that of beasts is felt as degrading, precisely because a beast's pleasures do not satisfy a human being's conception of happiness. Human beings have faculties more elevated than the animal appetites and, when once made conscious of them, do not regard anything as happiness which does not include their gratification. I do not, indeed, consider the Epicureans to have been by any means faultless in drawing out their scheme of consequences from the utilitarian principle. To do this in any sufficient manner, many Stoic, as well as Christian, elements require to be included. But there is no known Epicurean theory of life which does not assign to the pleasures of the intellect, of the feelings and imagination, and of the moral sentiments a much higher value as pleasures than to those of mere sensation. It must be admitted, however, that utilitarian writers in general have placed the superiority of mental over bodily pleasures chiefly in the greater permanency, safety, uncostliness, etc., of the former—that is, in their circumstantial advantages rather than in their intrinsic nature. And on all these points utilitarians have fully proved their case; but they might have taken the other and, as it may be called higher ground with entire consistency. It is quite compatible with the principle of utility to recognize the fact that some kinds of pleasure are more desirable and more valuable than others. It would be absurd that, while in estimating all other things quality is considered as well as quantity, the estimation of pleasure should be supposed to depend on quantity alone.

If I am asked what I mean by difference of quality in pleasures, or what makes one pleasure more valuable than another, merely as a pleasure, except its being greater in amount, there is but one possible answer. Of two pleasures, if there be one to which all or almost all who have experience of both give a decided preference, irrespective of any feeling of moral obligation to prefer it, that is the more desirable pleasure. If one of the two is, by those who are competently acquainted with both, placed so far above the other that they prefer it, even though knowing it to be attended with a greater amount of discontent, and would not resign it for any quantity of the other pleasure which their nature is capable of, we are justified in ascribing to the preferred enjoyment a superiority in quality so far outweighing quantity as to render it, in comparison, of small account.

Now it is an unquestionable fact that those who are equally acquainted with and equally capable of appreciating and enjoying both do give a most marked preference to the manner of existence which employs their higher faculties. Few human creatures would consent to be changed into any of the lower animals for a promise of the fullest allowance of a beast's pleasures; no intelligent human being would consent to be a fool, no instructed person would be an ignoramus, no person of feeling and conscience would be selfish and base, even though they should be persuaded that the fool, the dunce, or the rascal is better satisfied with his lot than they are with theirs. They would not resign what they possess more than he for the most complete satisfaction of all the desires which they have in common with him. If they ever fancy they would, it is only in cases of unhappiness so extreme that to escape from it they would exchange their lot for almost any other, however undesirable in their own eyes. A being of higher faculties requires more to make him happy, is capable probably of more acute suffering, and certainly accessible to it at more points, than one of an inferior type; but in spite of these liabilities, he can never really wish to sink into what he feels to be a lower grade of existence. We may give what explanation we please of this unwillingness; we may attribute it to pride, a name which is given indiscriminately to some of the most and to some of the least estimable feelings of which mankind are capable; we may refer it to the love of liberty and personal independence, an appeal to which was with the Stoics one of the most effective means for the inculcation of it; to the love of power or to the love of excitement, both of which do really enter into and contribute to it; but its most appropriate appellation is a sense of dignity, which all human beings possess in one form or other, and in some, though by no means in exact, proportion to their higher faculties, and which is so essential a part of the happiness of those in whom it is strong that nothing which conflicts with it could be otherwise than momentarily an object of desire to them. Whoever supposes that this preference takes place at a sacrifice of happiness—that the superior being, in anything like equal circumstances, is not happier than the inferior—confounds the two very different ideas of happiness and content. It is indisputable that the being whose capacities of enjoyment are low has the greatest chance of having them fully satisfied; and a highly endowed being will always feel that any happiness which he can look for, as the world is constituted, is imperfect. But he can learn to bear its imperfections, if they are at all bearable; and they will not make him envy the being who is indeed unconscious of the imperfections, but only because he feels not at all the good which those imperfections qualify. It is better to be a human being dissatisfied than a pig satisfied; better to be Socrates dissatisfied than a fool satisfied. And if the fool, or the pig, are of a different opinion, it is because they only know their own side of the question. The other party to the comparison knows both sides.

It may be objected that many who are capable of the higher pleasures occasionally, under the influence of temptation, postpone them to the lower. But this is quite compatible with a full appreciation of the intrinsic superiority of the higher. Men often, from infirmity of character, make their election for the nearer good, though they know it to be the less valuable; and this not less when the choice is between two bodily pleasures than when it is between bodily and mental. They pursue sensual indulgences to the injury of health, though perfectly aware that health is the greater good. It may be further objected that many who begin with youthful enthusiasm for everything noble, as they advance in years, sink into indolence and selfishness. But I do not believe that those who undergo this very common change voluntarily choose the lower description of pleasure in preference to the higher. I believe that, before they devote themselves exlusively to the one, they have already become incapable of the other. Capacity for the nobler feelings is in most natures a very tender plant, easily killed, not only be hostile influences, but by mere want of sustenance; and in the majority of young persons it speedily dies away if the occupations to which their position in life has devoted them, and the society into which it has thrown them, are not favorable to keeping that higher capacity in exercise. Men lose their high aspirations as they lose their intellectual tastes, because they have not time or opportunity for indulging them; and they addict themselves to inferior pleasures, not because they deliberately prefer them, but because they are either the only ones to which they have access or the only ones which they are any longer capable of enjoying. It may be questioned whether anyone who has remained equally susceptible to both classes of pleasures ever knowingly and calmly preferred the lower, though many, in all ages, have broken down in an ineffectual attempt to combine both.

From this verdict of the only competent judges, I apprehend there can be no appeal. On a question which is the best worth having of two pleasure, or which of two modes of existence is the most grateful to the feelings, apart from its moral attributes and from its consequences, the judgment of those who are qualified by knowledge of both, or, if they differ, that of the majority among them, must be admitted as final. And there needs be the less hesitation to accept this judgment respecting the quality of pleasures, since there is no other tribunal to be referred to even on the question of quantity. What means are there of determining which is the acutest of two pains, or the intensest of two pleasureable sensations, except the general suffrage of those who are familiar with both? Neither pains nor pleasures are homogeneous, and pain is always heterogeneous with pleasure. What is there to decide whether a particular pleasure is worth purchasing at the cost of a particular pain, except the feelings and judgment of the experienced? When, therefore, those feelings and judgment declare the pleasures derived from the higher faculties to be preferable *in kind,* apart from the question of intensity, to those of which the animal nature, disjoined from the higher faculties, is susceptible, they are entitled on this subject to the same regard.

I have dwelt on this point as being a necessary part of a perfectly just conception of utility or happiness considered as the directive rule of human conduct. But it is by no means an indispensable condition to the acceptance of the utilitarian standard; for that standard is not the agent's own greatest happiness, but the greatest amount of happiness altogether; and if it may possibly be doubted whether a noble character is always the happier for its nobleness, there can be no doubt that it makes other people happier, and that the world in general is immensely a gainer by it. Utilitarianism, therefore, could only attain its end by the general cultivation of nobleness of character, even if each individual were only benefited by the nobleness of others, and his own, so far as happiness is concerned, were a sheer deduction from the benefit. But the bare enunciation of such an absurdity as this last, renders refutation superfluous.

According to the greatest happiness principle, as above explained, the ultimate end, with reference to and for the sake of which all other things are desirable—whether we are considering our own good or that of other people—is an existence exempt as far as possible from pain, and as rich as possible in enjoyments, both in point of quantity and quality; the test of quality and the rule for measuring it against quantity being the preference felt by those who, in their opportunities of experience, to which must be added their habits of self-consciousness and self-obervation, are best furnished with the means of comparison. This, being according to the utilitarian opinion the end of human action, is necessarily also the standard of morality, which may accordingly be defined "the rules and precepts for human conduct," by the observance of which an existence such as has been described might be, to the greatest extent possible, secured to all mankind; and not to them only, but, so far as the nature of things admits, to the whole sentient creation. . . .

I must again repeat what the assailants of utilitarianism seldom have the justice to acknowledge, that the happiness which forms the utilitarian standard of what is right in conduct is not the agent's own happiness but that of all concerned. As between his own happiness and that of others, utilitarianism requires him to be a strictly impartial as a disinterested and benevolent spectator. In the golden rule of Jesus of Nazareth, we read the complete spirit of the ethics of utility. "To do as you would be done by," and "to love your neighbor as yourself," constitute the ideal perfection of utilitarian morality. As the means of making the nearest approach to this ideal, utility would enjoin, first, that laws and social arrangements should place the happiness or (as, speaking practically, it may be called) the interest of every individual as nearly as possible in harmony with the interest of the whole; and, secondly, that education and opinion, which have so vast a power over human character, should so use that power as to establish in the mind of every individual an indissoluble association between his own happiness and the good of the whole, especially between his own happiness and the practice of such modes of conduct, negative and positive, as regard for the universal happiness prescribes; so that not only he may be unable to conceive the possibility of happiness to himself, consistently with conduct opposed to the general good, but also that a direct impulse to promote the general good may be in every individual one of the habitual motives of action, and the sentiments connected therewith may fill a large and prominent place in every human being's sentient existence. If the impugners of the utilitarian morality represented it to their own minds in this its true character, I know not what recommendation possessed by any other morality they could possibly affirm to be wanting to it; what more beautiful or more exalted developments of human nature any other ethical system can be supposed to foster, or what springs of action, not accessible to the utilitarian, such systems rely on for giving effect to their mandates.

The objectors to utilitarianism cannot always be charged with representing it in a discreditable light. On the contrary, those among them who entertain anything like a just idea of its disinterested character sometimes find fault with its standard as being too high for humanity. They say it is exacting too much to require that people shall always act from the inducement of promoting the general interests of society. But this is to mistake the very meaning of a standard of morals and confound the rule of action with the motive of it. It is the business of ethics to tell us what are our duties, or by what test we may know them, but no system of ethics requires that the sole motive of all we do shall be a feeling of duty; on the contrary, ninety-nine hundredths of all our actions are done from other motives, and rightly so done if the rule of duty does not condemn them. It is the more unjust to utilitarianism that this particular misapprehension should be made a ground of objection to it, inasmuch as utilitarian moralists have gone beyond almost all others in affirming that the motive has nothing to do with the morality of the action, though much with the worth of the agent. He who saves a fellow creature from drowning does what is morally right, whether his motive be duty or the hope of being paid for his trouble; he who betrays the friend that trusts him is guilty of a crime, even if his object be to serve another friend to whom he is under greater obligations. But to speak only of actions done from the motive of duty, and in direct obedience to principle: it is a misapprehension of the utilitarian mode of thought to conceive it as implying that people should fix their minds upon so wide a generality as the world, or society at large. The great majority of good actions are intended not for the benefit of the world, but for that of individuals, of which the good of the world is made up; and the thoughts of the most virtuous man need not on these occasions travel beyond the particular persons concerned, except so far as is necessary to assure himself that in benefiting them he is not violating the rights, that is, the legitimate and authorized expectations, of anyone else. The multiplication of happiness is, according to the utilitarian ethics, the object of virtue: the occasions on which any person (except one in a thousand) has it in his power to do this on and extended scale—in other words, to be a public benefactor—are but exceptional; and on these occasions alone is he called on to consider public utility; in every other case, private utility, the interest or happiness of some few persons, is all he has to attend to. Those alone the influence of whose actions extends to society in general need concern themselves habitually about so large an object. In the case of abstinences indeed—of things which people forbear to do from moral considerations, though the consequences in the particular case might be beneficial—it would be unworthy of an intelligent agent not to be consciously aware that the action is of a class which, if practiced generally, would be generally injurious, and that this is the ground of the obligation to abstain from it. The amount of regard for the public interest implied in this recognition is no greater than is demanded by every system of morals, for they all enjoin to abstain from whatever is manifestly pernicious to society. . . .

Again, utility is often summarily stigmatized as an immoral doctrine by giving it the name of "expediency," and taking advantage of the popular use of that term to contrast it with principle. But the expedient, in the sense in which it is opposed to the right, generally means that which is expedient for the particular interest of the agent himself; as when a minister sacrifices the interest of his country to keep himself in place. When it means anything better than this, it means that which is expedient for some immediate object, some temporary purpose, but which violates a rule whose observance is expedient in a much higher degree. The expedient, in this sense, instead of being the same thing with the useful, is a branch of the hurtful. Thus it would often be expedient, for the purpose of getting over some momentary embarrassment, or attaining some object immediately useful to ourselves or others, to tell a lie. But inasmuch as the cultivation in ourselves of a sensitive feeling on the subject of veracity is one of the most useful, and the enfeeblement of that feeling one of the most hurtful, things to which our conduct can be instrumental; and inasmuch as any, even unintentional, deviation from truth does that much toward weakening the trustworthiness of human assertion, which is not only the principle support of all present social well-being, but the insufficiency of which does more than any one thing that can be named to keep back civilization, virtue, everything which human happiness on the largest scale depends—we feel that the violation, for a present advantage, of a rule of such transcendent expediency is not expedient, and that he who, for the sake of convenience to himself or to some other individual, does what depends on him to deprive mankind of the good, and inflict upon them the evil, involved in the greater or less reliance which they can place in each other's word, acts the part of one of their worst enemies. Yet that even this rule, sacred as it is, admits of possible exceptions is acknowledged by all moralists; the chief of which is when the withholding of some fact (as of information from a malefactor, or of bad news from a person dangerously ill) would save an individual (especially an individual other than oneself) from great and unmerited evil, and when the withholding can only be effected by denial. But in order that the exception may not extend itself beyond the need, and may have the least possible effect in weakening reliance on veracity, it ought to be recognized and, if possible, its limits defined; and, if the principle of utility is good for anything, it must be good for weighing these conflicting utilities against one another and marking out the region within which one or the other preponderates.

Again, defenders of utility often find themselves called upon to reply to such objections as this—that there is not time, previous to action, for calculating and weighing the effects of any line of conduct on the general happiness. This is exactly as if anyone were to say that it is impossible to guide our conduct by Christianity because there is not time, on every occasion on which anything has to be done, to read through the Old and New Testaments. The answer to the objection is that there has been ample time, namely, the whole past duration of the human species. During all that time mankind have been learning by experience the tendencies of actions; on which experience all the prudence as well as all the morality of life are dependent. People talk as if the commencement of this course of experience had hitherto been put off, and as if, at the moment when some man feels tempted to meddle with the property or life of another, he had to begin considering for the first time whether murder and theft are injurious to human happiness. Even then I do not think that he would find the question very puzzling; but, at all events, the matter is now done to his hand. It is truly a whimsical supposition that, if mankind were agreed in considering utility to be the test of morality, they would remain without any agreement as to what *is* useful, and would take no measures for having their notions on the subject taught to the young and enforced by law and opinion. There is no difficulty in providing any ethical standard whatever to work ill if we suppose universal idiocy to be conjoined with it; but on any hypothesis short of that, mankind must by this time have acquired positive beliefs as to the effects of some actions on their happiness; and the beliefs which have thus come down are the rules of morality for the multitude, and for the philosopher until he has succeeded in finding better. That philosophers might easily do this, even now, on many subjects; that the received code of ethics is by no means of divine right; and that mankind have still much to learn as to the effects of actions on the general happiness, I admit or rather earnestly maintain. The corollaries from the principle of utility, like the precepts of every practical art, admit of indefinite improvement, and, in a progressive state of the human mind, their improvement is perpetually going on. But to consider the rules of morality as improvable is one thing; to pass over the intermediate generalization entirely and endeavor to test each individual action directly by the first principle is another. It is a strange notion that the acknowledgement of a first principle is inconsistent with the admission of secondary ones. To inform a traveler respecting the place of his ultimate destination is not to forbid the use of landmarks and direction-posts on the way. The proposition that happiness is the end and aim of morality does not mean that no road ought to be laid down to that goal, or that persons going thither should not be advised to take one direction rather than another. Men really ought to leave off talking a kind of nonsense on this subject, which they would neither talk nor listen to on other matters of practical concernment. Nobody argues that the art of navigation is not founded on astronomy because sailors cannot wait to calculate the Nautical Almanac. Being rational creatures, they go to sea with it ready calculated; and all rational creatures go out upon the sea of life with their minds made up on the common questions of right and wrong, as well as on many of the far more difficult questions of wise and foolish. And this, as long as foresight is a human quality, it is to be presumed they will continue to do. Whatever we adopt as the fundamental principle of morality, we require subordinate principles to apply it by; the impossibility of doing without them being common to all systems, can afford no argument against any one in particular; but gravely to argue as if no such secondary principles could be had, and as if mankind had remained till now, and always must remain, without drawing any general conclusions from the experience of human life is as high a pitch, I think, as absurdity has ever reached in philosophical controversy. . . .

Questions of ultimate ends do not admit of proof, in the ordinary

214 Philosophical Explorations

acceptation of the term. To be incapable of proof by reasoning is common to all first principles, to the first premises of our knowledge, as well as to those of our conduct. But the former, being matters of fact, may be the subject of a direct appeal of the faculties which judge of fact—namely, our senses and our internal consciousness. Can an appeal be made to the same faculties on questions of practical ends? Or by what other faculty is cognizance taken of them?

Questions about ends are, in other words, questions about what things are desirable. The utilitarian doctrine is that happiness is desirable, and the only thing desirable, as an end; all other things being only desirable as means to that end. What ought to be required of this doctrine, what conditions is it requisite that the doctrine should fulfill—to make good its claim to be believed?

The only proof capable of being given that an object is visible is that people actually see it. The only proof that a sound is audible is that people hear it; and so of the other sources of our experience. In like manner, I apprehend, the sole evidence it is possible to produce that anything is desirable is that people do actually desire it. If the end which the utilitarian doctrine proposes to itself were not, in theory and in practice, acknowledged to be an end, nothing could ever convince any person that it was so. No reason can be given why the general happiness is desirable, except that each person, so far as he believes it to be attainable, desires his own happiness. This, however, being a fact, we have not only all the proof which the case admits of, but all which it is possible to require, that happiness is a good, that each person's happiness is a good to that person, and the general happiness, therefore, a good to the aggregate of all persons. Happiness has made out its title as *one* of the ends of conduct and, consequently, one of the criteria of morality.

But it has not, by this alone, proved itself to be the sole criterion. To do that, it would seem, by the same rule, necessary to show, not only that people desire happiness, but that they never desire anything else. Now it is palpable that they do desire things which, in common language, are decidedly distinguished from happiness. They desire, for example, virtue and the absence of vice no less really than pleasure and the absence of pain. The desire of virtue is not as universal, but it is as authentic a fact as the desire of happiness. And hence the opponents of the utilitarian standard deem that they have a right to infer that there are other ends of human action besides happiness, and that happiness is not the standard of approbation and disapprobation.

But does the utilitarian doctrine deny that people desire virtue, or maintain that virtue is not a thing to be desired? The very reverse. It maintains not only that virtue is to be desired, but that it is to be desired disinterestedly, for itself. Whatever may be the opinion of utilitarian moralists as to the original conditions by which virtue is made virtue, however they may believe (as they do) that actions and dispositions are only virtuous because they promote another end than virtue, yet this being granted, and it having been decided, from considerations of this description, what *is* virtuous, they not only place virtue at the very head of the things which are good as means to the ultimate end, but they also recognize as a psychological fact the possibility of its being, to the individual, a good in itself, without looking to any end beyond it; and hold that the mind is not in a right state, not in a state conformable to utility, not in the state most conducive to the general happiness, unless it does love virtue in this manner—as a thing desirable in itself, even although, in the individual instance, it should not produce those other desirable consequences which it tends to produce, and on account of which it is held to be virtue. This opinion is not, in the smallest degree, a departure from the happiness principle. The ingredients of happiness are very various, and each of them is desirable in itself, and not merely when considered as swelling an aggregate. The principle of utility does not mean that any given pleasure, as music, for instance, or any given exemption from pain, as for example health, is to be looked upon as means to a collective something termed happiness, and to be desired on that account. They are desired and desirable in and for themselves; besides being means, they are a part of the end. Virtue, according to the utilitarian doctrine, is not naturally and originally part of the end, but it is capable of becoming so; and in those who live it disinterestedly it has become so, and is desired and cherished, not as a means to happiness, but as a part of their happiness.

To illustrate this further, we may remember that virtue is not the only thing originally a means, and which if it were not a means to anything else would be and remain indifferent, but which by association with what it is a means to comes to be desired for itself, and that too with the utmost intensity. What, for example, shall we say of the love of money? There is nothing originally more desirable about money than about any heap of glittering pebbles. Its worth is solely that of the things which it will buy; the desires for other things than itself, which it is a means of gratifying. Yet the love of money is not only one of the strongest moving forces of human life, but money is, in many cases, desired in and for itself; the desire to possess it is often stronger than the desire to use it, and goes on increasing when all the desires which point to ends beyond it, to be compassed by it, are falling off. It may, then, be said truly that money is desired not for the sake of an end, but as part of the end. From being a means to happiness, it has come to be itself a principal ingredient of the individual's conception of happiness. The same may be said of the majority of the great objects of human life: power for example, or fame, except that to each of these there is a certain amount of immediate pleasure annexed, which has at least the semblance of being naturally inherent in them—a thing which cannot be said of money. Still, however, the strongest natural attraction, both of power and of fame, is the immense aid they give to the attainment of our other wishes; and it is the strong association thus generated between them and all our objects of desire which gives to the direct desire of them the intensity it often assumes, so as in some characters to surpass in strength all other desires. In these cases the means have become a part of the end, and a more important part of it than any of the things which they are means to. What was once desired as an instrument for the attainment of happiness has come to be desired for its own sake. In being desired for its own sake it is, however, desired as *part* of happiness. The person is made, or thinks he would be made, happy by its mere possession; and is made unhappy by failure to obtain it. The desire of it is not a different thing from the desire of happiness any more than the love of music or the desire of health. They are included in happiness. They are some of the elements of which the desire of happiness is made up. Happiness is not an abstract idea but a concrete whole; and these are some of its parts. And the utilitarian standard sanctions and approves their being so. Life would be a poor thing, very ill provided with sources of happiness, if there were not this provision of nature by which things originally indifferent, but conducive to, or otherwise associated with, the satisfaction of our primitive desires, become in themselves sources of pleasure more valuable than the primitive pleasures, both in permanency, in the space of human existence that they are capable of covering, and even in intensity.

Virtue, according to the utilitarian conception, is a good of this description. There was no original desire of it, or motive to it, save its conduciveness to pleasure, and especially to protection from pain. But through the association thus formed it may be felt a good in itself, and desired as such with as great intensity as any other good; and with this difference between it and the love of money, of power, or of fame— that all of these may, and often do, render the individual noxious to the other members of the society to which he belongs, whereas there is nothing which makes him so much a blessing to them as the cultivation of the disinterested love of virtue. And consequently, the utilitarian standard, while it tolerates and approves those other acquired desires, up to the point beyond which they would be more injurious to the general happiness than promotive of it, enjoins and requires the cultivation of the love of virtue up to the greatest strength possible, as being above all things important to the general happiness.

It results from the preceding considerations that there is in reality nothing desired except happiness. Whatever is desired otherwise than as a means of to some end beyond itself, and ultimately to happiness, is desired as itself a part of happiness, and is not desired for itself until it has become so. Those who desire virtue for its own sake desire it either because the consciousness of it is a pleasure, or because the consciousness of being without it is a pain, or for both reasons united; as in truth the pleasure and pain seldom exist separately, but almost always together—the same person feeling pleasure in the degree of virtue attained, and pain in not having attained more. If one of these gave him no pleasure, and the other no pain, he would not love or desire virtue, or would desire it only for the other benefits which it might produce to himself or to persons whom he cared for.

We have now, then, an answer to the question, of what sort of proof the principle of utility is susceptible. If the opinion which I have now stated is psychologically true—if human nature is so constituted as to desire nothing which is not either a part of happiness or a means of happiness—we can have no other proof, and we require no other, that these are the only things desirable. If so, happiness is the sole end of human action, and the promotion of it the test by which to judge of all human conduct; from whence it necessarily follows that it must be the criterion of morality, since a part is included in the whole.

And now to decide whether this is really so, whether mankind do desire nothing for itself but that which is a pleasure to them, or of which the absence is a pain, we have evidently arrived at a question of fact and experience, dependent, like all similar questions, upon evidence. It can only be determined by practiced self-consciousness and self-observation, assisted by observation of others. I believe that these sources of evidence, impartially consulted, will declare that desiring a thing and finding it pleasant, aversion to it and thinking of it as painful, are phenomena entirely inseparable or, rather, two parts of the same phenomenon—in strictness of language, two different modes of naming the same psychological fact; that to think of an object as desirable (unless for the sake of its consequences) and to think of it as pleasant are one and the same thing; and that to desire anything except in proportion as the idea of it is pleasant is a physical and metaphysical impossibility.

So obvious does this appear to me that I expect it will hardly be disputed; and the objection made will be, not that desire can possibly be directed to anything ultimately except pleasure and exemption from pain, but that the will is a different thing from desire; that a person of confirmed virtue or any other person whose purposes are fixed carries out his purposes without any thought of the pleasure he has in contemplating them or expects to derive from their fulfillment, and persists in acting on them, even though these pleasures are much diminished by changes in his character or decay of his passive sensibilities, or are outweighed by the pains which the pursuit of the purposes may bring upon him. All this I fully admit and have stated it elsewhere as positively and emphatically as anyone. Will, the active phenomenon, is a different thing from desire, the state of passive sensibility, and, though originally an offshoot from it, may in time take root and detach itself from the parent stock, so much so that in the case of a habitual purpose, instead of willing the the thing because we desire it, we often desire it only because we will it. This, however, is but an instance of that familiar fact, the power of habit, and is nowise confined to the case of virtuous actions. Many indifferent things which men originally did from a motive of some sort they continue to do from habit. Sometimes this is done unconsciously, the consciousness coming only after the action; at other times with conscious volition, but volition which has become habitual and is put in operation by the force of habit, in opposition perhaps to the deliberate preference, as often happens with those who have contracted habits of vicious or hurtful indulgence. Third and last comes the case in which the habitual act of will in the individual instance is not in contradiction to the general intention prevailing at other times, but in fulfillment of it, as in the case of the person of confirmed virtue and of all who pursue deliberately and consistently any determinate end. The distinction between will and desire thus understood is an authentic and highly important psychological fact; but the fact consists solely in this—that will, like all other parts of our constitution, is amenable to habit, and that we may will from habit what we no longer desire for itself, or desire only because we will it. It is not the less true that will, in the beginning, is entirely produced by desire, including in that term the repelling influence of pain as well as the attractive one of pleasure. Let us take into consideration no longer the person who has a confirmed will to do right, but him in whom that virtuous will is still feeble, conquerable by temptation, and not to be fully relied on; by what means can it be strengthened? How can the will to be virtuous, where it does not exist in sufficient force, be implanted or awakened? Only by making the person *desire* virtue—by making him think of it in a pleasurable light, or of its absence in a painful one. It is by associating the doing right with pleasure, or the wrong with pain, or by eliciting and impressing and bringing home to the person's experience the pleasure naturally involved in the one or the pain in the other, that it is possible to call forth that will to be virtuous which, when confirmed, acts without any thought of either pleasure or pain. Will is the child of desire, and passes out of the dominion of its parent only to come under that of habit. That which is the result of habit affords no presumption of being intrinsically good; and there would be no reason for wishing that the purpose of virtue should become independent of pleasure and pain were it not that the influence of the pleasurable and painful associations which prompt to virtue is not sufficiently to be depended on for unerring constancy of action until it has acquired the support of habit. Both in feeling and in conduct, habit is the only thing which imparts certainty; and it is because of the importance to others of being able to rely absolutely on one's feelings and conduct, and to oneself of being able to rely on one's own, that the will to do right ought to be cultivated into this habitual independence. In other words, this state of the will is a means to good, not intrinsically a good; and does not contradict the doctrine that nothing is a good to human beings but insofar as it is either itself pleasurable or a means of attaining pleasure or averting pain.

But if this doctrine be true, the principle of utility is proved. Whether it is so or not must now be left to the consideration of the thoughtful reader.

[13]

Psychological Egoism

James Rachels

IS UNSELFISHNESS POSSIBLE?

Morality and psychology go together. Morality tells us what we *ought* to do; but there is little point to it if we are not *able* to do as we ought. It may be said that we should love our enemies; but that is empty talk unless we are capable of loving them. A sound morality must be based on a realistic conception of what is possible for human beings.

Almost every system of morality recommends that we behave unselfishly. It is said that we should take the interest of other people into account when we are deciding what to do: we should not harm other people; in fact, we should try to be helpful to them whenever possible—even if it means forgoing some advantage for ourselves.

But are we capable of being unselfish? There is a theory of human nature, once widely held among philosophers, psychologists, and economists, and still held by many ordinary people, that says we are not capable of unselfishness. According to this theory, known as *Psychological Egoism*, each person is so constituted that he will look out only for his *own* interests. Therefore, it is unreasonable to expect people to behave "altruistically." Human nature being what it is, people will respond to the needs of others only when there is something in it for themselves. Pure altruism is a myth—it simply does not exist.

If this view is correct, people are very different from what we usually

Reprinted from *The Elements of Moral Philosophy* (New York: Random House, 1986), by permission of the publisher.

James Rachels (b. 1941) is University Professor of Philosophy at the University of Alabama at Birmingham.

suppose. Of course, no one doubts that each of us cares very much about his own welfare. But we also believe that we care about others as well, at least to some extent. If Psychological Egoism is correct, this is only an illusion—in the final analysis, we care nothing for other people. Because it so contradicts our usual conception of ourselves, this is a shocking doctrine. Why have so many believed it to be true?

THE STRATEGY OF REINTERPRETING MOTIVES

Psychological Egoism seems to fly in the face of the facts. It is tempting to respond to it by saying something like this: *"Of course* people sometimes act unselfishly. Jones gave up a trip to the movies, which he would have enjoyed very much, so that he could contribute the money for famine relief. Brown spends his free time doing volunteer work in a hospital. Smith rushed into a burning house to rescue a child. These are all clear cases of unselfish behavior, and if the psychological egoist thinks that such cases do not occur, then he is just mistaken."

Such examples are obvious, and the thinkers who have been sympathetic to Psychological Egoism were certainly aware of them. Yet they have persisted in defending the view. Why? Partly it is because they have suspected that the "altruistic" explanations of behavior are too superficial—it *seems* that people are unselfish, but a deeper analysis of their motives might tell a different story. Perhaps Jones gives money for famine relief because his religion teaches that he will be rewarded in heaven. The man who works as a hospital volunteer may be driven by an inner need to atone for some past misdeed, or perhaps he simply enjoys this work, as other people enjoy playing chess. As for the woman who risks her life to save the child, we all know that such people are honored as heroes; perhaps she is motivated by a desire for public recognition. This technique of reinterpreting motives is perfectly general and may be repeated again and again. For any act of apparent altruism, a way can always be found to eliminate the altruism in favor of some more self-centered motive.

Thomas Hobbes (1588-1679) thought that Psychological Egoism was probably true, but he was not satisfied with such a piecemeal approach. It is not theoretically elegant to deal with each action separately, "after the fact." If Psychological Egoism *is* true, we should be able to give a more general account of human motives, which would establish the theory once and for all. This is what Hobbes attempted to do. His method was to list the possible human motives, concentrating especially on the "altruistic" ones, and show how each could be understood in egoistic terms. Once this project was completed, he would have systematically eliminated altruism from our understanding of human nature. Here are two examples of Hobbes at work:

1. *Charity*. This is the most general motive that we ascribe to people when we think they are acting from a concern for others. *The Oxford English Dictionary* devotes almost four columns to "charity." It is defined variously as "The Christian love of our fellowman" and "Benevolence to one's neighbors." But for the psychological egoist, such neighborly love does not exist, and so charity must be understood in a radically different way. In his essay "On Human Nature," Hobbes describes it like this:

> There can be no greater argument to a man, of his own power, than to find himself able not only to accomplish his own desires, but also to assist other men in theirs: and this is that conception wherein consisteth *charity*.

Thus charity is a delight one takes in the demonstration of one's powers. The charitable man is demonstrating to himself, and to the world, that he is more capable than others. He can not only take care of himself, he has enough left over for others who are not so able as he. He is really just showing off his own superiority.

Of course Hobbes was aware that the charitable man may not *believe* that this is what he is doing. But we are not the best judges of our own motivations. It is only natural that we would interpret our actions in a way that is flattering to us (that is no more than the psychological egoist would expect!), and it is flattering to think that we are "unselfish." Hobbes's account aims to provide the *real* explanation of why we act as we do, not the superficial flattering account that we naturally want to believe.

2. *Pity*. What is it to pity another person? We might think it is to sympathize with them, to feel unhappy about their misfortunes. And acting from this sympathy, we might try to help them. Hobbes thinks this is all right, as far as it goes, but it does not go far enough. The *reason* we are disturbed by other people's misfortunes is that we are reminded that the same thing might happen to us! "Pity," he says, "is imagination or fiction of future calamity to ourselves, proceeding from the sense of another man's calamity."

This account of pity turns out to be more powerful, from a theoretical point of view, than it first appears. It can explain very neatly some peculiar facts about the phenomenon. For example, it can explain why we feel greater pity when a good person suffers than when an evil person suffers. Pity, on Hobbes's account, requires a sense of identification with the person suffering—I pity you when I imagine *myself* in your place. But because each of us thinks of himself or herself as a good person, we do not identify very closely with those we think bad. Therefore, we do not pity the wicked in the same way we pity the good—our feelings of pity vary directly with the virtue of the person suffering, because our sense of identification varies in that way.

The strategy of reinterpreting motives is a persuasive method of reasoning; it has made a great many people feel that Psychological Egoism might be true. It especially appeals to a certain cynicism in us, a suspicion that people are not nearly as noble as they seem. But it is not a conclusive method of reasoning, for it cannot *prove* that Psychological Egoism is correct. The trouble is, it only shows that it is *possible* to interpret motives egoistically; it does nothing to show that the egoistic motives are deeper or truer than the altruistic explanations they are intended to replace. At most, the strategy shows that Psychological Egoism is possible. We still need other arguments to show it is true.

TWO ARGUMENTS IN FAVOR OF PSYCHOLOGICAL EGOISM

Two general arguments have often been advanced in favor of Psychological Egoism. They are "general" arguments, in the sense that each one seeks to establish at a stroke that *all* actions, and not merely some limited class of them, are motivated by self-interest. As will be seen, neither argument stands up very well under scrutiny.

1. The first argument goes as follows. If we describe one person's action as selfish and another person's action as unselfish, we are overlooking the crucial fact that in both cases, assuming the action is done voluntarily, *the person is merely doing what he most wants to do.* If Jones gives his money for the cause of famine relief rather than spending it on the movies, that only shows that he wanted to contribute to that cause more than he wanted to go to the movies—and why should he be praised for "unselfishness" when he is only doing what *he* most wants to do? His action is being dictated by his own desires, his own sense of what *he* wants most. Thus he cannot be said to be acting unselfishly. And since exactly the same may be said about *any* alleged act of altruism, we can conclude that Psychological Egoism must be true.

This argument has two primary flaws. First, it rests on the premise that people never voluntarily do anything except what they want to do. But this is plainly false; there are at least two kinds of actions that are exceptions to this generalization. One is actions that we may not want to do but that we do anyway as a means to an end that we want to achieve—for example, going to the dentist to stop a toothache. Such cases may, however, be regarded as consistent with the spirit of the argument, because the ends mentioned (such as stopping the toothache) are wanted.

Still, there are also actions that we do not because we want to nor even because they are means to an end we want to achieve, but because we feel that we *ought* to do them. For example, someone may do something because she has promised to do it, and thus feels obligated, even though she does not want to do it. It is sometimes suggested that in such cases we do the action because, after all, we want to keep our promises; so even here we are doing what we want. However, this will not work. If I have promised to do something and I do not want to do it, then it is simply false to say that I want to keep my promise. In such cases we feel a conflict precisely because we do *not* want to do what we feel obligated to do. If our desires and our sense of obligation *were* always in harmony, it would be a happier world. Unfortunately, we enjoy no such happy situation. It is an all too common experience to be pulled in different directions by desire and obligation. Jones's predicament may be like this: he *wants* to go to the movies, but feels he *should* give the money for famine relief instead. Thus if he chooses to contribute the money, he is not simply doing what he wants to do. If he did that, he would go to the movies.

The argument has a second flaw. Suppose we were to concede, for the sake of argument, that all voluntary action is motivated by desire, or at least that Jones is so motivated. Even if this were granted, it would not follow that Jones is acting selfishly or from self-interest. For if Jones wants to do something to help starving people, even when it means forgoing his own enjoyments, that is precisely what makes him *unselfish*. What else could unselfishness be, if not wanting to help others, even at some sacrifice to oneself? Another way to put the point is to say that it is the *object* of a want that determines whether it is selfish or not. The mere fact that I am acting on *my* wants does not mean that I am acting selfishly; it depends on *what it is* that I want. If I want only my own good and care nothing for others, then I am selfish; but if I also want other people to be happy and I act on *that* desire, then my action is not selfish.

Therefore, this argument goes wrong in just about every way that an argument can go wrong: the premises are not true, and even if they were true, the conclusion would not follow from them.

2. The second general argument for Psychological Egoism appeals to the fact that so-called unselfish actions produce a sense of self-satisfaction in the person who does them. Acting "unselfishly" makes people *feel good* about themselves. This has often been noted and has been put in various ways: "It gives him a clear conscience" or "He couldn't sleep at night if he had done otherwise" or "He would have been ashamed of himself for not doing it" are familiar ways of making the same point. This sense of self-satisfaction is a pleasant state of consciousness, which we desire and seek. Therefore, actions are "unselfish" only at a superficial

level of analysis. If we dig deeper, we find that the *point* of acting "unselfishly" is really to achieve this pleasant state of consciousness. Jones will feel much better about himself for having given the money for famine relief—if he had gone to the movies, he would have felt terrible about it—and that is the real point of the action.

According to a well-known story, this argument was once advanced by Abraham Lincoln. A nineteenth-century newspaper reported that

> Mr. Lincoln once remarked to a fellow-passenger on an old-time mud coach that all men were prompted by selfishness in doing good. His fellow-passenger was antagonizing this position when they were passing over a corduroy bridge that spanned a slough. As they crossed this bridge they espied an old razor-backed sow on the bank making a terrible noise because her pigs had got into the slough and were in danger of drowning. As the old coach began to climb the hill, Mr. Lincoln called out, "Driver can't you stop just a moment?" Then Mr. Lincoln jumped out, ran back, and lifted the little pigs out of the mud and water and placed them on the bank. When he returned, his companion remarked: "Now, Abe, where does selfishness come in on this little episode?" "Why, bless your soul, Ed, that was the very essence of selfishness. I should have had no peace of mind all day had I gone on and left that suffering old sow worrying over those pigs. I did it to get peace of mind, don't you see?"

Lincoln was a better President than philosopher. His argument is vulnerable to the same sorts of objections as the previous one. Why should we think merely because someone derives satisfaction from helping others, that this makes him selfish? Isn't the unselfish person precisely the one who *does* derive satisfaction from helping others, whereas the selfish person does not? If Lincoln "got peace of mind" from rescuing the piglets, does this show him to be selfish or, on the contrary, doesn't it show him to be compassionate and good-hearted? (If a person were truly selfish, why should it bother his conscience that others suffer—much less pigs?) Similarly, it is nothing more than sophistry to say, because Jones finds satisfaction in giving for famine relief, that he is selfish. If we say this rapidly, while thinking about something else, perhaps it will sound all right; but if we speak slowly and pay attention to what we are saying, it sounds plain silly.

Moreover, suppose we ask *why* Jones derives satisfaction from contributing for famine relief. The answer is, it is because Jones is the kind of person who cares about other people: even if they are strangers to him, he doesn't want them to go hungry, and he is willing to take action to help them. If Jones were not this kind of person, then he would take no special pleasure in assisting them; and as we have already seen, this is the mark of unselfishness, not selfishness.

There is a general lesson to be learned here, having to do with the nature of desire and its objects. If we have a positive attitude toward the attainment of some goal, then we may derive satisfaction from attaining it. But the *object* of our attitude is *the attainment of that goal;* and we must want to attain the goal *before* we can find any satisfaction in it. We do not first desire some sort of "pleasurable consciousness" and then try to figure out how to achieve it. Rather, we desire all sorts of different things—money, a new car, to be a better chess player, to get a promotion in our work, and so on—and because we desire these things, we derive satisfaction from getting them. And so if someone desires the welfare and happiness of other people, he will derive satisfaction from helping them; but this does not mean that those good feelings are the *object* of his desire. *They* are not what he is after. Nor does it mean that he is in any way selfish on account of having those feelings.

These two arguments are the ones most commonly advanced in defense of Psychological Egoism. It is a measure of the weakness of the theory that stronger arguments have not been forthcoming.

CLEARING AWAY SOME CONFUSIONS

One of the most powerful theoretical motives is a desire for simplicity. When we set out to explain something, we would like to find as *simple* an explanation as possible. This is certainly true in the sciences—the simpler a scientific theory, the greater its appeal. Consider phenomena as diverse as planetary motion, the tides, and the way objects fall to the surface of the earth when released from a height. These appear, at first, to be very different; it would seem that we would need a multitude of different principles to explain them all. Who would suspect that they could all be explained by a single simple principle? Yet the theory of gravity does just that. The theory's ability to bring diverse phenomena together under a single explanatory principle is one of its great virtues. It makes order out of chaos.

In the same way, when we think about human conduct, we would like to find one principle that explains it all. We want a single simple formula, if we can find one, that would unite the diverse phenomena of human behavior, in the way that simple formulas in physics bring together apparently diverse phenomena. Since it is obvious that self-regard is an overwhelmingly important factor in motivation, it is only natural to wonder whether all motivation might not be explained in terms of it. And so the idea of Psychological Egoism is born.

But, most philosophers and psychologists would agree today, it is stillborn. The fundamental idea behind Psychological Egoism cannot even be expressed without falling into confusion; and once these confusions have been cleared away, the theory no longer seems even plausible.

The first confusion is between selfishness and self-interest. When we think about it, the two are clearly not the same. If I see a physician because I am feeling poorly, I am acting in my own self-interest, but no one would think of calling me "selfish" on account of it. Similarly, brushing my teeth, working hard at my job, and obeying the law are all in my self-interest, but none of these are examples of selfish conduct. This is because selfish behavior is behavior that ignores the interests of others, in circumstances in which their interests ought not to be ignored. The concept of "selfishness" has a definite evaluative flavor; to call people selfish is not just to describe their action but to criticize it. Thus you would not be called selfish for eating a normal meal in normal circumstances (although this would surely be in your self-interest); but you would be called selfish for hoarding food while others are starving.

A second confusion is between self-interested behavior and the pursuit of pleasure. We do lots of things because we enjoy them, but that does not mean we are acting from self-interest. The man who continues to smoke cigarettes even after learning about the connection between smoking and cancer is surely not acting from self-interest, not even by his own standards—self-interest would dictate that he quit smoking at once—and he is not acting altruistically either. He *is*, no doubt, smoking for the pleasure of it, but this only shows that undisciplined pleasure seeking and acting from self-interest are very different. This is what led Joseph Butler, the leading eighteenth-century critic of egoism, to remark, "The thing to be lamented is, not that men have so great regard to their own good or interest in the present world, for they have not enough."

Taken together, the last two paragraphs show (*a*) that it is false that all actions are selfish and (*b*) that it is false that all actions are done from self-interest. When we brush our teeth, at least in normal circumstances, we are not acting selfishly; therefore not all actions are selfish. And when we smoke cigarettes, we are not acting out of self-interest; therefore not all actions are done from self-interest. It is worth noting that these two points do not depend on examples of altruism; even if there were no such thing as altruistic behavior, Psychological Egoism would, according to these arguments, *still* be false!

A third confusion is the common but false assumption that a concern for one's own welfare is incompatible with any genuine concern for others. Since it is obvious that everyone (or very nearly everyone) does desire his or her own well-being, it might be thought that no one can really be concerned for the well-being of others. But again, this is surely a false dichotomy. There is no inconsistency in desiring that everyone, including oneself *and* others, be happy. To be sure, it may happen on occasion that our interests conflict with the interests of others, in the sense that both cannot be satisfied. In these cases we have to make hard choices. But even in these cases we sometimes opt for the interests of others, especially when the others are our friends and family. But more important, not all cases are like this. Sometimes we are able to promote the welfare of others when our own interests are not involved at all. In those circumstances, not even the strongest self-regard need prevent us from acting considerate toward others.

Once these confusions are cleared away, there seems little reason to think Psychological Egoism is a plausible theory. On the contrary, it seems decidedly implausible. If we simply observe people's behavior with an open mind, we find that much of it is motivated by self-regard, but by no means all of it. There may indeed be one simple formula, as yet undiscovered, that would explain all of human behavior—but Psychological Egoism is not it.

THE DEEPEST ERROR IN PSYCHOLOGICAL EGOISM

The preceding discussion may seem relentlessly negative—even objectionably so. "If Psychological Egoism is so obviously confused," you may ask, "and if there are no plausible arguments in its favor, why have so many intelligent people been attracted to it?" It is a fair question. Part of the answer, I think, is the almost irresistible urge toward theoretical simplicity; another part is the attraction of what appears to be a hard-headed, deflationary attitude toward human pretensions. But there is a deeper reason: Psychological Egoism was accepted by many thinkers because it appeared to them to be *irrefutable*. And in a certain sense, they were right. Yet in another sense, the theory's immunity from refutation is its deepest flaw.

To explain, let me first tell a (true) story that might appear to be far from our subject.

A few years ago a group of investigators led by Dr. David Rosenham, professor of psychology and law at Stanford University, had themselves admitted as patients to various mental institutions. The hospital staffs did not know there was anything special about them; the investigators were thought to be simply patients. The investigators' purpose was to see how they would be treated.

The investigators were perfectly "sane," whatever that means, but their very presence in the hospitals created the assumption that they were mentally disturbed. Although they behaved normally—they did nothing to feign illness—they soon discovered that everything they did was interpreted as a sign of some sort of mental problem. When some of them were found to be taking notes on their experiences, entries were made in their records such as "patient engages in writing behavior." During one interview, one "patient" confessed that although he was closer to his mother as a small child, he became more attached to his father as he grew older—a perfectly normal turn of events. But this was taken as evidence of "unstable relationships in childhood." Even their protestations of normalcy were turned against them. One of the real patients warned them: "Never tell a doctor that you're well. He won't believe you. That's called a 'flight into health.' Tell him you're still sick, but you're feeling a lot better. That's called insight."

No one on the hospital staffs ever caught on to the hoax. The real patients, however, did see through it. One of them told an investigator, "You're not crazy. You're checking up on the hospital." And so he was.

What the investigators learned was that *once a hypothesis is accepted, everything may be interpreted to support it.* The hypothesis was that the pseudopatients were mentally disturbed; once that became the controlling assumption, it did not matter how they behaved. Everything they did would be construed so as to fit the assumption. But the "success" of this technique of interpretation did not prove the hypothesis was true. If anything, it was a sign that something had gone wrong.

The hypothesis that the pseudopatients were disturbed was faulty because, at least for the hospital staffs, it was *untestable*. If a hypothesis purports to say something about the world, then there must be some conditions that could verify it and some that conceivably could refute it. Otherwise, it is meaningless. Consider this example: suppose someone says "Kareem Abdul-Jabbar cannot get into my Volkswagen." We know perfectly well what this means, because we imagine the circumstances that would make it true and the circumstances that would make it false: to test the statement, we take the car to Kareem, invite him to step inside, and see what happens. If it turns out one way, the statement is true; if it turns out the other way, the statement is false. The problem with the hypothesis about the pseudopatients' mental health, as it was applied within the hospital setting, was that nothing could have refuted it. Such hypotheses may be immune from refutation, but their immunity is purchased at too dear a price—they no longer say anything significant about the world.

Psychological Egoism is involved in this same error. All our experience tells us that people act from a great variety of motives: greed, anger, lust, love, and hate, to name only a few. Sometimes, people think only of themselves. At other times, they do not think of themselves at all and act from a concern for others. The common distinction between self-regard and unselfishness gets its meaning from this contrast. But then Psychological Egoism tells us that there is *really* only one motive, self-regard, and this seems a new and fascinating revelation. We must have been wrong. But as the theory unfolds, it turns out that we were not wrong at all. The psychological egoist does not deny that people act in the variety of ways they have always appeared to act in. In the ordinary sense of the term, people are still, sometimes, unselfish. In effect, the psychological egoist has only announced his determination to *interpret* people's behavior in a certain way, *no matter what they do.* Therefore, *nothing that anyone could do could possibly count as evidence against the hypothesis.* The thesis is irrefutable, but for that very reason it turns out to have no factual content. It is not a new and fascinating revelation at all.

I am not saying that the hypothesis of the pseudopatients' mental illness or the hypothesis of Psychological Egoism are meaningless in themselves. The trouble is not so much with the hypotheses as with the people who manipulate the facts to fit them. The staffs of the mental institutions, and the estimable Hobbes, *could* have allowed some facts to count as falsifying their assumptions. Then, their hypotheses would have been meaningful but would have been plainly false. That is the risk one must take. Paradoxically, if we do not allow some way in which we might be mistaken, we lose all chance of being right.

ABOUT THE AUTHOR

STEVEN M. CAHN is Professor of Philosophy at the Graduate School of The City University of New York, where he serves as Provost and Vice-President for Academic Affairs. He received his B.A. from Columbia College and his Ph.D. from Columbia University. He previously taught at Dartmouth College, Vassar College, the University of Rochester, New York University, and at the University of Vermont, where for seven years he headed the Department of Philosophy. He is President of The John Dewey Foundation and chairs the American Philosophical Association's Committee on the Teaching of Philosophy.

Dr. Cahn is the author of *Fate, Logic, and Time, A New Introduction to Philosophy, The Eclipse of Excellence, Education and the Democratic Ideal* and *Saints and Scamps: Ethics in Academia.* He has edited or co-edited eight other volumes, including *Classics of Western Philosophy, Contemporary Philosophy of Religion, New Studies in the Philosophy of John Dewey, The Philosophical Foundations of Education,* and *Philosophy of Art and Aesthetics: From Plato to Wittgenstein.*